Martin Bucer: Unsung

"David Lawrence has a Ph.D. in European History from the University of Kansas and has taught History of Greece, History of Rome, Medieval Europe, Renaissance and Reformation, as well as several other courses for over twenty years at Lipscomb University in Nashville, Tennessee. His doctoral dissertation was on Erasmus, and he has published articles on him and the Protestant Reformation. David is eminently qualified to analyze and interpret the period, including the role of Martin Bucer, and I often say that he has forgotten more than I have ever learned."

Jerry L. Gaw, Ph.D.
Professor of History, Lipscomb University

"Martin Bucer is the premier unsung hero of the Protestant Reformation. A modern, accessible, biography of Bucer is long overdue. I am delighted that historian Dr. David Lawrence has undertaken this work. I know of no one better suited for the task. Like his subject, he is passionate about theology and worship, and thorough in his scholarship. His book is a must read for anyone interested in understanding and advancing the cause of Christ."

Rev. Charles Bradley
Pastor, Hopewell Presbyterian Church, Columbia, Tennessee

"Martin Bucer's significant role in the Reformation Movement has often been overlooked and neglected by historians. The lack of historical studies about this sixteenth century German reformer has left a major void in Reformation scholarship. David Lawrence has rendered a valuable service by providing his account of Bucer's life. Professor Lawrence is a dedicated historian, a longtime student of the German Reformation, and a skillful writer who is eminently qualified to pursue this study. His research in both Europe and the United States will add to the respect that his book is sure to garner."

Timothy Johnson, Ph. D.
Professor of History, Lipscomb University

Martin Bucer:
Unsung Hero of the Reformation

David Lawrence

WESTVIEW PUBLISHING CO., INC., NASHVILLE, TENNESSEE

First Edition, January 2008

Printed in the United States of America on acid-free paper.

ISBN 1-933912-09-X

Cover design by Landon Earps

Typography by Mary Catharine Nelson

Prepress by Westview Book Publishing, Inc.

Bob Allen, Author Representative

WESTVIEW PUBLISHING CO., INC.
P.O. Box 210183
Nashville, Tennessee 37221
www.westviewpublishing.com

Table of Contents

Preface

It doesn't seem a long time ago, but it has been, since I sat in a classroom at Wichita State University hearing the lectures of my esteemed professor and personal mentor, Kelley Sowards. I was a young graduate student aspiring for a degree in history and bringing to the table a passion for Christian theology. Dr. Sowards was a world-renowned scholar and authority on Erasmus, who persuaded me to pursue Erasmian studies through my master's and doctoral studies, which I did, on and off, for the next fifteen years. It was a glorious time in my life, when the history of the church was being unfolded to me day by day.

However, this course was the Reformation, and as Dr. Sowards explained how Martin Luther came to his understanding of the doctrine of forensic justification, *soli fide,* I can say with John Wesley that "my heart was strangely warmed," and I can say with Martin Bucer that I came to that class an Erasmian and left a "Martinian." I was, at least, a "Martinian" in heart, although I continued my studies in the life and work of Erasmus.

It was another unforgettable day in that class when Dr. Sowards lectured on "the other Martin," Martin Bucer. I was deeply moved and impressed by Bucer's commitment to a formula for unity, and by his indefatigable efforts in working with church leaders, both Catholic and Protestant, and with the great princes of his day to bring about a united church that would embrace Biblical teaching. His "doctrine of essentials" fascinated me, and his arrangement of the debate at Marburg between Luther and Zwingli over the Lord's Supper appeared to me as a pivotal moment in church history.

In the intervening years the idea of writing a biography of Bucer, to try to get out the story of his prodigious accomplishments, has grown. It is the idea that would not go away. In the meantime, my own knowledge of and commitment both to Reformation history and to the theology of the Reformation has grown and matured. In the last few years, the seed of an idea has developed into a passion.

My university, Lipscomb University in Nashville, Tennessee, was gracious enough to award me a sabbatical in the spring of 2003 to do the initial research, and they have supported me financially in traveling to Europe to visit sites of Bucer's preaching. Additionally, I have received considerable encouragement from my university colleagues, both in faculty and administration, from close friends who are pastors, from family, from students, and a whole host of wonderful people who have given me the incentive to pursue the work.

The story of "the other Martin" needs to be told. It needs to be known. Unfortunately, the knowledge of our history, the history of the Church of Christ, is sadly neglected today in the Christian community. Few Christians have more than a passing knowledge of the better known Martin, and most Christians think of October 31st in terms of pumpkins and trick-or-treat or some scary movie. When Martin Bucer is mentioned, people usually have a blank expression on their faces, for it is obvious they have no idea who he was. Many of them who are polite enough to ask me about my work on the book soon discover that they have learned far more about Martin Bucer than they ever intended to hear. I have found it very difficult to inform people of the significance of his life in a few minutes of explanation; they need the whole story.

Roman Catholics need to hear the story of the Protestant leader who, until the emperor put a definite end to his efforts, continued to work tirelessly to establish a basis for reunification. His attitude toward Catholics was far from condemning, although he had contempt for the abuses of the leadership of the Roman Church and its traditions that developed into what he called "superstitions". Catholics will find his overall attitude and efforts for unity encouraging, especially in these days when Catholics and Protestants are making serious efforts to rediscover common ground.

Reformed Christians need to be aware that John Calvin was not the primary architect of the Reformed faith, but rather Bucer's protégé. And that comment is written with no discredit to the genius and significant contributions of Calvin. Reformed people need to understand the tremendous contributions made by Bucer in the formation of the doctrines, points of emphasis, organization, liturgy, and overall approach to theology that came to be known as Reformed. To call him the father of the Reformed faith is not at all an exaggeration, although he certainly lacked the ability to systematize and to express doctrine in the succinct way that Calvin did.

Non-Reformed Christians, those who may call themselves, or be called, Arminians, or those who may find themselves even more distant to the doctrines of the Reformation, need to know Bucer and appreciate his passion for unity and his willingness to consider what any group of Christian believers had to offer. He was impressed by the piety of the Moravian Brethren and even of the Anabaptists. And even though he strongly disagreed with the latter, he was willing to listen to what they had to say about personal faith and piety.

In a way, Bucer is representative of all Christians, as he drew on several sources for his own beliefs and encompassed generally that which was of Christ, rather than of a specific group. Bucer borrowed from Erasmus an influence on piety and learning, a need to bring about reform in Christian living and to end the abuses of corrupt church leadership. As a one-time Dominican monk, Bucer was influenced by Thomas Aquinas to visualize theology in its widest terms and to seek documentation and authority for beliefs. And Bucer was certainly influenced by Martin Luther to embrace salvation by grace through faith and to affirm the final authority of Holy Scripture.

In a day when concern for our lack of piety and weak Christian commitment, for church unity, and better communication among the saints is awakening anew, and in a time when there is increasing awareness that we do have problems in these areas, and that the church needs to face what Christ is really about and what the church should really be, Bucer's life and teaching become increasingly relevant.

In recent years there has been considerable work done in Bucer studies, and I have tried to avail myself of the literature. However, there is no recent biography that incorporates recent scholarship, the only English biography of significance having been written by Hastings Eells in 1931. I have tried to tell the story of Bucer's life, aided greatly by Eell's book, although it is rather tedious for readers today, and to include thoughts that have been supplied by a host of competent Bucer scholars who have focused on specific areas of his work. Bucer's *Opera Omnia*, partly in Latin and partly in old German, is extremely lengthy, but I have consulted it, though will freely admit that I have not translated all of it. To do so would require so much time that this book would never have been written, but the work is available to be consulted by the serious student. My objective is to reach the literate Christian public, not necessarily the scholars of church history, because it is the general Christian public who truly need to hear this story.

I dedicate it to the glory of God with the sincere prayer that the information that follows may not only be interesting and informative, but truly a blessing to the reader and an encouragement for him or her to pursue matters of the faith, doctrine, the disciplined life, the way of love, and unity without compromise, and certainly to pursue the absolutely wonderful joy of our salvation!

Soli Deo Gloria

David Lawrence

Chapter 1

The World of Martin Bucer

The Protestant Reformation did not burst into the context of Christian history as a self-contained phenomenon like aliens invading from outer space. It came as a result of events that had developed over a long period of time. In one sense it was inevitable; in another, it was the result of the confluence of key persons and events that were unique to the time. The story of the Reformation and its great leaders cannot be told without placing it in the flow of a story that began centuries earlier.

The early church was not the pristine pattern for emulation that we would like to believe it was. Confusion, division, and constant persecution characterized those beginning times. After the age of the apostles who planted churches and wrote the letters, prophecies, biographies, and histories that became the New Testament, leadership passed to well-educated former pagans, most of whom had literary and political training, and now as Christians, wrote to the scattered churches to encourage order and discipline. These writers were known as the *Fathers*, who, claiming no inherent authority but citing copiously from New Testament Scriptures, wrote passionately and persistently to Christians to endure persecution, maintain moral order, and respect the leadership of the local church, which consisted of either a board of elders or a single bishop. Fathers in the West traditionally condemned or discouraged study of Greek philosophy and stressed strict morality and church authority. Eastern Fathers reflected the mystical mind of their milieu and often tried to harmonize philosophy and the Christian faith, tending to deal with the more spiritual and esoteric aspects of the faith. Neither set concentrated on what we might call "systematic theology," for there were more pressing needs.

After the conversion of Constantine in 312 and the end of persecution, Christians had the leisure and opportunity for the first time to turn to definition of doctrine. And by this time, Christians felt the need for understanding the workings of their salvation. Thus, the Fathers of this period, known as *Post-Nicene*, turned their attention to the development of a systematic theology. The term *Ante-Nicene* indicates that they preceded in time the first ecumenical council held at Nicea in 325 and *Post-Nicene* to those who came after 325, which certainly called to attention the need of definition of true doctrine. An elder from Libya by the name of Arius challenged the Trinity by citing Psalm 2 to prove that there was a time when the Son was not. A scholar by the name of Athanasius rose to the occasion and capably defined and defended the doctrine of the Trinity, leading eventually to the formation of the Nicene Creed, after the second ecumenical council at Constantinople in 381.

It would seem that challenges to Christian belief, what orthodox Christian thought would call *heresy*, was the catalyst that occasioned definition of doctrine. When Pelagius, a British monk living in Italy, feared that Augustine's beliefs as expressed in his *Confessions,* that God must grant that which he commands us to do, would lead to loose living, he developed a doctrine that to this day bears his name. Pelagius taught that God would never command that which man lacks the ability to perform, thus the doctrine of original sin could not be true, for to believe in the Fall would be to believe that man lost his moral ability as a result of another's sin. Pelagius taught that Adam's sin affected only Adam, that man is born in a neutral state with total free will, and that his salvation depends on his choice and performance of good over evil. His was a works-based salvation where grace was nebulous if not unnecessary.

Augustine, bishop of Hippo and author of the autobiography that incensed Pelagius, responded. He had been requested by a Christian Roman official to write an apology of Christianity that would answer the charges of pagans that ceasing sacrifices to the old deities had infuriated the gods so that they brought about the sacking of Rome by the Visigoths in 410. Augustine answered both challenges in his monumental work *City of God.*[1] It was the act of a sovereign God that caused the sacking of Rome, as God carried out his eternal purpose to remove the City of Man and replace it with the City of God. And salvation within the City of God is a matter of sovereign grace, not works. Man's will is fallen as a result of

---

[1] Augustine, however, also wrote a specific denunciation of Pelagius' doctrines in a separate work.

Adam's transgression, man has come under condemnation, and he lacks the ability to come to God unless God restores his will. This God will do for his elect, and he will give them the ability to persevere to eternal life. With the work of Augustine, the Church of Christ had a theology, a soteriology, based on the New Testament and especially the work of Paul. The theology was clear, simple, and straightforward. We are saved by grace through faith. Original sin, predestination, the perseverance of the saints, the sovereignty of God, and the authority of Holy Scriptures were established, particularly in the Western Church, as the statement of Christian faith.

Augustinian theology was accepted as the norm for the next five centuries without serious question. Most of the missionaries and scholars of the Middle Ages not only accepted Augustine's thinking, but often made advances on it. For instance, Anselm of Canterbury furthered Augustinian thought on the nature of the atonement, pointing out in his *Cur Deus Homo?* That Christ died to satisfy the justice of God so that the elect of God could receive mercy and salvation from Him. Bernard of Clairvaux showed the aspect of God's love as the motivating factor, and brought many of Jesus' teachings on sovereign grace to bear alongside with the Pauline theology developed by Augustine. His lectures on the Song of Solomon come as close to a systematic theology as Bernard would produce.[2]

However, there were some changes introduced that did not build on the Augustinian foundation but rather began to erode it. John Cassian posited a concept that came to be known as *Semi-Pelagianism.* Contemporary with Augustine, he did not presume to deny the truths Augustine set forth regarding the fall and the necessity of supernatural grace in salvation. However, Cassian argued that, although the will of man was fallen, God preserved the capacity within the fallen will to choose to come to Christ. This concept logically meant that salvation was ultimately the decision of the human will and thus based on human performance. Though many of the theologians in the universities rejected Semi-Pelagianism, it was a convenient doctrine for the developing papacy

---

[2] J. David Lawrence, "Medieval Refinements in Augustinian Theology: Scholastic Foundations of the Reformation," *Fides et Historia,* XXXIII:2, Summer/Fall 2001.

to embrace, for it enabled them to make demands on the people which carried the weight of salvation in their performance.

Judging the motivations of people is a dangerous and difficult task. It is easy to note that Semi-Pelagianism gave the popes power over the souls of the people, for they could make demands and threaten eternal punishment if they were disobeyed. Thus, we conclude that the popes were driven by a lust for power and they accepted an interpretation of Christianity that facilitated that lust. However, the pope who made the first small departure from Augustinianism in the direction of Semi-Pelagianism, was hardly driven by a lust for power. That pope was Gregory I (590-604), and in this humble Christian there are no evidences of anything but the highest motives. Gregory was unwilling even to be called pope and disdained honors and titles. He was passionately concerned about the conversion of English children whom he saw in the slave market, and sent missionaries to that island to convert the populace. He worked very hard to inculcate high moral standards in clergy and people. We may reasonably conclude that Gregory's emphasis on works and downplaying of grace was in a sincere effort to enhance morality, as it was for Pelagius. But Gregory set in motion a trend that was followed in increasing measure by successive popes. And successive popes were not as humble and Christ-like as Gregory and tended to exploit the developing works system to full advantage.

The next significant pope of the early Middle Ages was Nicholas I (856-867) who enunciated the concept that the pope had the right to rule the secular powers, that church always prevailed over state, priests over kings, and the religious over the worldly. Nicholas did not live long enough to consolidate the political strength he had assumed in the West, and the Roman senate regained control over and dominated the papacy for the duration of the ninth century. Then the rising German Empire, correctly understanding the papacy as a rival, gained control of papal appointments and quite deliberately selected the most immoral, lazy, and profligate men they could find to the Holy See. Bill Austin has called this period of the papacy the "pornocracy."[3]

---

[3] Bill R. Austin, *Austin's Topical History of Christianity* (Wheaton, IL: Tyndale House Publishers, Inc., 1983), p. 148.

With the advent of the new millennium came changes in the basic structure of Medieval civilization, and the papacy was no exception. Leaders came to the fore, like Hildebrand, who became Pope Gregory VII, Peter Damian, Bruno of Joul (Pope Leo IX), and Humbert, products of the Cluny monastic reform movement, committed to creating a strong papacy capable of resisting the German Empire, and determined to enact fundamental reforms in the Church. They moved quickly to wrest the election of popes from other bodies who controlled it in the past such as the Roman senate and the German emperor, and created the College of Cardinals, the Papal Curia, to select popes. In essence, the ancient Roman curia (Senate) that had assumed the prerogative in the early days of the papacy was now restructured as the *Papal* Curia, its members appointed by the pope himself.

The movement succeeded marvelously. The papacy emerged into the High Middle Ages of the twelfth century well-organized and disciplined and ready to take on any challengers, including both the German Empire, now claiming to be the true successor to Rome and renaming itself in 1155 as the Holy Roman Empire, and the Byzantine Empire, the legitimate successor to Rome, who looked to the emperor, not the pope, as the head of the church. The real architect of the policy was Hildebrand who reigned as Gregory VII from 1073-1085, although he had been the power behind the throne for a quarter century. His *Dictatus Papae* made absolutely clear that only the pope could select bishops, only the pope could depose emperors, and that the pope was the supreme political power in Christendom. Although rejected by the kings of Europe and the two rival emperors, Gregory was able to force the German emperor Henry IV to stand as a penitent outside his lodgings at Canossa for three days beginning to be pardoned, for Gregory held enough power to call a council of German nobles to depose the rebellious emperor. Although Gregory failed to force the conqueror of Anglo-Saxon England, William I, to bow to his will and swear fealty to the pope, and he died in exile in Salerno after the Germans sacked Rome in 1054, Gregory left behind a strong paper structure that could not be resisted except by the strongest secular rulers.

The Medieval papacy reached its political apex of power in the reign of Innocent III (1198-1216) who was able to name two

German emperors, force King John of England to surrender his realm as a fief to the pope, lead an inquisition against heretics in the south of France, call two crusades, invoke the interdict fifty-three times, and excommunicate anyone who opposed his will. His greatest triumph came in 1215 when the Fourth Lateran Council approved all his proposals, including the defining of the seven sacraments, transubstantiation, and a number of other doctrines that developed within the context of Medieval Christianity and have come to be known as the distinctively Catholic dogmas. The political factor present in the development of these distinctive doctrines is undeniable at this point. And it is these doctrines that came to be the nemesis of the great, universal Latin Church.

The outstanding theologians of the Medieval universities, especially Paris, continued to base their reasoning on Augustinian doctrines; however, the concept of sacraments was especially useful to the hierarchy, and they clung to definitions that gave them power over the people. As finally defined at Fourth Lateran, and later upheld by the Council of Trent, the sacraments became channels of grace. Assuredly, man is saved by grace alone, and God has his elect. The Fall corrupted man beyond his ability to recover, so that he is dependent on God's mercy for salvation. However, God appointed the Church as the guardian of truth and gave to the Church the power of administering God's grace. The seven sacraments became the channels through which saving grace flowed to the people. The clergy, who alone had the power to administer the sacraments, controlled them. Each sacrament required *form* (that which was said by the administering clergy), and *matter* (that which is done), and when properly applied, the result was forgiveness of sins. Baptism, properly administered, removed original sin, but not the sins of daily life. Forgiveness could be obtained through the Eucharist, another of the sacraments, and Extreme Unction just prior to death. But for the ongoing daily sins the sacrament of *Penance* was of the utmost importance. In order for sins to be remitted, the sinning Christian must confess the sin, have a contrite heart, be absolved by a priest, and do a work of atonement for that sin. The unlikelihood that all four of these conditions could be adequately met in every sin in a person's life removed any possibility of real assurance of salvation.

Transubstantiation was the concept that in the Eucharist the bread and wine were changed into the literal body and blood of Christ when the priest elevated the host and said the words *"Hoc est Corpus meum."* Additionally, only the bread was distributed to the laity, the cup being reserved for the clergy. The area of the altar in a church became sacred territory that only priests could enter, separated from the area where the congregation gathered in front of an altar rail. Every refinement of sacramental theology reinforced the separation of clergy from laity and the consequent dependence of the latter on the former for salvation.

However, there were other significant theological developments in the twelfth and early thirteenth centuries aside from sacramental theology and the political power of the hierarchy. The crusades that began in the late eleventh century had re-opened trade with the Middle East, and one item of great interest to the scholars of Western Europe was the availability of ancient manuscripts. The Islamic conquest of the seventh century meant that many of the great libraries of antiquity were in the hands of Muslims, and they made good use of them. Islamic scholarship led the world in the early Middle Ages, whereas the Christians, during their time of control of the Near East, disdained most of them as pagan and unworthy of Christian study. Now they fell into the hands of a more receptive Christian audience, centuries removed from pagan Rome and Athens, with a growing intellectual curiosity about ancient cultures. It was a time of nascent humanism that would later flower in Italy, but no doubt, it had its roots in the twelve century Renaissance. Interest in academic subjects was broad in spectrum, but one ancient scholar in particular became an object of renewed interest with scholars in the West, the pagan Aristotle.

Aristotle, with his concepts of relative truth, his denials of absolutes, and his inductive approach to ethics and knowledge, had long been regarded as dangerous for Christian minds. Augustine had praised the philosopher Plato as being closest to Christian truth, for Plato began with the assumption of God as the embodiment of absolute truth which flowed from him as forms. Although Augustine was careful to point out Plato's errors, such as the eternality of matter, he accepted his basic framework of thought, and it had become the norm for Christians from that time into the twelfth century. However, now a challenge appeared in the re-emergence of Aristotle from the Islamic world. At the same time, the Muslim scholar Averroës from Cordoba published his commentaries on Aristotle that greatly advanced Aristotelian studies in the West. Aristotelianism found its champion in the young teacher at the University of Paris, Peter Abelard. He advanced Aristotle's beliefs that all learning is beneficial, but all learning, including that of God, is based on man's examining evidence, specifically the particulars, and reaching a conclusion. Abelard was opposed by the equally brilliant, if not somewhat mystical, Bernard of Clairvaux, who saw the consequences of Abelard's reasoning and declared that Abelard would make faith merely an opinion, not a certitude.

The intellectual leadership of the Church was now divided between those who held to the old, Augustinian-Platonic idea of universal truth (realists), and those who accepted the Aristotelian-Averroean-Abelardian concepts of relative truth (nominalists). To reaffirm Augustine would imply that man cannot use his reason, nor that he could legitimately explore the broad spectrum of scientific knowledge, but to adopt the Aristotelian platform would deny the certainty of the Christian faith and allow every man to decide for himself what truth was, or if truth even existed or not. A young Italian Dominican monk by the name of Thomas Aquinas took it upon himself to resolve the dilemma, and he did so by the production of a monumental work, unquestionably one of the greatest systematic theological contributions ever written, his *Summa Theologica.*

Aquinas was determined to arrive at the conclusions of Augustine by the methods of Aristotle, that is, to use empirical evidence and human reason to postulate absolute truth. He did agree that there were limits to reason, for it could go only so far, and faith must take over where reason leaves off. His five reasons to believe in God provide excellent examples of his use of observation of material data to reach the conclusion that an invisible Deity exists and has created and now rules the universe. Aquinas saved the Christian religion from the threat of subjective empirical scientific investigation and from the threat of subjective human reason. His conclusions come back again and again to Scripture and are in line with Augustine's; however, in the process he examines every possibility and analyzes it. His methodology was that typical to the Medieval university, as it was to the ancient Greeks, especially Plato, that of *dialectic,* where one argument is presented as a *thesis,* its opposite stated as an *antithesis,* and through analysis a new position is achieved that embodies aspects of both, presumably closer to absolute reality, a *synthesis.*

As significant and worthy as Aquinas' work was, there were some dismal aspects for Christians. The Church took a long while before it finally accepted Thomistic theology as the standard for the church, and after that, the excitement of debate ended, and theologians were expected simply to accept Thomism. Scholasticism, the pursuit of truth in the university setting, which had been invigorating and exciting for students prior to Thomas' time, now became dull and rote. Students love debate and lively discussion, not imbibing unquestionably the conclusions of another. Their disdain for post-Thomas scholasticism was a factor in their interest in new ideas, particularly those coming from Italy in the fourteenth century.

The fact that Scholasticism became boring was only one factor. The delicate reasoning of Thomas in the *Summa* was difficult and tedious to follow, and it was dreadfully cold and impersonal. People longed for expressions of God's love, for the assurance of their salvation, for some kind of personal experience in religion that Thomism lacked with its cold, formal, scholarly approach to faith. All these intellectual concerns were compounded by external events in the fourteenth century that sent people in new directions, looking for new meaning in life and in God. The fourteenth century, an absolutely incredible time, brought down the Medieval world with its axioms of "Order, Authority, and Tradition," with its assumption that "God's in his heaven, all's right with the world," for the Bubonic Plague struck with a force in the mid century and from one third to one half of Europe's population was exterminated. Towns were ruined; some disappeared. The labor force was gone. A cathedral in Siena was under construction that would be the largest church in the world. The laborers died, and the church is unfinished to this day. Clergy either died from the plague or fled its victims in horror, and the people wondered where the Church was when they needed it. Without a priest to administer last rites, how could they face God in judgment?

The century brought also a terrible war between England and France that lasted over a century and devastated both countries, especially France. The nobility of France lay dead and bleeding at Crecy in 1346, ending forever Medieval knightly warfare. The English were embroiled in their own civil war during and after the conflict with France that decimated their own nobility. The war and its aftermath brought on uprisings of peasants against the nobility, something unheard of in the Middle Ages. Sometimes, as in the uprising in England in 1381, these had religious, even apocalyptic, overtones. All these events were combining rapidly to produce a feeling of anti-clericalism and suspicion of the authority and effectiveness of the Church, and there were those who even questioned if Rome and its Pope should have authority over the Christians of the world.

The Church had its own problems in this dark century. It had hardly begun when the King of France, Philip IV, sent his representative, Guillaume Nogaret, to arrest Pope Boniface VIII at his retreat at Anagny. Boniface was oblivious to the eroding of the papacy's temporal power since the days of Innocent III. What he did not realize was that in the titanic struggle between popes and German emperors, both sides had exhausted themselves. That conflict had reached its apex in the thirteenth century under the German emperor Frederick II. Frederick had been the ward of Innocent III, and Innocent named him as emperor to succeed his father, Henry VI, after a German interregnum civil war and the brief reign of another appointee of Innocent, Otto IV. Frederick was, however, the inveterate enemy of the papacy, and struggled against two of Innocent's successors, Gregory IX and Innocent IV. When Frederick died in 1250, the pope gave Sicily, the German capital since the days of Henry VI, to the French count of Anjou, Charles. Germany sank into a long interregnum from 1254 to 1273 with no ruler, until Rudolph of Hapsburg was elected, but the halcyon days when Germany could advance a meaningful claim to being the heir of the universal Roman Empire were over. When the papacy was unable to make good its establishment of the French in control of Sicily, and the Sicilians arose in revolt in 1282 and drove out the

French, it was apparent that neither could the pope. Boniface came to realize the real consequences of the Sicilian Vespers when he tried to prevent the kings of the rising and recovering national states of England and France from taxing the clergy. He was to be arrested and brought to France. However, he resisted, a scuffle ensued, the pope was struck, and soon died, not so much from injury but from humiliation. The papacy was then moved to France, and the days of the "Babylonian Captivity of the Church" at Avignon began.

With the popes in France, under the nose of the French king, and with all popes during that seventy-year period being French, the pope posed no political threat to France, or to any other power. The popes were consumed with raising money to offset the loss of revenues that the disruption of papal political control caused, and over two hundred new church taxes emanated from Avignon. But there were those, like Catherine of Siena, who believed the French exile was wrong and wanted the papacy back in Rome. When one of the popes died in Rome trying to secure the return, the Italian cardinals took the event as a sign that the papacy had returned to Rome, and they promptly met and elected an Italian pope and established him in Rome. The French cardinals retaliated by electing a French pope for Avignon, and the Church now had two popes. It was one body with two heads, a spiritual monstrosity. All knew it was untenable, but no one knew what to do about it, until the Church turned to its old answer for problems: the convening of a council. Several councils followed at Pisa, Constance, Basel, Florence, Ferrara, and other places. When the council elected a pope, neither the Italian pope nor the French pope was willing to step down, and now the Church had three popes! Finally, in 1415, after a fiasco with a completely corrupt council pope, John XXIII, newly elected and very capable council appointee Martin V was established in Rome as the one and only pope, and a second generation of rival popes resigned. The Great Schism that had bewildered, confused, and disgusted Christians all over Europe was over, but left in its wake additional anti-clerical sentiment and disillusionment with the Church's ability to oversee the souls of its people.

Now the question had to be addressed as to who had sovereign authority in the church: council or pope. Councils had been used in the past, but in the days of strong papal authority, such as Innocent

III and Fourth Lateran, they were the tools of the papal monarch. Now the councils had selected a pope, and if they could select popes, then they would be the ultimate authority in the Church. Thus, even popes who supported the council earlier had to turn on them and reassert papal supremacy. The Conciliar Movement itself contributed to the rising anti-clerical sentiment and inspired scholars such as Marsilio of Padua, writing in his *Defensor Pacis,* to suggest that Christians no longer needed a pope.

When Martin and his successor popes returned to Rome, they found it a very different place from what they had left seventy years before. In the interim strong Italian states arose that now challenged the very survival of the pope's own territories. The popes had to this point been able to manage the Patrimony of St. Peter, a section of mid-Italy given by the French duke Pepin III in 754 to the papacy in return for being named as the first Carolingian monarch of France. These lands had previously been invaded by the Lombards who were driven out by the French in 751, and then gladly given to the papacy, cementing a French-papal alliance. But the rest of Italy was weak during the middle ages and never participated fully in the great Medieval civilization of the north of Europe. However, Italians had been gradually drawn into maritime trade and were able to take advantage of loss of trade routes by the old Islamic Empire that eventually collapsed completely on the invasion of the Turks in 1055, and by the increasingly diminishing once-mighty Eastern Roman or Byzantine Empire, itself defeated in Anatolia by Turks in 1071 and losing territory continually over the next four hundred years until extinguished by the Ottomans in 1453. It was the states of Genoa, Pisa, Florence, Milan, Venice, Siena, and others who benefited from the misfortune of the decline of these two great trading empires. They had accumulated much wealth, and with their money hired mercenary armies to defend their lands, and often to invade their neighbors. Now the Papal States were vulnerable, and the pope was forced to defend his land by military force. No longer aspiring to be the sovereign of all Christendom, he was struggling to be the lord of his own territories in Italy!

Yet another circumstance was different. As a result of the trade in which Italians were heavily involved, manuscripts and art works from the Near East flowed into Italy. Many of these were of ancient

Roman and Greek origin, and the Italians were awakened to the fact that these ancient Romans were their ancestors. Roman ruins all around them now acquired great meaning. With their money they could buy art treasures and manuscripts, hire translators and teachers, and recover the learning of their ancestors. They could restore their heritage! The Italian Renaissance was born, and it became an obsession with upper class wealthy Italians. The purpose of the Renaissance was to learn, through a study of writings from the ancient world, great principles that would enhance their own lives. It was a moral purpose, but it was also outside of Christianity, and assumed that the ancient Romans, and later Greeks, had understanding of a good life that was lost to the Christians. While it was not an attempt to repudiate Christianity, it involved use of a pagan culture and its ideas, and it was clearly more secular. The popes who returned to Italy found themselves immersed in a society passionate about the rebirth of ancient civilization, and soon they became leaders of the movement. Pope Nicholas V established the Vatican Library that became a repository of ancient manuscripts and art treasures, and Pope Sixtus IV built the Sistine Chapel that became a showplace of Renaissance art. By 1492 with the accession of Pope Alexander VI, the Church was governed by Renaissance popes who were completely committed to the Renaissance and to the defense of their states. We then find that strange paradox, that supreme irony, known as *the total secularization of the papacy!*

The scandals of the Church, the failure of its leadership, the complexity and impersonal nature of Thomism, rising anti-clericalism for a number of reasons, and the sincere Christian impulses of so many Europeans, led to new expressions of religious sentiment. Some of these expressions were within the bounds of what the Church considered acceptable, some were not, but all were suspect by Rome.

One of these expressions, very suspect but never proven unorthodox, was *mysticism.* Mysticism by definition, in all philosophies and religions, is an attempt to experience a personal relationship with God through some kind of vehicle. Plato was a mystic, but so were Bernard of Clairvaux, St. Theresa of Avila, St. John of the Cross, and Ignatius Loyola. However, a new kind of mysticism developed, spawned by concerns over the lack of spiritual leadership from Rome and nurtured in a more sincerely Christian area along the Rhine River and in the Low Countries. This mysticism advocated discipleship, following Christ in a personal way, and thereby finding a union with God. It came to be known by the generic term of *devotio moderna*, the new devotion. Its leaders were men like John Tauler, Meister Eckhard, and Thomas à Kempis. Meister Eckhard filled his sermons with passionate appeals to follow Christ and develop the character of Christ. He stressed that in so doing, we can have fellowship with Christ. But fellowship is communion, joint participation, and according to the Church's defined theology, the Communion is the Eucharist, a sacrament dispensed by the clergy. Although Meister Eckhard never openly denounced Rome or its system, he by-passed it, ignored it, and proffered a way to God that did not specifically name the Church. His teaching was certainly implicit heresy, and the Church brought twenty-six counts of heresy against him, which they subsequently dropped. He was no explicit heretic, and explicit heresy was needed for conviction. But these mystics fell under the close scrutiny of Rome. Thomas á Kempis was the author of the well-known work *On the Imitation of Christ*, and became the primary exponent of the *devotio moderna*. In the Low Countries Gerhard Groote established a lay order to educate young people in the way of Christ, the Brethren of the Common Life.

Another expression of piety was what may be called Late Medieval Nominalism, of which William of Occam was the leading exponent. Although Nominalists never assembled a coherent system as such, Occam's thrust was to separate what God has done from what God has not done: God's ordained power from God's absolute power. His efforts gave rise to what has been called "Occam's razor," as he stripped away the speculative and superfluous and concerned himself with what we can know of a certainty. God's creation can be known, but so can the Bible, for it belongs to the realm of God's ordained power. Occam zealously guarded the concept that God, not man, is sovereign over creation, but so much so that he eschewed any kind of interpretation that would make God a slave to the system. Thus Occam taught that God *could* accept someone based on good works, whereas Thomistic theology taught that God gave the habit of grace to man, and with that grace he performed good works. Occam thus came dangerously close to a Pelagian view. While Reformers like Luther, who read his works, appreciated his firm assertion of the sovereignty of God, they were quite suspicious of a Pelagian concept of earning grace by good works.

In addition to Mysticism and Nominalism, this fertile age produced another paradox in *Christian Humanism.* The ideas of the Christian humanists were clearly imported from Italian humanism of the Renaissance and a part of the general phenomenon known as the Northern Renaissance. As Italian ideas spread across the Alps, they encountered a naturally more Christian atmosphere, and of necessity they were adapted to that environment. But these ideas also intersected with the *devotio moderna,* and the result was a new movement that bore characteristics of both. From Italy these scholars imported the concept of "back to the sources" (*ad fontes*), using primary sources to create a dialogue with the author. They also had a moral end in view. However, with the Italians, that morality was more involved with proper etiquette and social behavior, while with the Northerners it was clearly the inculcation of Christian moral values and living the Christian way of life. In that regard it was certainly akin to the goal of the mystics of the *devotio moderna.* Thus these scholars used the Bible and the Fathers as their primary sources, taught them, urged their personal study, with a goal of learning Christ and his way. Yet the objective was the benefit of man more than the glory of God. It assumed that man was naturally good, in contradistinction to traditional Catholic views, and that his basic problem was ignorance. That ignorance could be corrected by knowledge, of which the Bible was the core in the curriculum, but involving the study of the classics, law, philosophy, science, and the whole gamut of knowledge. Ideas of sin, satisfaction of the justice of God, and eternal judgment were not relevant to the Christian humanists. God was seen as a perfect man; man as God's perfect creation.

The Christian humanist movement was suspect from its inception. The universities, all under Church control, refused to accommodate it. However, humanist students formed their own little extra-curricular study groups, and created underground movements in most major universities. Many students preferred the lively discussions of the humanist groups to the boring Scholastic lectures heard in class. Some of the Christian humanists were able to infiltrate the universities and have an influence. Jacques LeFévre d'Etaples taught the Bible directly at the University of Paris, and John Colet did so at Oxford. They saw the Bible as a primary source, and students who heard Christ and the apostles speak directly from the Word, not through commentaries and lectures filled with analogies and interpretations, would learn to live like Christ. A cardinal of the Church in Spain, Cardinal Ximines, became a humanist and founded the University of Alcala along humanist lines. Ximines also produced the Complutensian Polyglot translation of the Bible, an excellent work. Johann Reuchlin taught Hebrew in Köln, although the Church tried him for heresy on the basis that the study of Hebrew might cause a young Christian to convert to Judaism. Again, charges were dropped after the publication of a satirical pamphlet called *Letters of Obscure Men* setting forth the Roman Church as the champion of ignorance. But Christian humanists were now supremely suspect.

In this context arose the greatest of all Christian humanists, Erasmus of Rotterdam, the "Prince of Humanists." Erasmus, orphaned in his youth and brought up in an Augustinian monastery, soon developed an appetite for the classics. At the University of Paris he fell in with several humanist students and was even introduced to Neoplatonism, which was sweeping Italy and now entering the north. However, during his stay at Paris he made a trip to England that changed his life. He was invited there by William Blount, Lord Mountjoy, whom he met at Paris. William introduced him to his friends, a circle of humanist scholars meeting in the home of Thomas More at Chelsea in London. There he met, in addition to More, John Colet, William Grocyn, Thomas Linacre, and Prince Henry, the future King Henry VIII, who at this point in his life was committed to Christian humanism. Their program of reform of the Church by teaching its people the Bible and the whole of knowledge was instantly appealing to Erasmus. His scholarship now had a purpose. He would have every plowboy to read the scriptures in his own language so that he could learn to follow Christ. Erasmus developed what he called the *philosophia Christi,* the philosophy of Christ, meaning that the Christian way, the spiritual way, was simply the best way to live. The rest of his life was given to prolific writing of Christian texts, critical editions of Christian works, satires to point out the corruption of the church, and some classical works. Interestingly, his first work that gained him fame as a writer, was a distinctly secular and classical one, *The Agadia,* a book of quotable quotes from the classical authors which he revised and enlarged several times. It was Erasmus who gave the world the 1516 Greek New Testament text that became the basis both of Martin Luther's German Bible and the King James English Bible of 1611. Erasmus wrote the famous satire *Praise of Folly (Encomium Moriae),* as a house present to Thomas More. Later he was afraid it would offend Pope Leo X whose endorsement for his Greek text was needed. The book is still popular, and is a good evidence of the fact that Christian humanists produced much more scathing rebukes and exposés of clerical corruption than the Reformers ever did. But again, their purpose was *moral* rather than *redemptive*, and they reacted against any kind of corruption and immorality as barbaric and uncivilized.

Erasmus also produced *The Enchiridion Militis Christiani (Handbook of the Christian Soldier),* written on the request of a lady whose husband was abusive to her and did not conduct himself in a Christian manner. This book set forth in straightforward terms the superiority of the spiritual to the physical, of the Christian life to the worldly way. Erasmus went on to produce a critical edition of most of the Fathers, works advocating pacifism, commentaries and paraphrases on the Bible, statements of faith, and unceasing attacks on the ignorance and worldliness of the clergy. He became the most popular and sought-after of all writers. He was the confidant of princes, kings, emperors, popes, and the leading intellectuals of Europe. Certainly he was the most respected and influential man of his time, and his influence was felt mightily across the continent. However, his program was doomed to failure because it was acceptable neither to the old Church, now threatened from many directions, nor to the Reformers who could not accept the ideas of the goodness of man or morality as the supreme end of his existence. Erasmus finally bemoaned that he was a heretic to both camps; however, his influence on the rising Reformation cannot be overstated, as we have occasion to discuss later.

Finally, the reactions to the Church and search for a better way drive some totally outside accepted Catholicism. The line between heresy and orthodoxy was always crossed when one denied the authority of the Church itself. John Wyclif, professor at Oxford, was willing to do just that. Protected by the Duke of Lancaster, John of Gaunt, Wyclif was able to teach freely at Oxford University. In view of the confusion in the leadership of the Roman Church, Wyclif came to accept that the Scriptures alone were authority for the universal church, which he no longer equated with Rome. All the earth belongs to God, not to popes, emperors, or kings. He taught that we all hold ultimately from one sovereign Lord. Salvation, as well as the earth, is his domain, and it is based on his decree. God has his elect, chosen by grace, not those defined and approved by Rome. Thus Wyclif dismissed the pope, the sacraments, and church authority and reaffirmed an Augustinian theology of salvation by grace according to God's elective decree. Because the queen was from Bohemia, Jerome of Prague had occasion to hear Wyclif, accepted his teaching, and returned to inform Prague's greatest preacher, John Hus. Hus accepted these doctrines of grace and taught them at Bethlehem Chapel at Charles University in Prague. However, he had no such protector as Wyclif, for the King of Bohemia was a Hapsburg, linked to the emperor. Hus was condemned by the Council of Constance even though the emperor Sigismund had guaranteed him safe conduct, and was burned at the stake in 1415.

A century later a young student at the University of Erfurt in Germany, journeying back to campus and caught in a summer thunderstorm, was nearly killed by a lightning strike near him. This young man, Martin Luther, asked for protection from St. Anne, and promised if saved from the storm, to take holy orders and to become a monk. He kept his vow, entered the Augustinian monastery at Erfurt, the same order Erasmus joined, and, much to the dismay of his father, committed himself to rigorous monastic obedience and discipline. When these labors failed to produce peace in his heart, when even a trip to Holy Rome did not assuage his fears, his superiors sought to keep him so busy with his studies that he would have no time to worry about whether he was saved or not. Luther pursued the doctorate, and was given a position in the theology department of the new Wittenberg University established by Elector Frederick III of Saxony. But even here, Luther did not find the love of God. Rather, he said he hated God, because God hated him and tormented his soul. He knew God was holy, and he knew he was a sinner, and although he confessed every sin he could think of, he never felt forgiven. He had somehow not met the conditions of the sacrament of penance.

The solution for Luther came from his academic studies. He was preparing his notes for an upcoming class on the Pauline epistles, of which Romans would be the first. As he read a passage that he had read many times before, something clicked in his mind that he had overlooked. For one thing, he noticed the Greek word for *righteousness*, and he had been accustomed to reading Latin. Thus the humanist's insistence on reading the Bible in its original languages was a major factor in the Reformation, for Luther saw in Romans 1:17 that the righteousness revealed from heaven in the gospel is in fact an alien righteousness, it is a legal declaration of righteousness, according to the meaning of the Greek word. The Latin word *iustitia* suggests a personal righteousness, one that Luther had come by experience to know was beyond him. But the righteousness of which Paul writes is God's own righteousness, the righteousness of Christ, with which we are clothed when we trust in Christ; it is by faith that the just, those declared righteous, shall live. When Luther saw the concept of imputed righteousness by faith alone, he said a gate was opened to Paradise for him. Luther was changed. He knew he was saved. He preached his new-found understanding to his students who accepted it joyfully, and the Reformation was born.

The world into which Martin Bucer was born in 1491 was this world: the world of the humanist renaissance, the printing press, and the awakening to Biblical teaching. It was not disconnected from a long series of events that went back to the cross, actually that went back to creation. It was clearly an exciting time, a time of discovery, or perhaps rediscovery, of truth. It was a time of interchange of ideas. The dissatisfaction with the Roman Church that fueled the inquiry into a better way was now beginning to have unexpected results. Ideas of the Humanists, the Nominalists, the Mystics, and the "Heretics" like Wyclif and Hus, could now be examined and appropriated where they fit into a new approach to Christianity. But above all, the leaders of this movement were fundamentally committed to the Scriptures alone as the authority for their beliefs, and their dream was the reforming of the Christian world into a truly Godly community that would bring glory to Him alone. This was the world of Martin Bucer, and he found his introduction into it in the humanist academy at Schlettstadt and his matriculation into it when he journeyed to Heidelberg in 1518 and sat in the audience as Dr. Martin Luther expounded the biblical doctrine of justification by faith alone. Then Bucer would also be forever changed.

Chapter II

From "Erasmian" to "Martinian":

The Conversion of Martin Bucer

The Youth of Martin Bucer

Children grew up quickly in early modern Europe; childhood was not necessarily a happy experience. Plague and poverty disrupted many a household. The childhood of Martin Bucer (German: Butzer) fell into this all too common category. Martin was born on November 11, 1491 and named for that day's patron saint. Probably the only child of a shoemaker,[4] Claus Butzer, and a midwife, Eva Butzer, he entered this world in the small but cultured town of Schlettstadt, today known as Selestat. Interestingly, his cradle has survived and still may be seen in Selestat. However, little else remains except some of his possessions and manuscripts in the humanist library there.

Bucer was eight years younger than Martin Luther and Ulrich Zwingli, but he was eighteen years older than John Calvin, who was later to become his protégé. Like Luther, he came from a household of pious parents, and like Erasmus, he found himself bereft of their love and guidance during his youth. The comparisons with these two people is appropriate, for Erasmus of Rotterdam and Martin Luther were the two people who, more than any others, had a deep influence on Bucer's life and beliefs.

Schlettstadt boasted a Latin school of very high quality, and young Martin was able to study under its able headmaster Jerome Gebweiler, who introduced him to Erasmian humanism, which made the deepest kind of impression on the boy. Actually, the little town of Schlettstadt had quite a reputation as a center of humanist studies that dated back about a hundred years. The school at Schlettstadt became known for quality humanistic education under its first

---

[4] Many sources indicate that Claus Butzer was a Küfer, a cooper (cf., Friedrich Wilhelm Bautz, *Biographisch-Bibliographisches Kirchenlexicon,* Verlag Traugott Bautz, Band 1, p. 1)

rector, Ludwig Drinngenberg who had been trained by the Brethren of the Common Life at Deventer, where Erasmus also studied. Jerome Gebweiler in turn was the pupil of Faber Stapulensis, and these two men brought to the small town of Schlettstadt a world of practical piety and education in letters.[5]   The town boasted a humanist library that had acquired valuable classical and humanist manuscripts from other libraries, enabling students to spend many happy and profitable hours poring over the volumes. Many of the medieval manuscripts contained beautiful illuminated capitals, and some of the humanist works included Latin exercise books. The city contained two beautiful churches, each making its own architectural statement, one Romanesque and one Gothic.[6]

Martin was a good student under Jerome Gebweiler, but he also became, like Luther, a proficient musician. The appreciation both men had for music would have dramatic impacts on the introduction and development of congregational singing in the Evangelical church. Young Martin also loved art and became a talented painter; as well he acquired quite an interest in French cuisine.[7]

Selestat today lies in France, but it retains much of its earlier Alsatian-German character, with some buildings that date back to the time of Bucer still standing. Because Bucer came from such a poor family, the house of his birth is long gone, but the humanistic library remains, and today houses an impressive collection, including some of Bucer's manuscripts. It was particularly thrilling to be walking through the town and look up and see the name and picture of Beatus Rhenanus, another humanist scholar attached to the humanistic center in Schlettstadt.

However, Bucer was not allowed to enjoy the educational benefits of Schlettstadt for long.   The plague struck Erasmus'

---

[5] Willem van't Spijker, *The Ecclesiastical Offices in the Thought of Martin Bucer,* tr. John Vriend and Lyle D. Bierma (Leiden: E.J. Brill, 1996), p. 7. See also T.W. Röhrich, "Die Schule in Schlettstadt im 15ten Jahrhundert," *Mittheilungen aus der Geschichite der evangelischen Kirche des Elsasses* (Paris: 1855), and E.-W.Kohls, *Die Schule bei Martin Butzer* (Heidelberg: 1963).

[6] Haines, Alsace Untour Diary, www.untours.com. The library and the churches still may be found in Selestat.

[7] Joshua Clark, "Martin Bucer: The Reformation's Own Chesterton" in *Chasing Hats Magazine,* (online), Nov. 2002.

household and carried off his parents, leaving him in the care of guardians, while Bucer's parents had to leave town because of financial needs, move to Strasbourg, and leave Martin in the care of his grandfather, Nicholas Butzer. The practice of grandparents taking over the rearing of their grandchildren is certainly not just a contemporary situation. However, that relationship is never an easy one, given the separation in ages. Bucer's grandfather was not one to show tenderness and affection; rather, he was disciplined and committed to work. Very early young Martin developed an interest in both religion and learning, but his grandfather was concerned only that the boy contributed to the needs of the family, and those needs were real indeed. Nicholas forced Martin to work to pay for his keep, allowing him no opportunity to pursue his education. It was Nicholas' unwillingness or inability to aid Martin in the furtherance of his studies that pointed the young Bucer to the fulfillment of his destiny and calling as a minister of Jesus Christ and scholar of his word.

In the summer of 2004 as my wife and I traveled by train from Strasbourg to Selestat and then back to Strasbourg, I looked out the train window at the gently rolling hills of the countryside and thought of the journey of Bucer's parents from their home to the "big city" of Strasbourg. It probably would have seemed a long way, not only because of the fact that walking alongside a cart with all one's earthly possessions is far slower than riding a French train today, even given the fact that it was a local that stopped at every town between Selestat and Strasbourg, but more especially because they were now separated from their son, not to see him again for several years.

Bucer the Dominican Monk and Erasmian Scholar

Erasmus was another young man passionately interested in learning, and when his guardians were faced with the problem of what to do with him, the situation for them was to enroll him in an Augustinian monastery. The church was the route to learning for young men and women who lacked financial resources, but neither Erasmus nor Bucer was interested in taking the vows. However, both did. In Erasmus' case the Augustinian monastery of Steyn in the Low Countries was a wonderful place to learn. The monks had an excellent library, filled with humanist books, and they encouraged learning. But Bucer, on the recommendation of his parents who believed that the Dominicans were the only order well grounded in true Catholic doctrine that opposed heresy, joined the Dominican monastery in Schlettstadt and found a very different situation from that of Erasmus. The monks lured him there with promises that he could pursue his interests in humanist studies. They told him that the Virgin herself had assured the order that no Dominican would ever go to hell, although he might have to spend some time in Purgatory.

However, after entering the Novitiate at the young age of fourteen in 1506,[8] Bucer found he had been misled. The monks put him through a terrifying experience designed to break his will and force him into submission. They did not allow him to continue his humanist studies, but took his classical Latin books away from him, and forced on him a steady diet of Thomism. Martin Bucer came to loathe Thomas Aquinas as a result of this experience.[9] However, the intense study in scholasticism was of great benefit to Bucer later when, as a leader of the Protestant Reformation, his knowledge of the subtleties and logic of Thomistic theology was highly valuable, for it was a knowledge few Reformers possessed to that fine degree.[10] Lest he not proceed with his vows, the monks told him that if he did not take holy orders, he would fall under God's curse for the rest of his life.[11]

The reason for the disparate experiences of Erasmus and Bucer lay in the basic orientation of the two orders. Augustinians were always more favorable to learning in a broad sense. They tended to emphasize the teachings of their namesake, and thus grace and Christian freedom were not uncommon traits. Martin Luther was also an Augustinian, and although Luther had some very negative comments to make about them, a close examination of Luther's life

---

[8] Most accounts give fifteen as the year; however, as he was born late in the year 1491, unless he entered after Nov. 11, he would still have been only fourteen.

[9] Hastings Eells, *Martin Bucer*, (New Haven: Yale University Press, 1931), p. 2.

[10] C.H. Smith, p. 146.

[11] Bucer's *Verantwortung,* written in 1523, describes these painful scenes from his youth. It is also known as *Apologia pro vita sua.* Cf. BDS I, pp. 293-302.

as an Augustinian monk reveals that his superiors and his brothers encouraged and facilitated his education. Such was not the case with Dominicans generally, although they produced some great scholars of whom Thomas Aquinas is most notable. From their inception they were dedicated to protection of Catholic orthodoxy and rooting out all heresy. The irony of their name in Latin illustrates their nature: *Dominicanes*, Latin for Dominicans, if split into two words: *Domini* and *canes* would then translate "the hounds of the Lord."

Martin endured ten agonizing years at the monastery before being transferred to Heidelberg in 1515 to study theology, to Mainz in 1516, and then back to Heidelberg in 1517, the same year Martin Luther nailed his *Ninety-Five Theses* to the door of the castle church in Wittenberg. Bucer commented that it was certainly true in his case that "Despair makes a monk."[12] What is interesting is the fact that although Bucer was grieved by the situation at the Dominican monastery at Schlettstadt, the monks were impressed with his keen intellect and astute reason. Many of them thought of him, as the Augustinians early on thought of Luther that he would one day be an ornament to his order. His rapid mastery of the complex Thomistic theology earned him the position of professor of theology among the Dominicans. So impressed was his order with Bucer, that in their zeal for having Bucer utilize the great capacity of his mind they were motivated to send him to Heidelberg to study philosophy, theology, Greek, and Hebrew.[13]

The Dominican monastery in Heidelberg was an entirely different environment for Bucer than had been the one in his hometown. The monastery existed in close relation to the university, and the prior was a humanist who allowed Bucer to lecture on Erasmus' *Praise of Folly* and allowed his Greek tutor, Brentius, to lecture on Plato's *Symposium.* Although a definite tension existed between monastery and university over humanism which the university accommodated to a greater extent, the situation was still much more conducive to humanist study by this young

---

[12] C.H. Smith, p. 146, cf. *Verantwortung (Apologia pro vita sua),* Bucer's autobiography.
[13] Clark, loc. Cit.

Erasmian-Dominican than most monasteries of his order would have been. Bucer's deep interest in Erasmian humanism drew him to the university where in 1517 he took the degree of Bachelor of Theology and was appointed Master of the Students. By this time, Bucer's studies from books he could locate had made an Erasmian disciple of him, committed to a program of reform through learning that would enable Christians to live holy and disciplined lives that would bring glory to God, and this passion for focused Christian education, with an end in view of Christian piety, never left him. In one sense, Bucer remained an Erasmian all his life, and Bucer integrated fundamental Erasmian ideals of Christian piety growing from Christian education into his theology of grace. Thus Bucer took an interest in any activity at Heidelberg University that would advance his knowledge of humanism, its leaders, and their work.

However, even though Erasmus' influence would make a permanent impression on Bucer's thinking, the course for Bucer's life was to direct him away from the substance of humanism to something far different, to a new movement that had just arisen in Saxony and was about to threaten the very existence of the Roman Church and re-orient Western civilization forever. Martin Bucer the Dominican was about to meet "the other Martin", Martin Luther the Augustinian, and both of them were about to break with the Roman church to become the greatest leaders of what would be the Protestant Reformation.

Conversion at Heidelberg

The story of Luther is well known, and we have already noted most of the important aspects of his own conversion. However, here we need only to rehearse a few significant events in his life that brought him to his intersection with Martin Bucer. Luther was born in 1483, exactly eight years before Bucer, in the small German town of Eisleben, the son of Hans Luther, a copper miner who had become wealthy from his trade. Martin was his oldest child, intelligent and capable, and Hans planned for him to attend the best schools and become a lawyer.

Luther studied at the school in Magdeburg operated by the Brethren of the Common Life, the order founded by Gerhard Groote and belonging to the pietistic *devotio moderna* movement. Later he matriculated at the University of Erfurt; however, in 1505, after nearly being killed in a thunderstorm, he made a vow to God that, if God would save him, he would become a monk. Luther entered the Augustinian order at Erfurt and immediately committed himself fully to monastic life and discipline. But the more he worked at being obedient, the more he felt estranged from God. Sometime around 1513 he had a famous enlightening experience that we noted in the earlier chapter in which he came to understand the text of Romans 1:16-17 to mean that the gospel Paul preached revealed a salvation resulting from justification by faith, a forensic declaration of pardon from sin which clothes the Christian with a foreign righteousness, and the words Paul quoted from Habakkuk "the just shall live by faith," opened the doors of Paradise to Luther.

Soon after arose the controversy over the sale of indulgences to pay for the purchase of the Archbishopric of Mainz by the young Albrecht von Hohenzollern. Pope Leo X sold the office to Albrecht to provide funds to build St. Peter's Cathedral in Rome, a deal in which proceeds raised by the Dominican indulgence-seller, Johann Tetzel, would be split between them. When news of the sale of indulgences in Mainz reached Luther, he was stirred to action. Indulgences began after the crusades as a kind of substitute penance. Crusaders were given an indulgence, time out of Purgatory, for participation, but those who could not go were allowed to give money to the church instead. Indulgences would then take the place of the sacrament of penance as a way to reduce time in Purgatory, and the practice was always questionable at best but too financially profitable to be questioned too much.

However Luther saw the sale of indulgences as not only a violation of his newly-found principle of justification by faith alone, but an insult to the once and for all atonement of Jesus Christ, who has already paid for our sins. He drew up his *Ninety-Five Theses*, propositions for scholarly debate on the subject, written in Latin, and posted them on October 31, 1517 on the Castle Church door in Wittenberg, where he was pastor and professor of theology in the university. His zealous students took them down, translated them into German, and had them printed on the newly accessible presses, and distributed all over Germany. Immediately, Germany was on fire. Even those who did not understand the theology that was involved realized that a German had stood up to the pope, and the long smoldering resentment of papal interference in German affairs and German money flowing to Rome was kindled into a mighty conflagration.

Luther had hoped for a disputation on the subject of indulgences, but that never happened. Instead, the pope sought to silence him in the usual way of dealing with heretics: burning at the stake. He commissioned Gabriel della Volta (Venetus), general of the Augustinian Eremites, to take care of Luther, but Volta turned over this rather unpleasant task to Johann von Staupitz, vicar of the German congregation of the order, who happened to be a friend of Luther. Instead of death at the stake, Staupitz opted for allowing Luther to speak before the triennial meeting of the Augustinians in Germany scheduled for Jubilate Sunday, the third Sunday after Easter, which would meet on April 25 in Heidelberg. He cautioned Luther not to debate controversial subjects, but rather to prepare theses on sin, free will, and grace, topics that Luther had earlier addressed in his *Disputation Against Scholastic Theology*. In that way, scholastic theology became the focus of attack.[14]

Luther, armed with safe conduct from his Duke, Frederick the Wise, set out on foot with his fellow Augustinian, Leonhard Beier. Luther had prepared twenty-eight theological and twelve philosophical theses for the disputation. That the meeting of the Augustinians was held in Heidelberg was providential for a number of reasons. Heidelberg exercised an extensive influence over the west and south of Germany, and Luther saw an opportunity to extend the reform movement into churches in that area. Disputations were not unusual; on the contrary, they were the norm when matters of difference arose in theology. Luther, however, wanted to take full advantage of this opportunity to create a striking effect on the scholars who would be gathered there. The university, under the control of the church, could not allow this disputation involving Luther to take place in the great hall; the professors forbade it. However, the Augustinians proved to be more open and allowed the convent to be used, and the disputation began on the

---

[14] "Heidelberg Disputation," LW 31:37-45, also Augustana.edu (online sources).

twenty-sixth of April 1518. Indeed, this disputation probably bore fruit, for eventually Heidelberg embraced the Reformation.[15]

But the meeting was providential in an immediate result: three young men in the audience that day were converted to Evangelical beliefs, and they would exercise great influence and leadership in the new movement that Luther had spawned. One was Johann Brenz, later the leader of the Reformation in Swäbisch Hall, Erhard Schnepf (Theobald Dillichanus), Reformation leader in Württemberg, and Martin Bucer, who would later lead the Reformed church in Strasbourg.

The room was filled, for Luther's reputation had preceded him. There were professors, courtiers, burghers, and students in attendance. Luther liked to present truth in paradoxical form, as he thought the contrast illustrated the point better. Because of the significance of this disputation, we need to notice his twenty-eight theological theses:

1. The law of God is a salutary rule of life; and yet it cannot help man in the obtaining of righteousness; but on the contrary impedes him.
2. Much less can human works, which are done over and over again with the aid of natural precepts, so to speak, lead to that end.
3. Works of men, let them be as fair and good as they may, are yet evidently nothing but mortal sins.
4. Works that are of God, however unsightly and evil in appearance, have an endless efficacy.
5. The works of men are thus not mortal sins (we speak of works which are apparently good), as though they were crimes.
6. The works of God (we speak of those which he does through men) are thus not merits, as though they were sinless.

---

[15] Merle D'Aubigne, *History of the Great Reformation in the Times of Luther and Calvin* Milwaukee: A.A. Swanlund, 1901), pp. 96-97. Eventually many in the area embraced Reformed over Lutheran theology, leading to the *Heidelberg Catechism* as an attempt to reconcile the two viewpoints.

7. The works of the righteous themselves would be mortal sins, - if from a holy reverence of the Lord, they did not fear that their works might indeed be mortal sins.
8. By so much more are the works of man mortal sins when they are done without fear and in unadulterated, evil self-security.
9. To say that works done out of Christ are truly dead works, - but not mortal sins, is a dangerous forgetfulness of the fear of God.
10. Indeed, it is very difficult to see how a work can be dead and at the same time not a harmful and mortal sin.
11. Arrogance cannot be avoided or true hope be present unless the judgment of condemnation is feared in every work.
12. In the sight of God sins are truly venial when they are feared by men to be mortal.
13. Free will, since the fall of man, is but an empty word; and if man does all he can, he still sins mortally.
14. Free will, after the fall, has power to do good only in a passive capacity, but it can always do evil in an active capacity.
15. Nor could free will remain in a state of innocence, much less do good, in an active capacity, but only in its passive capacity.
16. A man who dreams he can attain to grace by doing all that is in his power, adds sin to sin, - and is doubly guilty.
17. Nor does speaking in this manner give cause for despair, but for arousing the desire to humble oneself and seek the grace of Christ.
18. It is certain that man must altogether despair of his own ability, if he would be made capable of receiving the grace of Christ.
19. That person does not deserve to be called a theologian who looks upon the invisible things of God as though they were clearly perceptible in those things which have actually happened (Rom. 1:20).
20. He deserves to be called a theologian, however, who comprehends the visible and manifest things of God seen through suffering and the cross.

21. A theology of glory calls good – evil, and evil – good; but a theology of the cross calls the thing what it actually is.
22. The wisdom which applies itself to learn the invisible perfections of God from his works, puffs up, blinds, and hardens men.
23. The law calls forth God's anger: slays, accurses, judges, and condemns, whatsoever is not *in Christ* (Rom. 4:15).
24. Yet this wisdom is not an evil; and the law is not to be rejected; but he who learns not the theology of the cross, turns to evil whatever is good.
25. That man is not justified who does many works; but he who, without having yet done works, has much faith in Christ.
26. The law says, "Do this," and what it enjoins is never done; Grace says, " Believe in him," and everything is already done.
27. Actually one should call the work of Christ an acting work and our work an accomplished work, and thus an accomplished work pleasing to God by the grace of the acting work.
28. The love of God finds nothing in man, but creates in him what He loves. Man's love is the gift of his well beloved.

In his twelve philosophical theses Luther condemned Aristotelianism. Following the disputation, five doctors attacked his theses as extravagant, but Luther listened with unusual patience and responded with unusual mildness to his opponents, but his answers were short and based on Scripture. He was able to answer quickly and well all the questions put to him.[16]

Before long all the adversaries left the room except one, Doctor George Niger, who alone remained to continue the contest with Luther. Niger was so alarmed at the boldness of this Augustinian, and lacking any adequate response, simply blurted, "If our peasantry heard such things, they would stone you to death!" This statement evoked a general round of laughter from the assembly. However, this congregation had listed with rapt attention to the words of Martin Luther, perhaps with more fixed concentration that at any

---

[16] Ibid.

other academic disputation they had ever attended; all appeared to be filled with the greatest interest and concern.[17]

There is no doubt that Luther used this presentation as an opportunity to discredit the Dominican concepts of theology. The old rivalries between Augustinians and Dominicans came to the foreground when Luther attacked the sale of indulgences led by a Dominican, John Tetzel. The Dominicans clearly wanted a fight, and for that reason Staupitz cautioned Luther to stay away from the subject of indulgences. However, his development of the theology of the cross and attacks on Aristotle, the Dominican favorite, undercut Dominican thought. In a deeper sense, however, it questioned the whole concept of medieval theology whereby grace is infused in consideration for a good work. Clearly Luther was presenting a radically different theology.

Of course, in the audience, and listening as intently as anyone present, was Martin Bucer. It might seem strange for a Dominican to attend the lectures of an Augustinian, especially if that Augustinian was already marked as heretical. However, Bucer had been reading some of Luther's writings and comparing them with Scripture. He had experienced some early misgivings about the papacy and the Roman system, all of which had been reinforced by his study of Erasmus who criticized the Roman corruption forcefully. When Bucer heard that Luther would be speaking at Heidelberg, he was joyful and excited and made immediate plans to attend. He was one of the first in the hall that day. He came equipped with paper, pen, and ink to take notes, which he did furiously, trying to get down every word Luther said. Although Bucer had a few prior misgivings about the Roman hierarchy and some familiarity with Luther, it was then and there that Bucer was converted to the Protestant faith. He may have walked in a Catholic Dominican, but he walked out an Evangelical! He said he was an Erasmian, but that day he became a "Martinian." How many great leaders of the Church of Christ, like Bucer and John Wesley, owe their understanding of the gospel to Luther![18]

---

[17] Ibid.

[18] Though not placing himself in the category with Bucer or Wesley, this old preacher, church historian, and would-be theologian thinks back on a time in 1968

It is really interesting to see Bucer's reaction. As he listened spellbound, he was especially impressed by the last thesis, as Luther explained that man's love is aroused by what man likes, but God finds nothing loveable in man. God creates in man what God loves. The love of the cross, born of the cross, is this: it transfers itself not when it finds some good to be enjoyed, but there where it may confer some good to a sinner or to an unfortunate.[19] Bucer immediately understood the radical inability of man, the grace of God, the power of the cross, and the focus on doing good to one's neighbor. All of these points, implicit in Luther's comments, became hallmarks of Bucer's theology.

So impressed and excited was Bucer that he ran up to him and talked with him a long time after the lectures, and Luther agreed to meet with him the next day. The two ate together, and Bucer was filled with questions. Luther shared with the young Dominican his general outline of his course on Romans taught at Wittenberg University in 1515 and 1516. Luther explained to Bucer how he taught that "the Christian acknowledges himself to be both a sinner and righteous at the same time: a sinner in reality, yet righteous according to the consideration and sure promise of God, and because of this, he is perfect, whole in hope, though in reality a sinner, but the Christian has the beginning of righteousness, that he may seek and ask more, always knowing himself unrighteous."[20] Luther described this truth in simple terms in Latin: *simul peccator et iustus, semper penitens.*[21]

Bucer was so impressed by this meeting with Luther that he wrote to his friend Beatus Rhenanus that "Luther solved all objections, not with the subtlety of Duns Scotus, but with the penetration of St. Paul; Luther's concise answers, drawn from the Word of God, astonished everyone. Luther very much resembled

---

when, in a graduate class on Reformation history, he heard Luther's concept of justification by faith explained, and his life, like those of Bucer and Wesley, was forever changed.

[19] *Bucer on Love,* tr. Paul Traugott Fuhrmann (Richmond, VA: John Knox Press), 1923, pp. 9-10.

[20] Ibid.

[21] "At the same time sinner and righteous, always repentant."

Erasmus but was superior to him inasmuch as Luther taught openly things which Erasmus had merely insinuated."[22]

The experience of those two days, hearing Luther expound the doctrines of grace and having supper with him the next day, changed Martin Bucer forever. From this point onward he never doubted the Evangelical doctrines, and that man is saved by the sovereign, elective grace of God, through the perfect atonement of Jesus Christ, the application of salvation by the Spirit, and justification by faith alone. However, he remained an Erasmian, and was able to incorporate Evangelical theology into Christian humanism, for Bucer held to the ideal of the complete Christian man or women, cultured, educated, pious, active in Christian community, and involved in good works that benefit one's neighbor. The two concepts made a perfect blend and balance in Bucer, and it is from this blend of Christian humanism and Evangelical theology that what the Christian world came to know as the Reformed Faith would develop, largely due to Martin Bucer.

---

[22] Ibid.

Chapter III

Heeding the Call:

The Formation of a Leader

Court Chaplain and Secular Priest: Ebernburg and Landstuhl

As a result primarily of the influence of Erasmus, Bucer had, particularly from his secret reading of Erasmus' *Praise of Folly,* serious misgivings about the papacy and corruptions within the Roman Church long before he went to Heidelberg, but he emerged from the meeting with Luther committed to the Protestant cause and a believer in the doctrine of justification by faith alone. At this point his theology was not fully developed, but it is safe to say that he had already formulated a view of the difference between the invisible church, the elect of God, and the visible church, that "multitudinous" mixture of hypocrites and true believers that made up the visible church. He knew that the church as defined by Rome was not the Church of Christ, and he realized that salvation was a matter of the mercy, love, and grace of God rather than the efforts of man. He had come to reject the Roman system of penance, which never enabled people to have assurance of their salvation, and he held firmly to an Erasmian view of piety and godly Christian living as the hallmark of a believer.

Bucer continued to advance in Dominican circles, being ordained as a priest in Mainz, awarded a bachelor of theology and made Master of Students, all in 1519. Despite his advancement, Bucer's newfound theological beliefs were not those that would be appreciated by the Dominicans, and they soon expressed to Bucer their extreme displeasure at his having adopted these Lutheran views. The Dominicans had a talent for making life unbearable for someone when they wanted to do so, and they chose to do so in Bucer's case. However, his newly granted position qualified him to read Bible, and doing so only fortified his convictions. He became the leader of a study group at Heidelberg and used Erasmus and

Luther as models. Bucer obtained a copy of Luther's commentary on Galatians and was deeply impressed by Luther's exegesis of Pauline theology, which he commented was "replete with wholesome precepts." He even sought to get the commentary printed in Schlettstadt and widely circulated, and he wrote his first letter to Luther.[23] But in the summer of 1519 he was nearly stoned for a speech made in a disputation, and his letters were constantly being opened.

Bucer continued to make and meet new friends during this critical time in his life. In the same year he made a trip to Basel and met the famous humanist printer Johann Froben and the Protestant pastor who would later be his colleague in Strasbourg, Wolfgang Capito. Their friendship was life long and close. Capito had already gained a reputation as a Hebrew scholar and a person of influence, and Bucer was already manifesting his talent for recognizing people of greatness and winning their friendship. His 1519 journey to Basel, a city where humanism and Protestantism had now joined forces, allowed him to expand his circle of influential friends that now included people like Jacob Wimpfehling, John Witz, and Otto Brunfels.[24]

In 1520 Bucer wanted to meet Erasmus at Louvain, but the inquisitor at Köln, Jacob Hoogstraten, summoned him to appear before him on the charge of teaching Latin and Greek to some of the younger brethren. The situation was so intolerable that he left for Strasbourg, his parents' home, in September of 1520 to be a guest of another Erasmian humanist who turned Protestant, Ulrich von Hutten. Von Hutten considered any enemy of Hoogstraten to be a friend of his.[25] Bucer served for a time as von Hutten's secretary. In enthusiastic defense of his position against the charges of Hoogstraten, Bucer wrote, "For to speak only for myself now, when I first learned from the books of Erasmus, then from those of Luther, next from the exhortations and writings of the Holy Fathers, most especially from the divine writings, what true religion is and what things pertain to it, I felt compelled to confess them thus and, being

---

[23] Eells, pp. 5-6.
[24] Eells, p. 5.
[25] Smith, p. 147.

given an opportunity to teach publicly, and to teach and to profess them openly."[26]

Finally, in 1521, through the influence of a friend, he requested and received by papal dispensation release from monastic vows on the basis of the fact that he had been coerced into taking them. Bucer was also motivated by the famous Reuchlin case in which a learned Hebrew scholar was brought before the inquisition in Köln for teaching Hebrew to his students and supposedly subverting their faith from Christianity to Judaism. He remained under holy orders as a part of the secular clergy, for according to the sacramental definition Rome assigned to orders, they were permanent, but he became a secular priest rather than one living under the discipline of his Dominican order. This change allowed him the freedom he needed to pursue his interests but brought him under increased scrutiny by Rome and its representatives.

Ulrich von Hutten had connections; he was a man with friends in high places, and he was able to put Bucer in touch with Franz von Sickengen who offered Bucer refuge at his court, as he had already offered refuge to a number of Protestants, and later set Bucer up at Landstuhl as a priest. The connection with von Sickengen was a momentous and pivotal one for Bucer for a number of reasons. First, it represented a change of position from being the brunt of abuse from the Dominicans to emerging as a leader among the Protestants, but secondly, it set a precedent for Bucer's milieu for the rest of his life: he would be involved with rulers and dignitaries and become eventually the diplomat par excellence for the Protestants, and thirdly, it represented the first of a series of exiles for Bucer. He was forced to take refuge with Franz von Sickingen for his own safety, and such moves would happen again and again as the apostle of peace was pursued by his adversaries.

He felt safe under Frank von Sickengen's protection at Ebernburg, but he was soon involved in negotiations with the Roman confessor Glapion in attempting to arrange a meeting with Luther at Ebernburg. Bucer met Luther at Oppenheim on April 15, 1521, and, sensing that the meeting at Ebernburg was a trick, urged him not to go, and that meeting never occurred. Bucer also urged

---

[26] Bucer, *De vere ecclesiarum reconciliatione)* in Spijker, p. 10.

Luther not to go to Worms, nor to trust the emperor's safe conduct. Luther's reply was typical, "If all the tiles on the houses of Worms were devils," he would still go.[27] Already Bucer was manifesting his keen powers of perception. Seeing that Luther was resolute, Bucer decided to accompany him, was in attendance at Worms, and heard Luther's impassioned appeal to Scripture that ended with the famous words, "Here I stand, I can do no other. God help me. Amen." Bucer was one of the first to know about Luther's being taken into protective custody at the Wartburg and to rejoice that Luther was safe.[28]

Now Bucer's involvement with Luther and von Hutten and his theological stance had drawn the attention of the notorious papal legate to Germany, Jerome Aleander, who perceived that Bucer was as dangerous as Luther, was another Hutten, and urged he should be recalled at once and taken out of Germany. Aleander also tried to prevent Bucer's being granted the release from his monastic vows, but he failed on both counts to stop the rising leader of the Protestant cause. Aleander was even more alarmed when Bucer accepted a position as court chaplain to the Elector Frederick of the Palatinate, fearing his influence on the young nobleman and tried unsuccessfully to get him fired. Failing in that endeavor, Bucer's enemies made life difficult for his friends in the monastery.

Ulrich von Hutten tried to dissuade Bucer from accepting Frederick's offer, accusing him of being carried away by the luxurious life in the Palatine court and engaging in worldly vanities. Bucer saw the move as an opportunity for advancement, but Hutten reminded him that the way to succeed in God's kingdom was not in worldly riches and ease but by the hard work of study and preaching.[29] When the count found himself in trouble for housing "Lutherans" under his roof contrary to the Edict of Worms, Bucer regretted ever having left Franz von Sickingen and asked Hutten to use his influence with Franz to find him a parish. Through von Hutten's efforts Frank von Sickingen awarded Bucer the parish of Landstuhl with permission for a year's leave of absence to study in

---

[27] "Martin Bucer: Ecumenicist of the Reformation," online souce (rsglh.org/bucer).
[28] Eells, p. 10.
[29] Eells, p. 11.

Wittenberg with Luther. He left the court of Frederick with good relations and took up his first true pastorate at Landstuhl, a small town at the foot of Sickingen's castle.

Elizabeth Silbereisen

Bucer had already reached the conclusion that mandatory clerical celibacy was an evil that could not longer be tolerated. It was contrary to nature, for Scripture taught that only those with the gift of celibacy could be expected to exercise it. In his mind the concepts of Christian family and community to replace the centrality of the medieval monastery were taking shape. Marriage was to Bucer more a duty and principle than an expression of passion, and the concept of marriage, including clerical marriage, became a centerpiece of his system of theology.

While he was serving in Landstuhl, he met a young nun whose father died, and whose relatives, greedy for her inheritance, had forced her into a convent in order to appropriate it. Her experience in the convent was so miserable that physicians said she would have soon died had she not left it. Bucer was filled with pity for her and deep resentment of the system that had victimized her, and advised by his friends to marry her, decided in 1522 to take her as his wife.[30] It is interesting that Bucer was married some time before Luther's famous marriage to Katherine von Bora.

Not much is known about Elizabeth Silbereisen. She was born in Mosbach-on-the-Neckar, the daughter of upper middle class parents Jacob Silbereisen and Anna Pallas. The exact date of her birth is unknown, but around 1511 she arrived at the Lebelfeld Convent in Krachgau southeast of Heidelberg. She remained there for twelve years until her parents died, at which time her family insisted she join the convent so that they would not have to look after her, and they could seize her parents' estate. What was left of her inheritance seems to have been acquired by the convent, and Elizabeth resided there like a prisoner, timid, afraid, sick, and learning very little. Her physician told her that she could not recover as long as she stayed there, and she came to believe that the

---

[30] Eells, p. 12.

monastic life hindered her from obeying Christ and living fully a Christian life, thus, in 1522, she simply left. The convent was not consulted, as Elizabeth did not seek their permission. To cover her disappearance, they left the impression that she had been abducted. In some unknown way she and Martin met when he was pastor at Landstuhl. By that time Bucer was convinced that God did not intend for him to remain unmarried, that he did not have the gift of celibacy, and that marriage would be for him more conducive to the Christian life. Thus in the summer of 1522, Martin Bucer and Elizabeth Silbereisen were married.[31]

Bucer knew the risk; he had broken his monastic vow of celibacy. Such a move was probably viewed with greater horror by the Roman Church than a change in theology. Bucer would be the object of persecution, abuse, calumny, and rejection, yet he acted deliberately and with great assurance and conviction. Elizabeth was convinced that her life in the convent had been anything but conducive to her spiritual development and saw an opportunity now to live a godly life as the wife of a Protestant theologian and pastor. She would bear him thirteen children before she and several of the children would die during a terrible outbreak of the plague in Strasbourg. Martin and Elizabeth stayed for a while in the home of Bucer's parents, while his accusers called him illegitimate and the son of a Jew who beat his wife and had a child by another woman. Bucer denied these absurd charges and wrote that "we have yet to have our first quarrel...Her morals and conduct, for that matter, are of such a nature that I do not doubt but that I will want to live with her without any reservations for as long as the Lord God permits us to stay together."[32]

There existed absolutely no precedent for married priests, and Bucer would find his marriage a genuine hindrance to his work. Even those who were coming to question the authority of Rome and the scholastic system of theology did not know how to assimilate a

---

[31] H. J. Selderhuis, *Marriage and Divorce in the Thought of Martin Bucer,"* tr. John Vriend and Lyle Bierma, in *Sixteenth Century Essays and Studies,* XLVIII (Kirksville, Mo: Thomas Jefferson University Press at Truman State University, 1999), pp. 116-117.

[32] Bucer BDS 1.183 in Seldenhuis, p. 118.

married priest. It was only through consummate patience and uncompromising adherence to his beliefs on the matter that Bucer was able to persuade magistrates, laity, and fellow clergy that what he had done was godly, Scriptural, and necessary for the advancement of the Kingdom of God on earth.

Weissembourg

Politicians have a way of involving themselves in matters that do not exactly coincide with those concerns of the Kingdom that preoccupied Bucer. Franz von Sickingen decided on war against the Elector of Treves, and against the background of civil upheaval, Bucer found it difficult to continue his studies and work in Landstuhl. Both he and Elizabeth found their lives unhappy, hardly a way to begin an unprecedented marital relationship successfully. Franz needed Bucer's developing diplomatic skills, and he sent him on missions to Brabant, Saxony, and other places. News of the war reached Strasbourg, and Bucer's parents thought that he had perished in the conflict. The war dragged on without much being accomplished until Franz decided to give Bucer a leave of absence until it ended. Martin and Elizabeth Bucer were relieved to get away from the violence and set a course for Wittenberg. However, it always seemed that Bucer was never able to make it to Wittenberg to study with Luther, even though he tried several times. He stopped at Weissembourg and met Heinrich Motherer who urged him to stay and help him with the reformation in that city.

The scenario sounds strikingly similar to one played out fourteen years later when young John Calvin, his heart set on returning to Basel, stopped off in Geneva and met the reformer Guillaume Farel who persuaded Calvin to remain in Geneva and help him with the reformation efforts there. And very soon the lives of these two great reformers would be brought together for a lifetime of mutual friendship and cooperation. .

Bucer undertook helping Motherer in Weissembourg with the same kind of reluctance as Calvin did with Farel in Geneva, and met with similar results. Motherer was the pastor of St. John's Church in Weissembourg, had accepted Luther's theology, was trying to preach the doctrines of grace there, and desperately needed help.

Bucer agreed and dedicated himself to the task of preaching, debating, organizing, and defending the faith. His talents in these areas, already evident, matured and developed during this experience. Weissembourg became a model of the Reformation that would be used again and again as Reformed communities sprang up all over Germany.[33] And Bucer was personally responsible for many of these Reformed communities!

Bucer had the gift of preaching. He was passionate and well read; he effectively stirred his audiences as he introduced them to Luther's doctrine of justification by faith alone and the all sufficiency of the atonement of Christ. His methodology was much the same as Luther's: rather than attack a practice simply because it was Roman in origin, he encouraged his audiences to see the reality behind the practice. What was important, Bucer taught, was the spiritual meaning rather than the outward form of a ceremony. He did not advocate doing away with fasts and vigils, but urged the importance of Bible study and prayer instead. He told people they could pray to saints if they wished, but they needed to remember that only Christ was their mediator. They could go on a pilgrimage, but it would be better to stay and home and take care of their families, for the grace of God is available everywhere.[34] His was not a radical approach that swept away everything Catholic just because it was Catholic, but an approach that sought to lead people gradually and meaningfully to a religion of grace and Spirit rather than works and outward ceremonies. It was characteristic of Bucer always to emphasize the necessity of people in a congregation understanding what they were doing and understanding the message of the gospel. Understanding came, Bucer reasoned, far easier in an atmosphere of quiet transition and patient teaching than in one of radical upheaval created by instantaneous and wholesale rejection of the whole Roman system. It was for this reason that Bucer was conciliatory rather than unyielding and stubborn, and many of his Protestant colleagues thought he was actually compromising of his convictions. However, Bucer had a focus on the unity of the church and the well being of the individual Christian even at this early

---

[33] Eells, p. 13.
[34] Eells, p. 14.

period in his ministry, and that focus would brighten and reach increasingly clearer definition as time went on.

It was at Weissembourg that Bucer publicly repudiated the mass. He argued that if the sacrifice of Christ on the cross was complete and sufficient, then man can do nothing in the furtherance of his salvation. In that context the idea of a priest offering the body and blood of Christ again and again in the mass is abomination and blasphemy. If faith is grounded in human activity, Bucer argued, then it is worthless and the free spiritual religion of Christ is turned into a worldly physical ritual, and the cross of Christ is robbed of its power. Bucer wrote of the mass that it is "the most horrendous, poisonous, and pernicious disgrace and blasphemy of Christ our Lord and Savior to think and to say that the priest offers him up in the mass."[35] He also commented that "Our syllogism still stands: If Christ has done and completed everything, then you do nothing."[36] Bucer was advocating not only reformation but restoration.[37]

The Weissembourg pastorate was another pivotal step in young Bucer's career, and the direction of his ministry was set, and he never swerved from that fundamental direction while maturing in his understanding both of theology and of methodology. But his work in Weissembourg caused increasing opposition from the monks. Bucer went time and again to them and asked for them to show him from the Bible where he was wrong. Like Luther, he posted his beliefs on the church door and sent copies to monks of various orders. Bucer even challenged his opponents to meet him in debate, set a time, and said that if he could not prove from Scripture that he was right, he would let them stone him to death.[38] Their response was not to discuss his theological concerns but to try to drive him out of the city. They simply appealed to the authority of the church which, for them, superceded personal interpretation of Scripture. Now Bucer was marked as a dangerous man.

---

[35] Bucer, *Grund und Ursach auss gotliche schrift der neüwerungen"* 1524. See BDS D1-2, Vol. I, pp. 210-213.

[36] Bucer, *Acta Bern* 1 and 3 in Spijker, p. 21.

[37] Bucer, "Reformatio alicuius rei, est eius ad pristinam suam formam et rationem restitutio," (Scr. Angl. 192) Spijker, p. 21.

[38] Eells, pp. 15-16.

By this time the bishop of Speyer, who had authority over Weissembourg, entered the conflict when Motherer asked the bishop to confirm Bucer's position as preacher of St. John's. The bishop refused and demanded that Bucer and Motherer appear before him to answer charges of heresy. They feared to go and refused, whereupon the bishop reminded the city council of Weissembourg of the provisions of the Edict of Worms refusing to allow Lutherans in the city and demanded that they expel Bucer. The council was not only sympathetic to Bucer but was really supportive, but they were placed in a dangerous situation by the turn of political events. Franz von Sickengen was defeated in battle in his war with the Elector of Treves, and now, without Franz's support, Weissembourg was vulnerable to attack from other cities in the Palatinate that resented the fact that Weissembourg harbored Protestants.

To add to Bucer's woes, the furious bishop of Speyer excommunicated Martin Bucer from the Roman Catholic Church in 1523. With his protector Franz von Sickengen imprisoned, an excommunicated and married priest became a serious liability to the city council of Weissembourg. Though satisfied with Bucer's teaching and respecting him personally, the council reluctantly and secretly asked both Bucer and Motherer to leave, at least until enemy armies were withdrawn. Bucer hated strife and certainly did not want to be the cause of it; thus, he and Motherer left as quietly as possible in May 1523 through one of the city gates, disappearing in the darkness. Bucer saw these events as defeat and misery; he saw the triumph of the Antichrist.[39] Once again Bucer was an exile. But he was an exile who yielded to the will of God.

The Journey to Strasbourg

Martin Bucer did not have many options open to him. He needed to seek a city that would offer him asylum, and given his circumstances, only one was clearly available; namely, the city to which his parents moved when he was a boy, the imperial free city of Strasbourg, a city that had followed a pattern of repudiation of the

---

[39] Eells, p. 17.

powers of the clergy since the thirteenth century.[40]   Bucer was not only a married and excommunicated priest; he was also almost penniless. His parents were now getting older and still were poor. As his parents were citizens of Strasbourg, Bucer was assured of protection there. It must have been an overwhelming surprise when, in May of 1523, Bucer appeared in Strasbourg. Claus and Eva Bucer had made a difficult decision when they left their only son in the care of his grandparents and moved to Strasbourg. They wholeheartedly supported his joining the Dominican order, knowing that the monks could provide the education that their son yearned for. He had stopped off to see them on his way to Heidelberg, surprising them then. They thought he had perhaps left the order, but he assured them he was being transferred to Heidelberg where he could advance his education. But now their son appeared broke, married, excommunicated, with his monastic vows broken and his ties to the order as well as the church severed. Parents do have a way of supporting their children even when they do not fully understand the reasons for their behavior, and such seemed to be the case with Bucer's parents. Their support was critical at this point, and Martin must have been quite grateful. When Bucer later was being attacked by the bishop who demanded that the council expel him, Martin's father appeared before the council pleading that his son be protected on the basis of the citizenship of his parents. The council agreed.

Another advantage to Strasbourg was the fact that the Reformation was already underway. Matthew Zell had accepted the teachings of Luther and was tirelessly implementing them as he had opportunity.   As Farel needed Calvin's help in Geneva, and as Motherer had requested Bucer's in Weissembourg, now Bucer found another reformer gladly welcoming assistance. Zell even took Bucer into his home in order to coordinate the leadership of the Reformation and to offer shelter to a fellow Protestant.

Zell actually found the groundwork laid by another reforming preacher, John Geiler, who even attracted the attention of the emperor Maximilian I by his forceful preaching. Geiler did not actually break with the Roman Church, but he advocated moral

---

[40] Spijker, p. 10.

reform among both clergy and laity and opposed the sale of indulgences. Matthew Zell came to Strasbourg with an impressive reputation as the rector at Freiburg to accept a position as the people's priest in the chapel of St. Lawrence in the cathedral. The Strasbourg cathedral was reputed to be the wealthiest in Europe, and the presence of many worshippers gave Zell an excellent opportunity to reach people with the gospel.

His initial approach was to declare, as had Geiler, moral reform, and he was able to conceal the fact that he was a Lutheran. Even though the city council had not suppressed Luther's writings, it was dangerous to come out openly as a Lutheran, as the church authorities still had great power. Eventually Zell gained the courage to preach from the text of Romans, and there was no doubt where he stood. The bishop attempted to silence him, but he rapidly gained popular support. The clergy even tried to assassinate Zell, but their actions simply contributed to his reputation, and more and more people flocked to the cathedral to hear him preach. The cathedral chapter, very much under Roman control, refused to allow him the use of the cathedral's pulpit, so the people constructed a temporary wooden rostrum, which they brought into the very nave of the cathedral without permission. The cathedral chapter ordered Zell to appear before them to answer for such actions, and then to appear before the vicar. Again the people reacted in defense of Zell and plastered the vicar's door with testimonies of their loyalty. At this point the bishop intervened and demanded that the council silence him, but the council similarly defended Zell by commissioning the people's priests to preach the gospel in their churches truthfully without fearing anyone, and the council promised to protect them. The bishop then demanded the Strasbourg council dismiss Zell, and they responded to the bishop that if he were put out of office, they would retain him at public expense. Faced with overwhelming opposition from both the populace and the magistrates, the bishop capitulated. Zell still needed to appear before the cathedral chapter to defend himself. Someone asked him if he were afraid, and he answered that "The Father of the family will certainly send me comrades. I wager they are already on their way." It was not long until Zell's expectations were fulfilled to a degree he could scarcely have imagined. Martin Bucer was on the way, and along with him came such great theologians and preachers as Capito, Firn, and Altbiesser.[41]

Bucer would soon become the foremost reformer of Strasbourg. This city, now selected as the capital of the European Union, has always enjoyed a position of importance and centrality. It was a great medieval city, ranking with populated, influential, and wealthy German cities like Augsburg and Nürnberg. Geographically, it was ideally situated at the crossroads of Europe. Aristotle would have admired its mixed constitution with elements of both democracy and aristocracy. The constitution as revised in 1482 called for a system of six councils: one was composed of the magistrates, another was called the Council of Twenty-One and was made up of seven nobles and fourteen citizens, the third was the Council of Fifteen, then the Council of Thirteen, the Council of Twenty-Two, and a senate-like council called "The Old Men." There was also an Assembly of three hundred aldermen, composed of fifteen deputies from twenty guilds. Though highly complicated, this intricate form of constitution was quite functional and tended to operate smoothly, precluding any power blocs that would impede justice.[42]

The general sentiment of the city government was favorable toward the Reformation but preferring a moderate approach that would avoid any mob uprising and disturb the peace. Like most German cities, Strasbourg entertained a deep resentment to clerical interference in local politics, which led to a church-state struggle. The head of the Strasbourg church was designated the bishop who bore the secular title of "count of Alsace." He in turn was subject to the Archbishop of Mainz, one of the seven imperial electors. Long before the Reformation the church-state struggle and resentment of Roman interference led to the council expelling the bishop from the city. He appointed a vicar to represent him in his absence. Smarting from a long tradition of resentment and rejection, the extreme reaction of the bishop against the Protestants would not be unexpected. As far as the council was concerned, they welcomed the opportunity to end papal and clerical interference once and for all, and the Reformation afforded them that opportunity. By

---

[41] Eells, pp. 22-24.
[42] Eells, p. 19.

backing the Reformation, and yet keeping it firmly under their control, they could avoid the kind of political struggles that had characterized their city for so long. It is important to note their general attitude toward the new ministers. They were happy to see them preach and unseat Roman authority, but they were not about to allow them to develop into a new clerical tyranny. Understanding their position helps in interpreting the rather bizarre and seemingly inexplicable behavior of the council after the Reformation was firmly established in Strasbourg.

It was into this situation that Martin Bucer walked in 1523. Once Matthew Zell was aware of Bucer's ability, he was willing to take the chance on this excommunicated and married Protestant priest. However, it required the interceding efforts of preachers Gerel, Brunfels, and Capito to persuade Zell to allow Bucer to preach. Capito had recently arrived in Strasbourg from Basel to become one of the canons at St. Thomas Church. Capito was in favor of Bucer's being allowed to preach but was too shy to take the initiative in open support for him. The city magistrates were suspicious of Bucer because of his association with Fritz von Sickingen and afraid of him because he was married.

To this point Zell had refused to answer Bucer's repeated written requests to preach. Finally, he allowed him to preach one hour a day on the book of John, and he became so popular that the magistrates forbade him to preach in German lest he cause an attack on the city. Bucer was allowed only to lecture in Latin on the Pastorals and in Zell's house where he was staying. Then Zell relented and allowed Bucer to preach on alternate days in the cathedral on the famous wooden pulpit, and the council kept silent.[43] Because Bucer felt the pressure from the council to state clearly what he believed, he chose to deliver a sermon on the subject of Christian love. The sermon was so popular that some of his audience urged him to publish it, and it became the first recognized publication of what would be over one hundred and fifty works of Bucer. Bucer realized that the publication of the sermon would establish in print what his views were, and so he consented. The work was called "Das ym selbs

---

[43] Eells, p. 25.

niemat/sonder anderen leben soll,"[44] and it established Bucer's reputation as a leader of the Reformation.

"Das Ym Selbs..."

The first work Bucer would produce dealt with the importance of living for one's neighbor rather than for oneself. The pastoral theme of ministering to the people of God became a theme that would endure throughout Bucer's life. The Church of Christ should be nurtured and cared for, and the people should live lives of mutual love and fruitfulness for Christ. He was greatly concerned that the clergy fulfill its responsibilities in guiding the Church to these ends, that the state perform its responsibilities in providing an environment where such Christian nurture could take place, and that the individual members of the Church should take seriously their responsibilities to live in love toward one another and to walk disciplined, orderly lives.

It was the meeting with Martin Luther at Heidelberg in 1518 that drew Bucer's attention to the subject of Christian love as Luther explained the doctrine of justification by faith. In his defense of his position Luther stated, with Bucer in the audience, that "man's love is aroused by what man likes, but God finds nothing loveable in man. God creates in man what God loves...the love of the cross, born of the cross, is this: it transfers itself not where it finds some good to be enjoyed, but there where it may confer some good to a sinner or to an unfortunate."[45] As Luther went on to explain to Bucer in their private meeting where he gave him the outline to his course on Romans, the Christian acknowledges that he is truly a sinner and at the same time truly considered righteous by God, "whole in hope, though in reality a sinner, but the Christian has the

---

[44] The complete title is "Das ym selbs niemat/sonder anderen leben soll, und wie der mensch dahyn kommen mög," ("That no one should live for himself, but rather for his neighbor, and how men are able to come to this.") BDS Vol. I, pp. 44-67.

[45] Martin Bucer, *Instruction in Christian Love: 1523 (das ym selbs...)* tr. Paul Traugott Fuhrmann and published under title: *Bucer on Love* (Richmond, VA: John Knox Press, 1952), p. 10; BDS I, pp. 44-67.

beginning of righteousness, that he may seek and ask more, always knowing himself unrighteous" (simul peccator et iustus)[46]

If God sees nothing loveable in man, yet he does love man, justify him, and create in him the beginning of true righteousness that is like God, then the expression of that divine work would be that man would seek to act in love toward his neighbor, not because he found something loveable in his neighbor, but because of the work of God in him. Bucer was beginning to assemble his mature theological concepts, but love of man for man always was foundational to his thought, and it is this great concept that he sought to set forth when asked by the Strasbourg council and pastors to clarify his beliefs in his first published work in 1523. The common people were already solidly behind Bucer; soon he would have the council and pastors united with him in a great effort to produce a truly Christian community in Strasbourg.

Bucer begins with this forward: "Martin Bucer to his readers. May God our Father and our Lord Jesus Christ give you grace and peace. Through our Lord Jesus Christ I thank and highly praise God our Father that He has so kindled in you the love and desire for His Word that you now diligently seek and ask for it. Indeed, righteousness and salvation come to us through the Word which awakens faith. Hence St. Paul rightly calls the Word a power unto salvation to every one who believes in it (Rom. 1:16). Since you so eagerly listen to it and so earnestly enquire about it, you are certainly born of God (John 8:47), and constitute a true assembly of Christ. For just as a city which listens to the word of the emperor and keeps his commands belongs to the empire, so the Kingdom of Christ and the true Church are surely where the Word of Christ is heard with such pleasure and observed with such diligence (Isaiah 55:11). As the Word of God cannot return to Him void, but must always capture some, it will not fail among you. The reason for my writing you in the measure of grace granted me and for offering you my guidance out of our mutual obligation is that some of you, my dear brethren and co-citizens, not satisfied with my sketchy lectures, have asked me to write this little essay. And so according to the Scripture I exhort every one of you not to live for himself, but for

---

[46] *Ibid.*

his neighbor. I shall later show how to attain this ideal, for it can be realized in this world and life. Since the Kingdom of God consists not of words but of power, may the Father of every grace grant through our Savior, Jesus Christ, that this perfect state may not remain a matter of mere talk among us. May the Father also make it so that you do not stop at these and other merely human suggestions, but devote yourselves to the divine Scripture and, as loyal sheep of your true and only Shepherd, Jesus, listen to His voice so that you may therewith progress in faith, be perfected in all love, live not at all for yourselves but for your neighbor, and through your neighbor for Christ, and through Christ for the Father Almighty. Praise and glorify Him in eternity. Amen. Strassburg, August, 1523."

Bucer then proceeds to illustrate in the first part of his sermon how man may attain the ideal of living not for himself but for others. He points out the inherent inability of man, that the pot cannot help the potter, that the creature cannot help the Creator in divine things: "Nothing can help God to be God. Nothing can keep him from acting as God."[47] Though man cannot help himself to be this kind of person, he must recognize that he was created for just such a purpose: "God's reason for creating us and all creatures is to make His goodness known. He willed that whatever thing exists through His goodness should recognize it and rejoice over it."[48] In the creation mandate God gave man dominion over all that He made, and He also gave man freedom, skill, power, and understanding, with the intention that man use these gifts to perform good: "To use each thing for the purpose for which it was made by God is not only honorable and godly but brings honor and profit to the thing itself."[49]

However, sin has poisoned the nature of man and caused him to turn away from God and to become selfish. We now use the creation to selfish and harmful ends and lack the ability to use plants and other creations of God for good. Thus, as Paul states in Romans chapter eight, the whole creation is burdened by sin and awaits the time of glorious restoration. Given this end in view, Bucer states:

---

[47] das ym selbs, p. 21.
[48] *Ibid.,* p.22.
[49] *Ibid., p. 23.*

"From all this it is clear that no one should live for himself, because God created all things so that they might contribute not to their own good but to that of others, and be an instrument and evidence of the divine goodness which all things should express and spread forth."[50] Man must then take the love that his own poisoned nature had him to place on himself and place it on his neighbor. When a minister preaches the word of God, he is doing just that for the whole Christian community, working spiritual good to each member.[51] Bucer wrote: "He commits no sin, therefore, who loves God and desires to obtain this blessedness for his neighbors."[52] Even if they are unwilling to go to the point of sacrificing their own blessedness for their neighbors, they should at least be willing to impart the Gospel to them faithfully, without seeking shameful personal profits and vain honors. "May they draw near a little and have a bit of that apostolic disposition with the Law, the Prophets, Christ, and all the Apostles set forth...It cannot be denied that most churchmen, as one may sadly see, now everywhere seek their own interest and not the benefit and blessedness of those under them, except in the measure in which the others' benefit and blessedness bring them material advantages and subserve their prestige."[53]

Bucer goes on to discuss the failure of the clergy to seek the good of those under their charge through the faithful preaching of the Word and the pastoral care of souls. Here is the clear note of distinction Bucer sees in the Reformed ministry that sets it apart, and provides the basis of his life's work: to bless people by preaching the Gospel and nurturing souls and bodies of believers.

He went back into the Old Testament to show that the function of the office of king was to govern the people for their good, and thus he could make an application to the work of the Christian king or prince in his own day. But, he observed, the rulers of his day were not concerned with divine Law but were bailiffs of men rather

---

[50] *Ibid.,* p. 28.
[51] *Ibid.,* p. 30.
[52] *Ibid.,* p. 31.
[53] *Ibid.,* p. 33.

than of God.[54] Yet the heart of the ruler is in the hands of God, and thus we should pray for our rulers.

The law of practicing love is extended to the family, for Bucer urges parents to direct their children into professions that will produce good for others. He mentions agriculture, cattle raising, and such necessary occupations. Parents should not necessarily encourage them to become clergymen, given the godless position of the clergy, neither should they encourage them in the direction of business, for the desire to become rich leads to eternal death. Bucer was always disdainful of wealth for the Christian, and modeled that disdain in his own life.[55]

The change in man from one oriented to selfishness to the desire to do good to his neighbor comes only through faith, only when men place their trust in the blood of Christ. We must believe that God, by making Christ head of His community has reconciled and united all things through Him, brought all things back to their original character, living for the glory of God and the usefulness to all His creatures, especially to men. Only then will the true spirit of love certainly return to us. True faith can make it so that we completely believe all the words of God – that we are rescued from the power of darkness and through the grace of the Father placed in His Kingdom. Only faith can detach us from ourselves and make us give ourselves over to God the Father as children. As true children our highest concern must be to follow the will of this dearest and best of fathers and in all things to live according to His Law, which is fulfilled in the single commandment: "Love thy neighbor as thyself." We must hold that we shall receive all necessary things and consider ourselves as nothing else than already blessed, now in hope of eternal inheritance.[56]

Faith places us in touch with God's love for us so that we can understand it, and understanding it enables us to act in like manner to others. "If God has sacrificed what was most dear and precious to Him, which sin of ours will He not overlook? What good could he withhold from us? His love is too great. Hence as soon as, through

---

[54] *Ibid.*, pp. 36-37.
[55] *Ibid.*, pp. 39-40.
[56] *Ibid.*, pp. 43-44.

faith, the heart recognizes and holds this truth, so soon the heart is overflowed with love and thereby completely made ready to do good to all men, and eager first of all, by proclaiming to them the unspeakable goodness of God, to lead them to this blessed sense of security." Bucer said that the nature of goodness is that it cannot be kept to itself.[57]   A good tree cannot be without good fruit. "Knowing that we are children who shall never suffer want in the present nor in the future, we feel the further need to serve our brethren in all faithfulness and with unfeigned love which springs from faith. Bucer comments that it should cause us to rejoice in that we are allowed in serving our neighbor to show a little gratitude to our gracious Father.   The man of faith shall acquire the same disposition he sees in Christ. A believing heart, meditating on the humbling of Christ to become a servant shall be so completely kindled to love for his Savior that it will completely renounce itself, strip itself, and think if Christ so humbled himself and became a servant, "Oh, may I, at least a little, follow my Lord and Deliverer as a token of gratitude, I who am nothing and can do nothing? All I have is through Thee out of the grace of the Father. I will keep nothing for myself but with joy will put all I possess at the service of my brethren."[58] Bucer commented that faith takes away from us the love for the present life that hinders so many from exercising true love and service to their neighbor.[59] Only faith brings us back to our primeval right and godly disposition as God first created it, so we may be useful to all creatures. Faith is true righteousness in which a righteous man lives and walks. He gives to God the honor and praise due to Him, and practices toward his neighbor love which fulfills all commandments. Thus we show ourselves to be disciples of Christ, keeping His new commandment. Faith brings self denial, dedication of self to the service of other men, forgetfulness of self, and living wholly for others to the glory of God. Otherwise it is not true and legitimate faith but a dead faith.[60] Bucer said that to preach faith is to point out the spring of all good deeds. "As faith comes

---

[57] *Ibid.,* p. 45.
[58] *Ibid.,* p. 47.
[59] *Ibid.,* p. 48.
[60] *Ibid.*

from God's grace through hearing the Word of God, we must above all things adhere to the divine Word, hear it, read it, meditate on it with all diligence, and act accordingly. We must let no man keep us from the Word of God; for it we must risk honor, life, possessions, and all that which God has given us. The divine Word brings faith; faith brings love; love brings good deeds as its fruits – after which God gives us the eternal inheritance, a wholly divine and blessed life. Amen."[61]

The little sermon once published became a prospectus for the Reformation. Bucer demanded the freedom to preach the Word of God openly, which was, in effect, a mandate to the civil authorities. The clergy could hear from it their obligation to be faithful in its proclamation. The people could hear the necessity of hearing and believing the Word. Bucer illustrated that faith was the divine activating principle of love that resulted in good works to the glory of God, but faith came by the Word of God. The work is not of man, but rather the Christian is God's creation by His grace to good works ordained for him. The whole Reformation principle was here, with a practical emphasis on love – acting in love toward one's neighbor. The implication was clear that such love could not be practiced under a system where corrupt clergy neglected their charge and the Word was fettered. But Bucer was not using love merely as a wedge to gain acceptance for the open preaching of the gospel of grace; rather, he was thoroughly sincere in his desire to see Christian love implemented, and he manifested that sincerity in his own behavior. It was this little sermon, this little pamphlet, that gained for Bucer the credibility he needed to proceed with the Reformation in Strasbourg, and once Strasbourg was open to him, Europe would follow, and the single most influential architect of the Reformed Church had begun his arduous and tortuous work.

Saint Aurelia to St. Thomas: Bucer as Strasbourg Pastor

Bucer gained rapid and widespread popularity with the common people of Strasbourg through his lectures in St. Thomas on the famous wooden pulpit and his small group teaching in Zell's home.

---

[61] *Ibid.,* p. 52.

Once he published *Das Ym Selbs*.... his reputation increased all the more. The vicar of Strasbourg said nothing: he neither sanctioned nor condemned Bucer's sermon. The vicar wisely sensed Bucer's wide popularity with the people

However the bishop, William von Hohenstein, was quite disturbed about a married priest preaching and publishing and demanded that the council deny Bucer protection. He also expelled Bucer from the diocese of Strasbourg. The council, trying to avoid taking sides, merely handed the bishop's letter to Bucer and advised him to write a defense, which Bucer was delighted to do. Bucer believed, at least until his later days, that if the truth was given an opportunity to be brought into the realm of public attention, it would triumph over error. Thus, Bucer wrote for the council his defense, his answer, the *Verantwortung* which he read to the council on June 20, 1523.[62]

In his answer he argued that he had a right to the protection of the city on the basis of the fact that he was the son of a citizen. He had asked the council for the right to exercise the only means available to him to earn a living. He claimed that he had met all requirements laid on him by the council, such as to cease teaching in German, and that he had taught nothing contrary to the Scriptures. He claimed that his marriage was legal and open according to both imperial and divine law and was a benefit both to him and to his wife. He claimed that the sentence of excommunication was not justifiable in his case.[63] The council agreed to hear Bucer's father who appeared before them and plead for his son. The council concurred with Bucer and sent a notice to the bishop that it would not remove protection from Bucer on the basis of the fact that he was the son of a citizen, and because he had not been officially installed as a preacher, mandates against married clergy would not apply in his case. The council's decision was pivotal in the progress of the Reformation in Strasbourg.

Bucer wanted the protection provided by citizenship, and thus he appealed to the council for consideration of his request. By acquiescing, the council was effectively removing the distinction

---

[62] BDS Vol. I, pp. 293-302.
[63] Cf. Eells, p 27.

between clergy and laity in Strasbourg. Other preachers took wives, and the established Catholic clergy was helpless to prevent it.[64] The bishop simply reacted by excommunicating all the Strasbourg clergy. The Reformation was now established.

One of the churches in Strasbourg was in need of a pastor. It was a congregation peopled by common folk. Most of them made a living by selling their produce from their own gardens. Of course, Bucer was an excommunicated and married priest, and for that reason the Catholic cathedral chapter rejected the request of the people of St. Aurelia to have Bucer installed as preacher. The council, still wanting to mediate between Catholic clergy and Protestant pastors, tried to suggest a compromise, but finally yielded to the gardeners, lest they offend a sizeable number of citizens. The parishioners of St. Aurelia wanted Bucer as their pastor, and they got him as their pastor!

Bucer preached his first sermon for this congregation on March 31, 1524. The council had now established the precedent of installing its first Protestant pastor, and soon others were installed. Capito, for instance, was installed as the pastor of New St. Peter's. In these installations the churches actually selected their own pastor, thus beginning the Protestant practice of a church *calling* its pastor.

Bucer's time at St. Aurelia was pleasant and productive. His sermons were well received by the congregation. Because St. Aurelia was supposedly a virgin, one of 11,000, her bones were venerated at this church named for her. Bucer had her "bones" dug up and said that they looked more like animal bones than human bones, and he told the parishioners that he was concerned that when people made pilgrimages to such churches to venerate saints, they thought that God was somehow confined to their bones. What Bucer courageously began that day continued and resulted in the systematic removal of images from the churches of Strasbourg, beginning with St. Aurelia. Bucer was not a true iconoclast, for he did not see images as wrong in themselves, but claimed that they became wrong at the point that people actually worshipped them, and, in fact, Bucer claimed that such a practice he had witnessed. Bucer always drew the line when a practice became "superstition."

---

[64] Eells, p. 28.

While Bucer was pastor of St. Aurelia, Erasmus published his famous *Diatribe on Free Will* to see if he could provoke a reaction from Luther. Bucer was deeply saddened by Erasmus' rejection of God's prevenient grace expressed in predestination of the elect, and he thought the time had come to make his own break from his former mentor and those who followed him. He wrote to Luther and urged him to reply to the "pestiferous pamphlet of the unhappy slave of glory, who pushes forward to prefer the spit of his own opinion to Scripture."[65] We do not know if Bucer's encouragement had any effect on Luther's decision to reply; he would probably have done so anyway. However, we can note that Bucer would have stood firmly on Luther's side in the famous reply *On the Bondage of the Will,* which left no doubt where the Reformers stood on the subject of salvation by grace alone.

The journey to St. Thomas Church was a slow transition. Zell involved Bucer increasingly in working with him. Bucer had permission to lecture on alternate days from the wooden pulpit erected in St. Thomas. He also presented lectures in Capito's house, with Capito lecturing on the Old Testament and Bucer on the New Testament. The lectures were later moved to monastery buildings, after the orders had lost their control of religion in Strasbourg. Capito and Bucer were joined by Kaspar Hedio, and they worked through exposition of book after book of the Bible. Their lectures marked the beginning of what would become the University of Strasbourg.

From the outset, education was of great importance to Bucer and the other reformers of Strasbourg. Bucer believed strongly that the whole community should be governed by and should operate by the principles of the Christian faith, and such operation required people educated in the faith. Jacob Sturm, completely in favor of the Reformation, worked closely with the preachers in establishing the educational system for the city. The school board was composed of three councilmen and two pastors, and they set up twelve grammar schools: six for boys and six for girls.[66]

---

[65] Eells, p. 41.
[66] Eells, p. 47.

By 1527 Bucer's reputation as a leading reformer was well known, and in that year he published his *Enarrationum in evangelia Matthiae, Marci, & Lucae*, an excellent commentary on the synoptic gospels that would mark him as a first rate scholar, would publish his theological concepts openly, and would have a major impact on the development of the thought of the younger John Calvin.[67]

Bucer's Theology in Process

At this juncture it will be good to stop and review the development of Bucer's theological ideas. There is no doubt that Bucer's theology underwent development, but it was a dynamic period in which theologians interacted and reacted with each other, learned from each other, honed and refined ideas, and moved slowly, and not always completely in concert, toward the defining of Protestant theology.

With the reformers, as with all Christian thinkers, ideas usually are the result of challenge, and it was no different with Martin Bucer. At the point Bucer was pastor at St. Aurelia and ready to make his move to St. Thomas, he had not yet encountered the challenges of the "Supper Strife," that would motivate him to define his communion theology, nor had he had to confront the Anabaptists who would force him to think through the meaning of Christian community and baptism. However, what he had learned first from Erasmus and then from Luther, and the trials he had faced from Dominican opposition, had provided for him a sufficient basis for much of his basic belief system. Bucer never wavered from these basic beliefs; rather, he built upon them as he gleaned new insights from the events that were yet to happen. As Bucer moved from being an "Erasmian," through being a "Martinian," to the point of an independent Christian theologian, certain beliefs were well established:

The Fall. Bucer accepted the doctrine of original sin that had been the hallmark of orthodox Christianity since the time of the

---

[67] A good translation into French and analysis of this work has been done by Jacques Courvoisier (Paris: Pasteur Licenciè en Thèologia: Librairie Fèlix Alcan, 1933).

Pelagian controversy. He saw clearly the wide implications of the reality of original sin in the disruption of all of nature that now must look to Christ for redemption. His theology is, as with Luther and later Calvin, *per* the fall; that is, Christ's work is necessitated by the fall because man has lost the moral ability to redeem himself or even to come to God.

Salvation by God's grace. Erasmus exercised the primary influence on Bucer to direct him away from works toward salvation by grace alone, but Luther reinforced that concept in his mind. By the mid 1520's Bucer enunciated a doctrine of salvation by the grace of God alone to which man could contribute nothing by his good works.

Election. Erasmus disappointed Bucer by renouncing the doctrine of predestination, and there was no doubt as to the force with which Luther embraced it. Bucer stood squarely with Luther, and perhaps gave broader implications to the doctrine. Although Luther saw predestination as the hinge on which everything turned, Bucer documented the eternal decrees as fundamental in a very practical sense to every aspect of our lives and in the certainty of our salvation. Along with the other major Reformers, Bucer believed that the invisible church was made up of the elect, known only to God. Through the preaching of the gospel, the Holy Spirit would bring the elect to faith, and the invisible church would become the visible church. Bucer's whole theology grows out of the concept of the elective, predestining decrees of God. To fail to understand the significance of election in Bucer's theology would be to miss the whole of it.

The Holy Spirit. As election accounted for the fundamental direction and purpose of salvation, so the Holy Spirit became the instrumental means of its accomplishment. Bucer had a *pneumatology* so extensive that he saw the Holy Spirit as the power and source of all Christian activity. The church and all it does come under the supervisory work of the Spirit. The concept of the centrality of the Spirit is a primary characteristic of Bucer's theology[68]

---

[68] See W.P. Stephens, *The Holy Spirit in the Theology of Martin Bucer,* (Cambridge: At the University Press, 1970).

Justification by faith. From the time Bucer heard Luther at Heidelberg in 1518, he was firmly committed to the position of *sola fide*. Man is declared righteous by faith, and by faith alone. Justification involves the imputation of Christ's righteousness to man, and the imputation of man's sins to Christ.

Piety. Although Bucer was deeply impressed later by the piety of the Anabaptists and incorporated many of their ideas about Christian living, the primary impetus did not come from them, but from Erasmus. Bucer recognized that he was indebted to Luther for understanding the justification of the sinner, but he was equally indebted to Erasmus for understanding the concept of the sanctification of life. In that regard, he was able to fuse the two into a working synthesis that he retained for his entire life.[69] Bucer believed passionately in the necessity of a godly Christian life, so much so that he considered sanctification as a second justification, based on James chapter two. This "double justification" concept, however, did no violence to the doctrine of forensic justification as a once-and-for all act. The truly regenerate person who is justified by faith alone will be sanctified and live a life of Christian love and piety.

Love of Neighbor. Already evident in the publication of *Das Ym Selbs,* Bucer by this point was firmly committed to the rule that Christians must love their neighbors and seek their good above his own. This rule became central to the very view Bucer held of the Christian life. All theology and preaching should have in view the good of the Christian and the Christian community. Christians needed to live their lives with such a view paramount in their hearts.

Marriage. Bucer came to Strasbourg as a married clergyman and found himself in the posture of having to defend his marriage from the criticism of the bishop. Again, Erasmus had a great influence on Bucer, for Erasmus taught that true love was a necessary part of marriage, and Bucer rejected Thomas Aquinas' mechanical view. Luther influenced Bucer to believe in the freedom

---

[69] H. J. Selderhuis, *Marriage and Divorce in the Thought of Marin Bucer,* tr. John Vriend and Lyle D. Bierma, in *Sixteenth Century Essays and Studies,* XLVIII (Kirkville, Mo: Thomas Jefferson University Press and Truman State University, 1999), p. 52.

of a Christian, and Erasmus in the importance of piety. These concepts came together in Bucer's mind as he came to understand that the rule of clerical celibacy forced priests and monks to take concubines because they lacked the gift to remain celibate. He was horrified that the church thought it was better for a priest to keep a whore than to be married.[70] He came to see the doctrine of forced clerical celibacy as wrong and immoral, and appealed to Scripture to support the belief that unless one had the gift of celibacy, it was the will of God to marry, whether lay or clergy. He wrote of his own marriage: "God has joined us together, he has helped us, and it is not true that one has craftily persuaded the other to take this step."[71]

---

[70] *Ibid.,* pp. 68-69.
[71] BD 51.175 in Selderhuis, p. 61.

Chapter IV

Bucer "The Fanatic for Unity"

The Separatist Controversy

The first problem with which Bucer had to deal in Strasbourg, which became only a gentle prelude to the vicissitudes of the "Supper Strife," concerned the Separatists. This group, along with those called "Enthusiasts," was convinced that the Reformation had not advanced far enough, and that a more thorough break with Rome and all its traditions was in order. There were no core doctrinal statements to bind these scattered groups together, but generally they disavowed a Christian community in favor of "gathered" churches, congregations composed of people who formed voluntary associations. Several terms came to be applied to these groups, such as "The Radical Reformation," "The Left-Wing of the Reformation," and "Anabaptists," because most chose to manifest their disdain for Christian community by abandoning infant baptism in favor of believers' baptism exclusively.

The movement seemed to have its genesis in Zürich with two of Zwingli's former pastors, Conrad Grebel and Felix Manz. They came to disagree fundamentally with Zwingli's involvement in the city government and the close cooperation between city council and the pastors. Their complete separation from any kind of identification between church and state and, therefore, repudiation of the very concept of Christian community beyond the gathered church, was a concept that orthodox Christians had never entertained since the fall of the Roman Empire. The church believed that Christ would rule over the nations, and they saw the conversion of Constantine as the outworking of that divine prophecy and promise. Since the early fifth century Christians labored to actualize Augustine's "City of God." Even though power politics and greed entered frequently into play on both the part of secular lords and church hierarchy, most affirmed that it was a dream worthy of continued effort. Protestants saw an opportunity to re-create a true Christian community purged from the corruption of

Rome's decadent and often vicious political machinations, and shaped and informed by Scripture alone. It was a golden opportunity that the Reformers welcomed but took seriously. Zwingli reacted in disbelief, anger, and finally in active opposition to these separatists in Zürich, and most of them fled elsewhere for safety.

Inevitably Separatists would make their way to Strasbourg, which already had a reputation for being a safe haven for the persecuted. Bucer and the other Strasbourg pastors were unwilling to treat them with inhospitality, but they asked for an opportunity to meet and dialogue with them over matters over which they differed. Very simply, Bucer found two areas of major disagreement with Separatists (Anabaptists), and one area for which he admired them greatly.

The latter positive reaction was over the Anabaptists' zeal and personal piety. Bucer still lived in the light of Erasmian pietistic influence, and he recognized and welcomed any individuals or groups committed to the godly Christian life. He also fought his whole life to stir up his brothers and sisters to passion and zeal over the gospel, and he appreciated such zeal in the Anabaptists. He would continue to talk with them, listen to them, and apply points he learned from them in this area, as he would dialogue with any such groups, including the Moravian Brethren.

Bucer could not, however, agree with the Anabaptists over the destruction of Christian community. More than any of the other Reformers, Martin Bucer was committed to the idea and ideal of the Christian community. He believed that the sovereign God reigned over all the earth, and that God would give his Son authority over the nations. The gospel rightfully belonged to all people, and the Christian civil authorities had the right and responsibility to protect and promote the preaching of the gospel in their cities. Coupled with these concepts was Bucer's deep conviction that Christians should act in love toward their neighbors, and the government should protect the opportunity for free and open practice of Christian charity. Church and state would work together to promote good morals and provide the environment in which the gospel of Christ could flourish and people practice love for each other. Government must be able to restrain and punish those who would not live in accordance with God's will, and this they did by making and enforcing laws. Their doing so allowed godly people to pursue service to God and each other without interference from wicked folk.

It was in the matrix of this shocking challenge to the very concept of Christian community that Bucer developed his own ideas, ideas that would grow and mature in the coming years, so that Bucer was identified with the very concept. His dedication to community would call forth some of his most noble and creative efforts.[72]

The Anabaptists discarded infant baptism because it was the symbol of Christian community. A child was born into the community and baptized as a sign of his belonging to it. In order to make sure that all commitments and identification were the results of mature, personal choices, the Anabaptists began the practice of re-baptizing people who had been baptized as infants.[73] Again, such a practice was a total innovation to orthodox Christians who practiced infant baptism from the beginning of the church. The notion of children deprived from baptism was a shocking if not frightening thought.

But again Bucer used the challenge as a catalyst to his thought. The argument for adult-only baptism could be made Biblically based on the fact that baptism was a sign of faith, and infants characteristically do not exercise faith. Also, there are no specific examples of infant baptism in Scripture. However, Bucer was convinced that it was clearly the will of the Lord that infants be baptized, because infants belonged to the kingdom. He referred to Jesus' prohibition to his disciples from preventing little children from coming to him. He took them in his arms and blessed them, and he said that "theirs is the kingdom of heaven," in other words, they belong to the kingdom.[74] The kingdom is a community, infants belong, and the visible mark of belonging to the community is baptism. The kingdom is manifested in covenant communities, and

---

[72] Bucer's work in building Christian communities is carefully analyzed in a series of essays edited by D.F. Wright and recently published under the title *Martin Bucer: Reforming Church and Community* (Cambridge: University Press, 1994)

[73] Hence the name *Anabaptist. Ana* in Greek means *again.*

[74] Matthew 19:13-15.

baptism is the sign of the covenant. Therefore, infants rightfully should be baptized.

Bucer became so passionate about the matter of infant baptism that he came to be called the "unparalleled master of a theology of infant baptism". He found over twenty reasons for the practice, and induced the city council to make parents' bringing of infants for baptism mandatory. "When paedobaptism was at issue, that tendency in Bucer's thought which assimilated the religious community to the civil was paramount."[75] It was this very assimilation of the religious community to the civil that caused the Anabaptists, the Separatists, to react. Their intention was to separate the religious community from the civil, and create a religious community based entirely on the volition of individual Christians. But for Bucer, or for any of the Reformers, to entertain such an idea would be a rejection of the reign of Christ over the nations. At stake was the whole vision of Christian community as well as the precious act of identifying an infant with that community and the Lord of that community. Because these two concepts were interrelated, an attack on one was an attack on the other, and to defend one was to defend the other. Bucer chose to defend infant baptism with all his energy, knowing that in so doing he was defending as well the concept of Christian community.

Bucer's concept of the relationship of church to state is summarized well in this excerpt from his articles for discussion at the Strasbourg Synod in 1533:

The civil authorities, who exercise the sword and the highest outward power, are servants of God; they ought, therefore, to direct all their abilities, as God in his law has commanded and as the Spirit of Christ himself teaches and urges in all whom he leads, to the end that through their subjects God's name be hallowed, his kingdom extended and his will fulfilled, so far as they can serve thereto by virtue of their office alone. Therefore the spirit of those who want the authorities not to concern themselves at all with

---

[75] David Wright, "Infant Baptism and the Christian Community in Bucer," in *Reforming Church and Community,* p. 96.

Christian activity, is a spirit directed against Christ our Lord, and a destroyer of all good.[76]

Americans pride themselves on Jefferson's "wall of separation between church and state," but that idea was both foreign and anti-Christian to the Reformers. Leaders of the state were to be subordinate to the ends of the church, but not to the church itself. Christians were obliged to obey the civil magistrates, but those magistrates in turn were obliged to be Christians, obey Christ, and rule in a way in keeping with Christ's directives.[77]

Bucer worked with the pastors of the church in Basel to produce in 1532 the *Confession of Basel*. In that confession, concerning magistrates, we read:

> *Moreover, God hath assigned to the magistrate, who is His minister, the sword and chief external power, for the defence of the good, and for the revenging and punishing of evil (Rom. Xiii.4; 1 Pet. Ii.14). Therefore every Christian magistrate doth direct all his strength to this: that among those which are committed to this charge, the name of God may be sanctified, his kingdom may be enlarged, and men may live according to his will, with an earnest rooting out of all naughtiness.*[78]

In the 1536 *Former Confession of Helvetia*, drawn up by Bucer and Wolfgang Capito and presented to the pastors of Wirtemburg, these words appear:

> *Seeing that every magistrate is of God, his chief durt (except it please him to exercise a tyranny) consisteth in this; to defend*

---

[76] BDS 5, p. 392. Cited also in Martin Greschat, "The Relation between Church and Civil Community in Bucer's Reforming Work," in Wright: *Martin Bucer: Reforming Church and Community.* For further discussion of Bucer's view of Christian community, see later chapter in this book on *De Regno Christi,* written for the expressed purpose of providing guidance for King Edward VI of England in setting up a true Christian state.

[77] David Hall, *Savior or Servant, Putting Government in Its Place,* cited from capo.org/premise/96/mar/p960304.

[78] Confession of Basel, Article VII: Of Magistracy.

and protect religion from all blasphemy, and as the prophet teacheth out of the word of the Lord, to put it in practice, so much as in him lieth (Ezek. Xiv.9). In which part truly the first place is given to the pure and free preaching of the word of God, the instruction of the youth of citizens, and a right and diligent teaching in schools; to lawful discipline, a liberal provision for the ministers of the Church and a provident care for the poor (unto which object tend all the faculties of the Church; secondly, to judge the people according to just and divine laws. That is, agreeably to equity and righteousness, and, to conclude, to the law of nature, whereof God himself is the author, to keep judgment and justice, to maintain the public peace, to cherish the commonwealth, and to punish offenders, according to the quality of the fault, in their estate, person, or life. Which things when he doth, he performeth a service due to God. We know that, though we be free, we both in our body, and in all our faculties, and with endeavor of mind also to perform faithfulness, and the oath which we made to him....so far forth as his government is not evidently repugnant to Him, for whose sake we do reverence the magistrate.[79]

Thus Bucer could not and would not agree to such a separation of church and state that would do violence to the very concept of a Christian ruler and his domain that Bucer and the other Reformers believed was entirely Biblical. All rulers, whether pagan, as in the time of the Roman Empire when Paul and Peter wrote, or Christian rulers, were established by God to be his instruments for order in the state. Christian rulers recognized the source of their power and mandate and held a golden opportunity to fulfill that mandate. To Bucer it would be absurd to deny that opportunity when God had graciously provided it. To separate church and state would be sheer madness.

But Bucer and Zwingli reacted quite differently to the Anabaptist/Separatist threat. Whereas Zwingli considered their doctrines heresy that should carry the traditional penalty of death,

---

[79] *Former Confession of Helvetia,* 1536, Article 26: Of the Magistracy.

Bucer followed, as he usually did, the conciliatory route. He engaged the Separatists in debate, treated them with the respect due to brothers in Christ, and tried to learn what he could from them that he could use in his own ministry. That is not to say that Bucer did not consider them a threat with which he had to reckon, but he regarded them as misguided Christians, not total heretics.[80]

The radicals flocked to Strasbourg for the simple reason that under the guidance of Bucer and Capito it had gained a reputation for tolerance; it had become a refuge for all those persecuted by the Roman Church for whatever reason. Bucer characteristically was irenic, and he and Capito genuinely wanted outcasts from other cities to feel welcome in Strasbourg and become a part of the religious community. The Anabaptists, on the other hand, were intransigent. They believed that their position was the truth and that they alone represented the true church. To them the Reformation was still too Roman to meet their approval, and their steadfast refusal to work with the Reformers of Strasbourg led to a gradual change of attitude on their part toward these newcomers. Eventually Bucer took a more forceful position against the Anabaptists, but only when he was convinced that reason and Biblical persuasion were insufficient to change them. Even when the Strasbourg city council was forced to respond to the attacks of Separatist leaders against them, retribution was light. (Only two Anabaptists were ever executed for heresy in Strasbourg, and one of them who was spared continued in an adulterous relationship.[81])

However, the involvement of Martin Bucer with the Anabaptists became a formative period in his life for a number of reasons. Although this involvement is usually overshadowed by the more

---

[80] Anabaptist scholars disagree on Bucer's reaction. Chris Good (*The Anabaptists and the Reformation*, ww.rbc.org.nz/library/anabap.htm) referred to Bucer as "The Gentle Reformer," and cited the fact that he and Capito were reluctant to use force, believing only that civil disobedience should be punished. However, John Howard Fowler (*The Historical Origins of Christian Non-Juration*, www.lafn.org/~az248/Oath.htm) described Bucer's hatred toward the Anabaptists that even Capito called "savage," and cited Bucer's demand that they should be condemned for denying God's order in the world of magistrates, oaths, and the sword. The contradiction is resolved by understanding the change in Bucer's attitude over time.

[81] Eells, p. 57.

dramatic and far-reaching controversy over the meaning of the Lord's Supper, Bucer's interaction with these Separatists led him to produce some of his most significant contributions to the developing Reformation. His attitude toward them was tempered also by his close friendship with Margaret Blaurer, sister of Ambrose Blaurer, Reformed pastor of Konstanz. Margaret came to embrace Anabaptist beliefs, but she never severed her friendship with Bucer. The other Strasbourg pastors sided with Bucer and followed the general rule that whoever confessed Christ as Lord should be regarded as a Christian and fellowship not withheld from him.

One of the first Anabaptists in Strasbourg, Clemens Ziegler, was a member of the gardeners' guild that had elected Bucer to the pastorate of St. Aurelia. Another, Jacob Gross, engaged Bucer in a disputation and was later exiled.[82] It was Hans Denck, who came to Strasbourg after having been exiled from Nürnberg and Augsburg, who offered Bucer the greatest challenge. Denck was a well-educated and highly moral leader among the Separatists, who took advantage of the open policy of Strasbourg for refuge and accepted Bucer's offer for an open disputation on four controversial doctrines: the freedom of the will, the negative character of sin, the sinlessness of true Christians, and universal salvation. When Bucer answered these positions with citations from the apostle Paul, he forced Denck to admit that he was willing to set Paul aside in favor of these beliefs. Denck was subsequently exiled from Strasbourg, and Bucer published a tract, *Getrewe Warnung,* providing his account of the disputation, attacking the teaching of Denck and other Anabaptists, and seeking to undermine their influence.[83] Denck and other Anabaptists now began a vicious attack on Strasbourg and her leadership, so vehement that the council regretted that it had been so mild, and on July 27, 1527, issued a mandate forbidding anyone to feed or give shelter to Anabaptists.

Yet Anabaptists still continued to come to Strasbourg and create turmoil.[84] By far the most radical was Melchoir Hoffman, who stirred up so much opposition along the lower Rhine region that he

---

[82] *Ibid.*
[83] Eells, p. 58; BDS Vol. II, pp. 234-258.
[84] Eells, p. 59.

was hounded by civil authorities everywhere. The disturbance that he caused in Strasbourg motivated the city council to imprison him in 1533.[85] Thus the irenic policy had failed, yet Bucer remained impressed with the commitment of these people to Christian piety and their emphasis on the personal guidance of the Holy Spirit. These points Bucer increasingly stressed in the development of his own theology and its implementation.

Some of the Anabaptists, like Michael Keller and Michael Sattler, possessed a more civil attitude, and Bucer and Capito became close friends with them. Sattler was close to the Reformers in his own beliefs, his primary point of departure being that he believed salvation was *promoted* by good works, true believers had to be separated from false ones in congregations (a denial of the traditional Augustinian *permixed* concept), and baptism marked the entrance by such true believers into these pure congregations.

Both Bucer and Capito were impressed with Keller's piety. Capito was so captivated by the man that he began to listen to his arguments against infant baptism, and gradually Capito embraced the Anabaptist adult-only view. Keller tried to leave the impression that Bucer agreed also, and Bucer dispelled any such thoughts by his publication of his commentary on the book of John in which he set forth his view that infant baptism was the clear will of God. Keller was furious with Bucer and began to drive a wedge between him and Capito, so much that Bucer consulted Zwingli and Oecolampadius on what his course of action should be. They wisely advised him to stay close to Capito, and although Capito continued to hold to Anabaptist views on baptism, the relationship with Bucer was healed. Bucer by this time came to regard the Anabaptists as dangerous, but he continued to meet them in public discussions.[86]

The confrontation with Anabaptists and the failure to win them by conciliatory means led Bucer to propose the Confession of 1533 that was adopted by the Strasbourg city council. The point that was clear by this time to Bucer was that doctrine needed to be well-defined by the pastors and defended by the city council. Reformation theology, as defined by Bucer, the other Strasbourg

---

[85] "The Anabaptists," spectrum.troyst.edu/~glitz/
[86] Eells, pp. 61-64.

pastors, and the Strasbourg city council, affirmed infant baptism, the permixed church, the fact that Christians continue the struggle against the sinful nature and its manifestations throughout life, that the Christian community with the relationship of church to state is right and needful, that man's will in bondage to sin precludes "free will," that the Old Testament is not inferior to the New and the Son did not change what the Father ordained in the law, for the Old and New Testaments represent a single, coherent law with no internal contradictions,[87] and that salvation is according to the predestining decrees of God.

The need for well-defined statements of faith also influenced Bucer in the direction of the development of the Protestant confirmation ceremony in which young people would state their beliefs publicly,[88] and the Tetrapolitan Confession. However, he was so impressed with the personal commitment of the Anabaptists to piety that he was determined to create small groups of Christians within congregations who would be dedicated to influencing the larger group toward Christian living. These contributions will be considered separately at a later point in this book, but for now we simply need to note the role that the Anabaptist interchange played with Bucer.

Another positive result of this interchange was the opportunity for Bucer and Zwingli to grow closer. The two leaders had been estranged during the initial stages of the controversy over the Lord's Supper, but the fact that Bucer consulted Zwingli for his advice on the Anabaptists helped Zwingli to restore his confidence in Bucer. That confidence would be largely maintained up to Zwingli's untimely death, but the less reasonable Heinrich Bullinger who succeeded Zwingli would prove beyond Bucer's reach.

Bucer's conciliatory attitude toward the Anabaptists was not without good results. He was known to visit them in prison in Strasbourg to plead with them patiently to return to the faith, and he

---

[87] Fowler, loc. cit.

[88] "His proposals for a public confirmation for baptized adolescents after they had been instructed in the faith came in response to Anabaptist demands for public profession of faith and surrender to Christ," Amy Nelson Burnett, "Confirmation and Christian Fellowship: Martin Bucer on Commitment to the Church," *Church History,* vol. 64, #2 (June 1995), p. 122.

listened to what they had to say about piety with interest and admiration. In his later years he was able to have sufficient influence to bring a number of Anabaptists, some of them leaders in the movement, back into the Reformed church. The most notable case is that of Peter Tesch whom he met during his work with the church in Hesse. Philip was concerned about the spread of Anabaptist doctrines and had invited Bucer to come there and organize the church in order to stop their progress. He debated with them during their imprisonment, sympathized with their concern for discipline, and won Tesch, who later sought out Bucer and expressed his desire to be reconciled with the church, feeling that the Anabaptists had created much offence and no real reformation by their separation. Tesch then sought to encourage other Anabaptists likewise to return.[89]

The Controversy over the Lord's Supper

The Origin of the "Supper-Strife"

Martin Bucer's ability as a peacemaker would be most severely tested by the tumultuous controversy that arose in Protestant ranks over the Communion and threatened to create warring denominations out of what could have been a united Reformed Church. The origins of the controversy really lay in the differences in background of the two great leaders, Martin Luther and Ulrich Zwingli. Luther had never had any involvement with humanism. His approach to theology reflected his peasant upbringing: he was down to earth and prosaic in everything. Luther came to see the Roman Church as guilty of corrupting the gospel by teaching salvation by works, and Luther came to understand that salvation was by God's grace through faith in Christ. The subject was redemption, and the question was whether it was by faith or works.

---

[89] Sebastian Franck, Kaspar Schwenckfeld, and Michael Servetus came to Strasbourg. Both men were hounded by Catholic and Protestant alike. Bucer asked Servetus to leave and wrote a refutation of his book on *The Errors of the Trinity*. Bucer considered Schwenckfeld a menace, and after driving him out set up a commission in Strasbourg to guard against further Anabaptists attempting to undermine their efforts.

To Luther the answer was crystal clear. He was not so concerned about total revision of all Roman practices as he was about reforming existing ones. He replaced monastery with family, chants by the choir with congregational singing, the Roman mass with its emphasis on offering Christ for an unbloody sacrifice for sins, with the German mass that would place as central the sermon that would set forth Christ and him crucified as the all-sufficient, once-and-for-all sacrifice for sins. As far as communion was concerned, Jesus said the bread was his body and the wine was his blood, and that is the way it was. Luther called it *consubstantiation* to distinguish his view from the Roman *transubstantiation,* which he called "priestly magic." To hold that the bread and wine were still the literal body and blood of Christ was no problem for Luther; it was enough that he had disconnected the communion from Roman perversions.

Ulrich Zwingli, like Bucer, was an Erasmian humanist before coming to Reformed views. He was born in early 1484 in Wildhaus, a small village in Switzerland, just weeks after Luther,. He was educated both at Vienna and Basel for the priesthood, but at an early age underwent a conversion after an illness. Quite apart from any influence from Luther, and applying the humanist maxim of *ad fontes,* Zwingli reached the same conclusions that Luther did regarding salvation: the sovereign God elects his people to salvation, thus there exists an invisible church known to God and determined by God, not the visible church as defined by Rome; justification is by faith alone; the Bible alone is the all-sufficient guide to faith and practice; clerical celibacy is a distortion of truth; all Christians are priests before God; and the Reformed community permits a close relationship of church and state. It is quite important to notice that there are no significant, observable disagreements in basic theology between Luther and Zwingli. Zwingli accepted a call to the pulpit at Glaurus, a small town in Switzerland, but soon after, in 1518, was called to the pulpit of Switzerland's largest church in her largest city: the Grossmunster Church of Zürich.

By 1523 the council authorized Reformed teaching, and Zwingli became foremost among a number of capable pastors in Zürich. But the subtle yet potentially troublesome differences between him and Luther soon began to surface. Humanists tend to be more spirit-oriented and less materialistic. They also tended to reflect the

Erasmian concern for moral reformation by extending the scope of their efforts in the direction of a total removal of all things Catholic, committed to the total removal of all corruption of the Roman Church. This broader objective in a more spiritual context enabled them to subject everything more exactingly to the scrutiny of Biblical authority. Zwingli recoiled from the idea of consubstantiation, not only because it failed to recognize the deeper spiritual meaning of Jesus' words, but also because it still too closely resembled Catholic practice. Zwingli came forth with what amounted to a third interpretation of the Lord's Supper: that it was only a memorial. He focused on Jesus' words, "This do in remembrance of me," and concluded that the bread and wine, which remain just that, serve to remind the believer of the great spiritual reality of the atonement.

Luther was understandably furious. He did not take well to anyone disagreeing with him, because Luther was characteristically convinced that he was right on whatever position he took. He had to be disappointed in one who could well be a colleague carrying forth the true gospel into Switzerland, now turning against him by perverting that gospel with such an innovative doctrine. Soon the preachers of Wittenberg and the preachers of Zürich squared off against each other, and the Reformed world was divided, much to the chagrin of Martin Bucer.

Bucer was so dedicated to Luther that he had not stopped to think other than that Luther's view was right. Zwingli disturbed him. But it was always in the heart of Martin Bucer to try to heal wounds and preserve unity. He was so committed to a united evangelical church, to the *need* of one united church in order to survive the attacks of Rome, that he strongly believed that division could not be tolerated. He always saw himself in the role of arbiter: perhaps because he felt that was his calling from God, perhaps because he saw no one else stepping forward to assume the responsibility.

The Supper controversy[90] came to Strasbourg in a strange fashion. Luther expelled his former colleague Andreas Karlstadt in 1522 after Luther returned from his confinement at the Wartburg to

---

[90] Frequently known by the German term: *der Abendsmahlstreit*

find that Karlstadt had turned his spiritual reformation into a violent social revolution. Karlstadt found refuge within the Anabaptists who at that time followed a violent agenda to implement their radical changes. As a part of his abandonment of everything Catholic, he turned from the sacramental view of Communion as well as the practice of infant baptism. He, like so many other Anabaptists, took advantage of the warm atmosphere of Strasbourg to take refuge, even though the authorities made known to him that he was not welcome. He arrived in October of 1524 and quickly assumed leadership of the Separatists. Even though the council ordered him to leave, Karlstadt continued to publish his views on the Supper to the extent that he caught the attention of the preachers, and they decided to review the matter.

Up to this point, as we saw, Bucer had simply assumed that Luther was correct in his interpretation; he had simply not given much thought to the meaning of the bread and wine. Bucer and the other Strasbourg preachers decided to send a questionnaire to pastors in other cities to gain their insights. Of course, they received very different responses. Bucer found himself impressed by Zwingli's defense of the concept that "is" means "signifies," which may be understandable when we remember that Bucer, like Zwingli, began as an Erasmian. Bucer did his own studying of Biblical texts and decided that Zwingli was essentially right, that the bread and wine held the same relationship to the reality of forgiveness that the water did in baptism. Obviously, Jesus is not physically present in the Communion service, but Bucer could find some statements in Luther's writings to justify his conclusions. However, Bucer never was fully a Zwinglian, for he always believed that it was more than just a memorial. It was Bucer who pointed out the concept that was later incorporated into the Heidelberg Catechism that as bread and wine nourish the body, so Christ continually nourishes his body, the Church. But for the time, Bucer essentially accepted Zwingli's interpretation of the Lord's Supper.

Prior to these events Bucer had begun a translation of Luther's exposition of the Gospels and Pauline Epistles for the benefit of Reformed brothers in non-German speaking lands. The fact that Bucer was doing so indicated the rapid spread of Reformation ideas, and the high esteem in which Bucer held Luther that he would want

Luther's sermons available to the expanding church. Bucer considered this work of Luther should be placed along with the Apostles' Creed and the Ten Commandments.[91] However, the last volume contained statements of Luther that would violate Bucer's convictions if he printed them, and yet he was under contract to continue with the translation. Bucer resolved the dilemma by adding a "Letter to the Christian Reader" acknowledging Luther's views and asking the reader to look at Oecolampadius' published comments on the Communion. Oecolampadius held the Zwinglian view. Understandably, Luther was furious and accused Bucer of crucifying his work. Bucer responded by writing a defense of what he did,[92] but the publisher removed Bucer's letter from further printings. Only one copy of the fourth edition that contained Bucer's letter is known to exist today.

At the same time Bucer wrote to both Oecolampadius and Zwingli urging them not to attack Luther so that the controversy would not rage any further. But he did urge both to write responses to Luther's consubstantiation views. Oecolampadius complied with a response in 1526. Bucer continued to write from a Zwinglian viewpoint as well during these years, as most of his commentaries, products of this time period, reflect. We may summarize Bucer's opinion of the Lord's Supper to this point by noticing that up to 1524 he simply accepted without question Luther's ideas, but from 1524 to 1528 he essentially agreed with Zwingli.

The Journey to Marburg

Everything changed for Bucer when in 1528 he read Luther's extensive defense of his position in *Von Abendmahl Christi Bekendnis Martin Luther*. Bucer suddenly awakened to the realization that Luther was not teaching the physical presence on Jesus in the Communion elements in the same sense that the Catholics do, but rather that there exists a "sacramental union" between the elements and Christ. Bucer concluded that Luther had simply failed to express himself accurately, and as a result, Bucer

---

[91] Eells discusses these events in pp. 70-86.
[92] *Praefactio M. Buceri in quartum tomum Postillae Lutheranae.*

had misunderstood him. He was excited and elated, and he could not wait to tell Zwingli and Oecolampadius that Luther did not actually disagree with them. Bucer saw hope for the unity he so much wanted for the Reformed Church, and for the next several years he worked arduously to bring it about. He was from that moment on convinced that he could find a formula on which Lutherans and Zwinglians would both agree that would preserve peace within evangelical ranks. He hurriedly wrote a treatise without even waiting to hear the response from Zwingli and Oecolampadius in which he showed that Luther actually was not the materialist that his opponents claimed he was. He was sure that fundamentally Luther and Zwingli believed the same thing.[93]

Without realizing it, Bucer was actually defining a new interpretation that was midway between Luther and Zwingli, the doctrine of the spiritual presence. Bucer sincerely thought that Luther believed this concept but had made some misinterpretations of Scripture and expressed himself poorly. Luther did not take such assumptions well, and the Zwinglians saw Bucer as defecting to the Lutheran camp. Actually, Bucer's comprehension of the Lord's Supper was closer to Luther's than to Zwingli's, although, as we noticed, Bucer always held to greater meaning in the elements than merely symbols. But now Bucer was enunciating an interpretation that held that we do indeed receive the body and blood of Christ in the Lord's Supper, not the physical body and blood, but the body and blood in a spiritual sense. Jesus is spiritually present in the elements, acting as mediator of salvation both in the Eucharist itself and in the hearts of believers. Bucer's understanding grew out of Luther's term "sacramental union," but it took shape in a somewhat different way. However, the doctrine of the spiritual presence became the fourth major interpretation of the Communion and the one that would be widely accepted by the Reformed Church, particularly by Calvin in Geneva, thus shaping the concept of communion in all areas influenced by Calvin, and also by Cranmer, and in so doing formed the view of the Church of England toward the Lord's Supper. Bucer first incorporated his views, his "formula" for unity, in his commentary on Ephesians published in 1528, in

---

[93] *Vergleichung D Luthers und seins gegentheyls, vom Abendmahl Christi,*

which he also lamented the division and strife over a minor point. Little did Bucer realize at the time that his formula for resolving this minor point, while not achieving the immediate unity he so desperately desired, would provide a means of understanding the Lord's Supper for millions to come in countless churches scattered over the whole earth.

Now it remained to see if Bucer could actually use his formula to bring about true unity within the divided church. Meanwhile, Philip of Hesse, alarmed by the Catholic majority assembled at the Diet of Speyer in 1529 in which evangelicals were told to cease appropriating ecclesiastical lands, sought to form a political alliance of Reformed cities to guard against increasing Catholic strength.[94] He had in mind an alliance of Electoral Saxony, Hesse, Nürnberg, and Ulm. Philip was also keenly aware that south Germany had returned to the Catholic camp after the disastrous peasants' revolt of 1525. The peasants were stirred up by Anabaptists, and Luther, although supportive of their cause, condemned their violence against their landlords. His denunciation of their uprising resulted in the evangelicals in south Germany becoming so upset with Luther that they returned to Rome. Their action meant that the Reformed areas of Switzerland, where Zwingli, Oecolampadius and other Swiss pastors preached, were sandwiched between layers of Catholics northward in south Germany and southward in the Catholic forest cantons of Switzerland. Philip foresaw a divide and conquer technique by the Catholics and the emperor, and he believed that only a strong union of Reformed princes could prevent their eventual annihilation. Religious unity would be a key to political unity, and for that reason Philip was quite willing to work with his good friend and confidant, Martin Bucer, to arrange a meeting to bring about the needed spiritual unity. Meanwhile, Luther had already turned down an appeal from Philip in 1527 to meet with Zwingli to discuss the possibilities of unity.

By this time Luther and Zwingli, with their respective colleagues Melancthon and Oecolampadius, were avowed enemies, suspicious

---

[94] It was the protesting of evangelical princes to this decree at the Second Diet of Speyer that led to their being marked as "Protestants," a term which obviously remained.

of each other. It required consummate diplomatic skill on the part of Bucer and the Strasbourg pastors to secure agreement from Luther, Melancthon, and Zwingli to meet at Philip's castle at Marburg on September 29, 1529. Both Zwingli and Oecolampadius agreed to come, but the fact that Zwingli was aware of imperial plans for the invasion of Switzerland may well have given him some incentive to agree. Zwingli journeyed from Zürich to Basel to pick up Oecolampadius, and both went on to Strasbourg where they were allowed to preach. Bucer and his colleague and fellow Strasbourg pastor Kaspar Hedio joined the group as representatives from Strasbourg. They all arrived at Marburg on September 22.

The Marburg Colloquy

When Luther arrived and met Bucer, his first words of greeting were, "You are a rogue!" Hardly a good way to start a meeting that would search for unity![95] The next day Luther was not any more civil as he told Bucer, "You are of the devil, and if you had a correct belief and the Scripture, you would not have betrayed me to Satan when I opposed your opinion." He ridiculed and mocked Bucer: "See Dr. Martin, see Dr. Philipp, how learned I am!"[96] Luther clearly had his mind made up before coming and saw little need of the meeting. It was Melancthon's concern for the possibility of unity that convinced him to go, but he was a reluctant participant. He wrote to Philip of Hesse prior to the colloquy: "I certainly know I am unable to give way just as I know that they are wrong. If we should meet and then part from one another in disagreement, then not only Your Sovereign Grace's expenses and troubles would be lost…but our opponents would continue their boasting."[97]

Philip was a gracious host, and his rich provisions and noble small talk amused Luther. The arrangement was to begin in small groups, which convened on the first day of October. Luther found

---

[95] The transcription of the procedure of the Colloquy, an unpublished manuscript, is found in BDS IV, pp. 323-364. The description of the arrival of the delegates is in German, and the text of the discussion itself is in its Latin form. The original is lost, but a transcription by Oseas Schaeäs exists.

[96] Eells p. 93.

[97] "Luther: A Life," www.religion-online.org

himself paired with Oecolampadius, probably to avoid as long as possible a direct confrontation with Zwingli, and Zwingli was assigned to Melancthon. But eventually a plenary session would be necessary, and the next two days the entire group met before the Landgrave Philip and his guest Duke Ulrich of Wurttemberg, with the focus being on the two major participants: Luther and Zwingli. Luther, as might be expected, found nearly everything Zwingli did or said to be irritating. He was bothered by Zwingli's speaking Greek and Hebrew, which Luther probably took as the demeaning attitude of the well-educated humanist looking down on the Saxon peasant.

However, Zwingli opened the session with a beautiful prayer, to whom Bucer must have said, if not outwardly, certainly inwardly, an "Amen." Zwingli prayed: "Fill us, O Lord and Father of us all, we beseech Thee, with Thy gentle Spirit, and dispel on both sides all the clouds of misunderstanding and passion. Make an end to the strife of blind fury. Arise, O Christ, Thou Sun of righteousness, and shine upon us. Alas! While we contend, we only too often forget to strive after holiness which Thou requirest from us all. Guard us against abusing our powers, and enable us to employ them with all earnestness for the promotion of holiness."[98]

There were fifteen points of disagreement, and they quickly resolved fourteen of them, leaving only the thorny issue of the Lord's Supper.[99] The Lord's Supper was the fifteenth article to be considered, and it contained six points. They actually agreed on five out of six points in that last article! The only point on which agreement could not be reached was the matter of the bodily presence of Christ in the Eucharist. All participants agreed that it was to be administered in both kinds (bread and wine), that the communion was not a means by which one could secure grace for someone else, that the sacrament of the Altar was indeed the true body and blood, that a spiritual partaking of the sacrament was necessary for every Christian, and that the sacrament, like God's

---

[98] www.prca.org/books/portraits/bucer.htm
[99] The others included topics relating to the Creator, the Trinity, the Son of God, Jesus, original sin, redemption, faith, the Holy Spirit, baptism, good works, confession, the state, and optional traditions.

word, was given by God so that weak souls could find faith through the Holy Spirit.[100]

On the point of the bodily presence, however, Luther was intransigent, and he intended to be so. While Zwingli was speaking, he took a piece of chalk and wrote on the table *Hoc est corpus meum* (this is my body), indicating that Zwingli's words were useless, for the matter was clear. Luther charged that Zwingli, in his opinion, did not know much about the gospel. When Zwingli asked Luther how Christ could be present in the bread and the wine, Luther replied that if the Lord commanded him to eat crab apples and manure, he would do it because it was a command.

At the end of the colloquy, when it was apparent that agreement was beyond reach, Martin Bucer, most anxious of all the reformers about unity, walked up to Luther and extended his hand. Said Bucer: "Will you recognize me as a brother, or will you show me my errors that I may overcome them?" Luther responded: "I am neither your Lord, nor your judge, nor your teacher. Your spirit and our spirit cannot go together. Indeed it is quite obvious that we do not have the same spirit. For there cannot be one and the same spirit where, on the one side, the words of Christ are accepted in sincere faith, and on the other side, this faith is criticized, attacked, denied, and spoken of with frivolous blasphemies. Therefore, as I have told you, we commend you to the judgment of God. Teach as you think you can defend it in the sight of God."[101] On October 4, Luther then wrote his comments on the colloquy to his wife, whom he tenderly addressed as "Sir Katie": "To my kind, dear lord, Katherine Luther, a doctor and preacher in Wittenberg. Grace and peace in Christ. Dear Sir Katie! You should know that our amiable colloquy at Marburg has finished and we are in agreement on almost all points, except that the opposition insists on affirming that there is only simple bread in the Lord's Supper, and on confessing that Jesus Christ is spiritually present there."[102]

---

[100] "Mending the Break," *op.cit.*

[101] "An Open Letter in Response to a Statement of Evangelical Concern," www.our redeemerlcms.org. Traditionally it has been assumed that Luther spoke these words to Zwingli, but recent Lutheran scholarship has established that it was Bucer to whom he was speaking. Cf. Sasse, *This Is My Body,* pp. 213-214.

[102] "Luther: A Life," *op. cit.* cf. Sasse, *This Is My Body,* pp. 213-216.

Following the discussions, Philip of Hesse asked the parties to meet together to see how, even though they did not agree, they could still live together as "members and brothers in Christ." Luther believed that because they rejected the truth on this point, they were outside the fellowship of the church and could not be recognized as members and brothers in the church.[103] Luther wrote again to Katie, "The Landgrave works hard on this item. But we do not want this Brother-and-member business though we do want peace and good will."[104]

Even though the Marburg conference failed to effect an actual union in the form of a common confession on the meaning of the Lord's Supper, the fact that agreement was reached on all the other matters is certainly significant. These issues on which consensus was reached were incorporated into a document, *The Marburg Articles,* written at the conclusion of the colloquy. The *Marburg Articles* in turn were used by Luther in his *Schwabach Articles,* by Melancthon in the 1530 *Augsburg Confession,* and by Bucer in the *Tetrapolitan Confession.* And Philip Melancthon was gained as a comrade in the struggle for unity. Of course, Melancthon shared a humanist background, a more ecumenical vision than Luther, and had always been interested in unity. Additionally, Melancthon was well on his way toward accepting Bucer's doctrine of the spiritual presence.[105] Like Bucer, as we shall soon see, he had not yet abandoned his hope for reunion with Rome, although the next year at Augsburg would represent a severe setback in those hopes. Also Luther was now aware that Bucer was not a Zwinglian. Bucer certainly did not see the bread as a "naked symbol" (only simple bread), and Luther realized that he was closer to him at this point than to Zwingli. Also, John Oecolampadius essentially came to agree with Bucer on the doctrine of the spiritual presence, leaving only the Zürich party to champion the "memorial-only" viewpoint.

Still, Zwingli was more willing to listen and be conciliatory than his successor, Heinrich Bullinger. The cause of unity suffered greatly when only two years later Ulrich Zwingli was killed in battle

---

[103] "Mending the Break," www.kingssing.com
[104] "Luther: A Life," *loc. Cit.*
[105] "The False 'Ecumenical' Attitude of Today."

at Kappel. That struggle with the Catholics was the inevitable result of a failure of the Reformed group to stand together, and fulfilled the fears of Philip of Hesse that led him initially to call the Marburg Colloquy.

The Marburg Colloquy, then, had genuine accomplishments that would be reflected in the ongoing development of the Reformation, especially of the Reformed churches. It had failed, however, to bring about a genuine unification of Reformed and Lutheran churches, and Bucer was all the more determined to keep pressing toward the elusive goal of the formula on which all dissident parties would agree. Additionally, Bucer's scholarship at Marburg won him the respect of the scholars who attended, and his reputation as a leader of the Reformation was spreading rapidly.

The castle of Philip of Hesse still stands today in Marburg and is used by Phillip's University as a museum. It is hard to describe the feeling I had when, in June of 2004, I stood in the very room where the religious disputation was held. Some young people were scurrying around setting up chairs and lighting for some kind of a performance and paid little attention to a wide-eyed American tourist with a camera. From the painting hanging in an adjacent hall showing all the participants listed above, it is obvious that the room has changed very little since 1529. As I stood before the portrait and looked at Luther pointing his finger at Zwingli, and Bucer and Melancthon sitting at the table talking to each other, probably about how the matter could ever be resolved, I felt a closeness to all of them, and later, reflected on the great importance of what they were doing.

Below the picture is posted the original document of the Marburg Articles signed by the participants: Martin Luther, Justus Jonas, Philipp Melancthon, Andreas Osiander, Stephen Agricola, John Brenz, John Oecolampadius, Ulrich Zwingli, Martin Bucer, Caspar Hedio and Philip of Hesse. These were men who had great reverence for God and his word, who loved the souls of people, and had a passion for truth!

The Tetrapolitan Confession[106]

Bucer truly believed that the formula of the spiritual presence that he had worked out and espoused at Marburg, with which Oecolampadius and Melancthon were in essential agreement, was Biblical, and that it incorporated the essence both of what Zwingli taught and what Luther taught. Zwingli and Luther were skeptical, both thinking Bucer had conceded too much to the other side. However, Bucer's wording that in the Lord's Supper one partook of the *true* body and blood of Christ as food for the soul, and the fact that Christ was present even if the participant lacked faith, convinced Luther that Bucer was sufficiently Christian to permit political alliance with him, while also convincing Zwingli that for the time he could accept the statement. Bucer moved quickly to gain the affirmation of Reformed churches throughout central Europe. He hoped to avoid irreparable division that would segment the Reformed church into sects, and Philip of Hesse hoped to avoid the political and military catastrophe that a divided evangelical church created for the Catholics.

The emperor had demanded to know what the evangelicals believed, and Philip Melancthon was at work drafting a confession to be presented at the Diet of Augsburg. Bucer sought to gain general assent to the spiritual presence interpretation of the Lord's Supper to be included in that confession, and he had little time to do it. He was unsuccessful in securing the support of major centers such as Wittenberg, Basel, and Zürich, but he was able to gain consent from Strasbourg, Konstanz, Memmingen, and Lindau. Bucer and Strasbourg hoped that they would be allowed to accept the Augsburg Confession with exception to its wording on the Lord's Supper. However, Wittenberg allowed no exceptions; one must sign on to all or not at all. For that reason his hastily composed confession was called the *Tetrapolitan Confession.* Bucer's confession contained twenty-three chapters and covered the essentials of the evangelical faith, as Bucer perceived them.[107] The

---

[106] For text see BDS Vol. III, pp. 35-185. The text is printed in parallel columns with German and Latin.

[107] BDS III, pp. 35-185.

language was not confrontational, but, in Bucer's typical style, sought to delineate the essentials in a way that all variations within the Reformed Church could accept them. Zwingli likewise drew up his own separate confession for the Diet.

Bucer presented his confession at the Diet of Augsburg, but it was given little notice, for the emperor showed contempt for it and refused a promised audience with Bucer, saying the Tetrapolitan Confession was filled with errors. It was later abandoned by the four cities in order to subscribe to the Augsburg Confession and gain acceptance to the Schmalkalden League. What is important is the fact that it represented Bucer's attempt to arrive at a *via media*, a "doctrine of essentials", that would provide a basis of unity without compromising scriptural truth. Perhaps more significant was the fact that Bucer now gained a prominent reputation as a leader who avoided extremes and as a peacemaker, and more and more cities were willing to have him come to them and help organize a Reformed community. Bucer would dedicate himself to this task in the next few years, being away from Strasbourg for long periods of time. His successes in these cities caused him to believe in the righteousness of his cause, and he labored all the more intensely. Bucer never abandoned the principles he expressed in the Tetrapolitan Confession of 1530, affirming it even on his deathbed.

The Wittenberg Concord

With Bucer there were two distinct but complementary aspects to his interpretation of the Lord's Supper. First, he saw it as the formula that would unite the Zwinglians and Lutherans, for he was firmly convinced that the two parties were saying essentially the same thing and simply did not understand each other. Second, Bucer, in the search for the acceptable formula that would preserve unity, came to believe sincerely that this middle position was scripturally correct. Thus he could approach the work of convincing the German and Swiss cities to accept this formula from a double motivation, both truth and unity.

Bucer traveled to Coburg, Ulm, Memmingen, Isny, Lindau, Konstanz, Zürich, Biberach, and Augsburg to secure support for the formula. While in these cities he worked as well to establish the

Reformation with both a truly Reformed church and a truly Reformed community. In 1531 he was quite successful at Ulm in this regard, as we shall note in greater detail later. At Lüneburg he gained the support of Duke Ernst of Brunswick. When he visited Zwingli in Zürich, he was able to convince him to sign on, though with some reluctance on Zwingli's part. However, when Zwingli learned that the Strasbourg city council was interested in a political alliance to stand against the Catholics, Zwingli came to suspect Bucer of acting primarily from base, political motives, which was certainly not the case. But at this point, Zwingli turned against Bucer. Also, Zwingli could not truly accept the idea, insisted on by Lutherans and included by Bucer, that the bread and wine were the true body of Christ to unbelievers. Bucer, in dismay and irritation, finally wrote to Zwingli: "I commit the cause to the Lord, and I will henceforth solicit nothing from you on behalf of concord, and I beg your pardon for having wearied you with my great expense, labor, and peril. Neither is Luther, nor are many of the Lutherans what you think. Often great error, also great vehemence in defending error, occupies the spirit even of the pious. I prefer to sin in innocent credulity than in wicked suspicion."[108]

The years of travel were most productive for Bucer and greatly enhanced his reputation and image as a leader of the Reformation. Not only did he work on behalf of unity on the Lord's Supper, but he would settle quarrels, establish clergy, help write constitutions for a Reformed community, preach evangelistic crusades, work with the political authorities, and help in composing confessions of faith. As we noticed, Ulm was one of the first cities where Bucer was able to bring about a thorough-going Reformation, and he was successful in strengthening the Reformed Church in Augsburg, Biberach, Esslingen, Memmingen, Kempter, and Reutlingen. Bucer was highly regarded for his wise judgment, moderation, concern for Christian people, and dedication to the principles of the Reformed faith. For this reason, he found increasing demand for his help from these and other cities. No other Reformer was "on the road" as much as Bucer, worked as extensively in so many different cities, and had this degree of influence. Though Calvin's writings made

---

[108] Eells p. 115.

him known to the entire evangelical world, and with greater lasting influence, Calvin remained physically tied to Geneva after 1541. Bucer, on the other hand, was the true traveling evangelist.

After Zwingli's death in 1531 and the accession to power in Zürich of Bullinger, Bucer found it increasingly difficult to placate the Swiss. The failure to achieve concord on the Supper controversy was hampering efforts at achieving a united stand against the Catholics, as a meeting at Schweinfurt in 1532 showed. The emperor and his forces were using the fact of division in Protestant ranks as a sign of their error, and were driving military and political wedges into theological crevices, as evidenced by their victory over Zwingli in 1531.

Bucer continued to try to moderate between the two opposing camps of Lutherans and Zwinglians, whose hatred and suspicion of each other resulted in continual violent rhetoric. Bucer tried to calm the situation by again and again pointing out to the parties that they failed to understand each other. He continued to appeal to the Tetrapolitan formula which the Lutherans had essentially accepted.

Philip of Hesse, still concerned about the strife, met with Melancthon at Wittenberg in August of 1534. There he suggested a conference among Bucer, Melancthon, and himself at his castle at Kassel at Christmas. Bucer was pleased, and set about to gain acceptance for the conference by the Zwinglians. He proposed a preconference so that he could meet with the Zwinglian leaders. Ambrose Blaurer of Konstanz was ensconced firmly in the Zwinglian camp and did not attend the preconference at Schaffhausen. It was thus moved to Konstanz, but boycotted by other Zwinglians including Bullinger. The Konstanz preconference agreed on Bucer's concepts, but the purpose of gaining acceptance from the Zwinglian camp was aborted.

The Kassel conference probably met about the twenty-eighth of December 1534. Melancthon was under strict orders from Luther not to compromise the fact that the body and blood of Christ were so united with the bread and wine that whatever movement or action one underwent, so would the other. But Bucer was able to moderate Luther's intransigence by convincing participants of what he truly believed, that Luther and Zwingli simply did not understand each other. The result was the Kassel formula on the Supper that was essentially a reiteration of the Tetrapolitan one. Luther was pleased, but the Zwinglians thought that Bucer had not entirely capitulated to Luther. At this point his friend Margaret Blaurer, Ambrose's sister, called him "A fanatic for unity!"

During the next year the Swiss cities turned increasingly against Bucer, and the cities of upper Germany toward him. It would seem that the time was right for a meeting with Luther himself at Wittenberg to see if a genuine agreement could be forged between the middle position of Bucer and the consubstantiation position of Luther. Luther shed tears of joy when he realized that the prospect of genuine unity without compromise might be present. Luther was eager to encourage other cities to participate and sent letters encouraging them. He wrote, "Now, Lord, let thy servant depart in peace, for I leave behind me peace in the church. This is the glory of God, the punishment of the Devil, and vengeance upon all enemies and opponents."[109]

Melancthon preferred to invite only those who were interested in peace so as to avoid arguments during the conference, but Bucer was not ready to give up on the Zwinglians, and again he tried to arrange a preconference with them to gain their assent to the meeting in Wittenberg. Blaurer responded that he was not interested and that the Zwinglians were having their own conference. This they held at Basel in February 1536 resulting in the Second Basel Confession. It was drafted by Bullinger, Myconius, and Grynaeus, and signed by representatives of Zürich, Schaffhausen, St. Gall, Muhausen, and Biel. Bern refused to sign.

Bucer left Strasbourg and journeyed through a number of cities picking up representatives as he went. And thus the party increased in size until it arrived at Wittenberg May 21, 1536. Luther had been ill, but the delegates found him eating supper that night and talked with him until after midnight.[110] The next morning Bucer and Capito met privately with Luther and showed him their documents. Luther refused to see one that the Zwinglians had sent, and spent the rest of the morning reading the materials given to him by Bucer and Capito. Luther was pleased with Bucer's work, but said he could

---

[109] Eells p. 191.
[110] Eells, p. 198.

never agree with Bullinger and the Zwinglians that the bread and wine were only empty symbols. Luther insisted that the concord include the statement that "in the holy Supper the true body and true blood of Christ are truly had and received even by the mouth, and that no less by the wicked than the good."[111] Bucer would rather Luther would have simply accepted the idea that the body and blood of Christ are *spiritually* eaten, but Bucer was willing to concede that sinful people also receive the body and blood of Christ. However, he insisted that truly wicked people who put no trust in Christ do not receive the sacrament and are the people to whom Paul referred when he said that those who do not discern the body of Christ eat and drink damnation to themselves.[112] Luther at that point grew too tired to continue, but they dismissed the session with Luther's expressing to Bucer that he thought him to be much closer to the truth than the Zwinglians.

The next afternoon the delegates met with Luther and convinced him that they did agree that there were two categories of sinners, and that they did not agree that the Supper was only bread and wine, and that it did not depend on either the belief or unbelief of man. They also assured him they had all so taught for a year and did indeed accept the Augsburg Confession. Then Luther and his colleagues retired to another room to confer and returned to say they were willing to accept what Bucer and his group taught and make no additional requirements. They all gave each other the right hand of Christian fellowship, and Bucer and Capito shed tears of joy. Melancthon was commissioned to draft a version of the accord that would be acceptable to all.

On Wednesday they discussed some other minor points, on which there was less disagreement, and on Thursday Luther was too ill to attend, and the preachers continued to discuss other matters among themselves for the next two days. They met again with Luther on Saturday, and he urged them to gain the support of the Swiss brothers. On Sunday Bucer preached in the afternoon service. It was significant that Zwinglians and Lutherans worshipped together and partook together of the Communion. The concord was

---

[111] *Ibid.*
[112] 1 Cor. 11:27-30.

signed by all but the delegate from Konstanz. The Wittenberg Concord did not mean the reconciliation of the extreme Zwinglians and Lutherans, but it did mean harmony between Lutherans and the middle element led by Bucer. It meant an end to attacks from the Lutheran camp on the others within the Reformed Church and marked the beginning of an era of peace and good relations in which the evangelical cause could prosper and advance. Most of the Reformed Church was now at peace on the matter of the Lord's Supper. Because a number of Zwinglians did accede to the Wittenberg Concord, it meant an isolation of the extreme viewpoint and paved the way for the gradual inclusion of the Swiss in one movement.[113]

Bucer left Wittenberg on May 29, 1536, and went from city to city gaining acceptance of the Wittenberg Concord. This document marked a high point for the "fanatic for unity."

Dialogue with the Catholics

Bucer did not confine his efforts at reconciliation only to the estranged camps of evangelicals; he continued to hold out the possibility of reunion with Rome, a dream shared by Melancthon as well. Both men held the optimum outcome to be that Rome would accept the gospel as understood by the Reformers, and there were all along indications that such might be the case. Cardinal Cajetan was willing to listen to Luther and admired his courage and sincerity, Cardinal Ximines, a humanist, and Cardinal Gasparo Contarini, leader of the reform movement under Paul III, all accepted the belief in justification by faith. Even at the Council of Trent there existed a substantial number of cardinals in agreement with the Reformation, but political concerns and the well organized efforts of the traditionalists claimed the day.

Even if Rome did not accept fully the beliefs of the Reformers, at least they might understand, stop the persecution and plans for war, and allow the evangelicals to worship and organize their churches as they believed to be right. Though the rhetoric was heated at times, the leaders of the Reformation never considered the

---

[113] Cf. Eells pp. 199-205.

Catholics to be other than their brothers in Christ. Their argument was with the leaders who had deceived the Catholic people, and at this juncture they still held to the possibility that even they might be reached. Bucer continued to hold longer than any of the other Reformers to this ever-diminishing possibility.

In the two years of 1540 and 1541 Bucer participated with Melancthon in three dialogues with Catholics exploring the possibility of reunion: at Hagenau, Worms, and Regensburg (Ratisbon). The primary issue throughout the entire Reformation era was that of justification by faith alone. Obviously, the Reformed church rejected papal authority in favor of the authority of Scripture; they rejected the abuses and excesses of the Roman Church, insisted on the possibility of marriage for clergy, and other matters. Many of the differences were ecclesiastical and external, but the theological issue of justification lay at the heart of the differences.

Catholics believed that God grants the habit of grace in a process of infusion, and the Christian must cooperate with this infused grace in order to reach a point of holiness or sanctification. The sacraments were defined as channels of grace, with baptism representing the initial experience, which forgave one of original sin and admitted him to the Church and Christian fellowship. The other six sacraments provided grace to deal with major aspects of life, so that true justification was the final result of the Christian life. In short, one was not justified until he was sanctified. Justification was based on the Christian himself being righteous.

Luther had defined the doctrine of forensic justification; that is, God justifies the sinner on the point of his faith as a court declaration. The act was external, and the sinner was imputed with the righteousness of Christ. Bucer, and all other Reformers, accepted the doctrine of forensic justification, but Bucer saw a further justification in the Christian life. Without at all contradicting Luther, Bucer's doctrine of "double justification" was simply the justification of Paul taken with the justification of James. Reformed theologians came to see James as speaking of the justification of one's faith; that is, faith being demonstrated by good works as a living faith as opposed to a dead faith. Reformers later coined the expression that "we are justified by faith alone, but not by a faith that remains alone." Justification from sin is not sanctification, but people who are justified will be sanctified. The one is a once-and-for-all act; the other a life-long process.

This point Bucer sought to communicate to Catholics at these meetings, and with some measure of success. He had initial success in persuading Cardinal Gropper to admit that we are justified by faith, but that faith will live itself out in good works. Gropper and Bucer produced an agreement that they called the Regensburg Book and presented it at the Regensburg Diet as a basis for reunion of the churches. Gropper later recanted his position and became an avowed enemy of Bucer. On the other hand, Cardinal Contarini, who was also present at Regensburg, held to his view of justification by faith that was not fundamentally different from that of the Reformers.[114]

The Haguenau Conference

Bucer moved to gain the initiative with the Catholics to counter the emperor who was calling assemblies and manipulating them for his own purposes to advance the Catholic cause over the Reformed. Bucer invited several leading Catholic theologians to meet with him at Haguenau, but the Catholics were under orders not to put themselves in a position to be persuaded by the Protestants, and they used the opportunity to demand the return of land and to make other unreasonable demands on the evangelicals that they could not accept. They even introduced an article that the Protestants had not seen before; thus, they effectively preempted the proceedings.

Bucer took the young John Calvin with him to Haguenau, as he took him along to a number of meetings that he attended in the years between 1538 and 1541. Calvin came to Strasbourg after being driven out of Geneva following the council's being taken over by a faction opposed to the preachers. Bucer was delighted to have the young French-speaking scholar in Strasbourg with him, and assigned him the responsibility of preaching to a congregation of French refugees. During the three years Calvin was there he

---

[114] Bucer's participation in the Diet of Regensburg and the various views on justification are discussed by R. Scott Clark in "Regensburg and Regensburg II," in *Modern Reformation,* published by the Alliance of Confessing Evangelicals.

preached, taught at the academy of John Sturm, got married, revised his *Institutes of the Christian Religion,* and came directly under Bucer's tutelage. Calvin learned from Bucer how to organize a Reformed community, and he returned to Geneva in 1541 with knowledge and skills that would equip him to lead the Reformation successfully there until his death in 1564.

Just before they left for Haguenau, Farel sent a notice to Calvin that the situation had changed in Geneva, and the council wanted the preachers back. Bucer protested that Calvin was profitable to him in Strasbourg, and he remained for a while longer. Later on that same year Farel prevailed, and Calvin left. But these three years were formative to Calvin, not only from the standpoint of learning the practical skills of organizing and overseeing the community, but of learning concepts and doctrinal insights from Bucer that Calvin incorporated into his own systematic theology. Much that is distinctively "Calvinistic" actually originated with Bucer, including the division of church offices, the view of the Lord's Supper, the centrality of election and the Holy Spirit in salvation, and the ability to think on universal rather than local terms.

The abortive Haguenau colloquy ended on July 28, 1540, but Bucer informed the emperor that he was summoning another meeting at Worms on October 28.[115] However, during this meeting at Haguenau, Bucer met Hermann von Wied, Imperial Elector and Archbishop of Köln, who was eager to reform his archdiocese and quite willing to listen to Bucer. Bucer formed a strong and lasting bond with von Wied, whom he highly respected. And Bucer held an advantage that the more extreme Protestants lacked in that he was willing to work toward a moderate Reformation that would be acceptable to both sides. When Hermann invited Bucer to his lodgings for an informal meeting, he introduced him to John Gropper, the Catholic theologian who was also interested in reform, at least for the moment.

---

[115] Bucer described the Haguenau conference in a report entitled Vom tag zu Haguenau, und verhinderet hab, das kein gesprach vom vergleichung der Religion, daselbst fürgangen ist.

The Worms Colloquy

Toward the end of 1540 Bucer was well aware of the "terrible things" the Catholics were planning, and knew the Protestants needed to have a decisive session that would produce accord on doctrine in order to avoid the coming catastrophe. By now Bucer could see that the emperor envisioned all-out war, and that his promise for councils and for providing opportunities for Catholics and Protestants to discuss on an equal basis was a ploy as he sought to gain time to build strength. For that reason Bucer was counting on Worms to offer the solution. "Bucer held in his hands the destinies of the French, the Swiss, and the Germans!"[116] Geneva by now was begging for Calvin to return, but the Strasbourg city council wanted Calvin to stay. Bucer told Calvin that Worms was so critical that he needed Calvin with him at this point, and promised him that after the conference he would return to Geneva with Calvin and help him to set up the Reformed community. Calvin later did return in 1541 to Geneva, but other matters prevented Bucer from honoring his promise.

Bucer counted much on the political support of Philip of Hesse, as his strength was sufficient to tip the political scales in favor of the Protestants. However, Philip's support for the Protestant cause was effectively lost because of his own personal problems: Philip was a bigamist. Bucer knew about it, and counseled Philip to keep the matter quiet, but it got out. In order to avoid punitive action from the emperor, Philip was forced to back down from his leadership of the Protestant cause. Also Philip did not agree with Bucer's negotiations with the French, as we shall see later. Thus, Bucer found himself without Philips's support, and the supporters of the emperor were aligned with the supporters of the pope against him. Soon after the conference opened on November 25, 1540, Bucer tried to arrange private meetings with the Catholic leaders Granvelle and Gropper. There were certain dangers in meeting privately, and Bucer knew not to trust Granvelle. The Strasbourg magistrates were staunchly opposed to the idea, and there was always the danger that if a secret colloquy worked out a solution, the emperor could say

---

[116] Eells, p. 278.

there was no need for an open, public one and send the envoys home. Yet Bucer felt he could handle Granvelle and gained Philip's help in authorizing the secret negotiations. Bucer's hope was to forge a coalition of moderate Catholics and Protestants that would withstand the extremists on either side.

This secret colloquy of Worms met off and on at Gropper's lodgings. They were able to reach some agreement on original sin and justification, but the Catholics were adamant in insisting on intercession of saints, transubstantiation, auricular confession, and prayers for the dead.[117] Bucer preferred to find whatever areas of agreement he could and build upon them. He proposed to Granvelle that in view of the fact that there could be no peace in Germany without theological accord, they submit their deliberations, drawn up as articles, to scholars for review and deliberation until they were acceptable, and then gain the political support they needed from the princes and electors. Bucer sent a copy of the articles to the Elector of Brandenburg, who, in turn sent them to Luther and Melancthon where they met with disfavor. Granvelle showed a copy to Contarini and Eck. Bucer tried unsuccessfully to discuss them with the moderate Catholic, the bishop of Vienna. Meanwhile the public colloquy was at a stalemate over the matter of original sin and had actually made no progress at all. At this point the emperor instructed Granvelle to end the colloquy, and Bucer left Worms on January 22, 1541 tired and discouraged.

The Diet of Regensburg

The third, and by far the most significant, meeting with the Catholics was held at the imperial city of Regensburg beginning January 6, 1541. By this time Bucer must have had a sinking feeling in his stomach that all was lost. Things were not going well on any front. He had heard that the plague was approaching Strasbourg; he knew that the Regensburg Diet would be dominated by the emperor and that he would manipulate it to advance his own agenda, which was to force some kind of unity in order to meet the threat of the Turks, as well he knew the papists would hold the advantage.

---

[117] Cf. Eells pp. 278-287.

Further, Luther had by this time condemned his Worms Articles. These articles appeared at the Regensburg Diet as *The Regensburg Book,* written by Gropper but incorporating Bucer's ideas.[118]

Calvin again accompanied Bucer, as did Jacob Sturm. Melancthon and some other Protestant leaders were there, as was Eck, Granvelle, Contarini, and Gropper for the Catholics. Eck and Melancthon were most opposed to concord; the others favored it. Discussions were underway by April 27, with the Count Palatine of the Rhine appointed as chairman. Jacob Sturm was to witness the proceedings. The emperor charged them to decide whether the Regensburg book was right or wrong, but only Granvelle could read it aloud, and after that the others were given only one hour to examine it. When the matter of justification came up, there was the expected disagreement between the two sides. Both Eck and Melancthon at this point wanted to end the colloquy, because neither intended to move at all on their respective positions.

Contarini and Bucer emerged as the leaders of the moderates on their respective sides, and both respected and admired the other. Had these two men had the authority and opportunity to continue working on accord, it possibly could have been achieved. Contarini's views, as we have noted, were not far from those of the Protestants, and he was highly impressed with Bucer. He wrote of him: "The Germans also have Martin Bucer, a man deeply learned in the principles of theology and philosophy, and in disputation. He shows such subtlety and ingenuity, that all by himself he was able to withstand our doctors."[119] Unfortunately, those who sought peace were in the minority at Regensburg. Soon Eck left the conference due to illness, and one by one others left, leaving only a rump diet to agree that it was hopeless to continue. Gropper also became ill, and relations worsened between Melancthon and the emperor, so that Charles dismissed the diet on May 22, 1541. Bucer's passionate work for unity brought him condemnation from both sides. Just as in the controversy over the Lord's Supper he found himself attacked both by Lutherans and Zwinglians, here he found himself accused of

---

[118] R. Scott Clark, "Regensburg and Regensburg II," *Modern Reformation* (Alliance of Confessing Evangelicals, online publication).
[119] Eells, p. 293.

compromise by his fellow Protestants and distrusted by Catholics. Even Calvin criticized Bucer for being overconfident in his own integrity and for disregarding the advice of his colleagues.[120] Philip disapproved of his conduct although he admired his sincerity. Granvelle, Gropper, and other Catholics condemned him. Bucer had worked assiduously to save the Reformation from certain violence and possible destruction at the hands of the imperialists and papists, and he was rewarded with near universal disdain and contempt. Bucer left Regensburg bitter, the first time we can note such a change in his attitude. It marked the end of conciliatory efforts toward the Catholics. From this point on Bucer would stand firmly against the Catholic Church and attempt to gain and retain as much territory for the Protestants as he could.

Eells comments that others on both sides opposed the concord but demanded peace without advancing a plan to obtain it. "He had failed while trying to do something; they had failed in not trying to do anything."[121] Bucer knew now that the failure at Regensburg meant war was inevitable. "Germany has fallen," he lamented.[122]

Soon after Regensburg, the emperor Charles defeated the French in battle, and Bucer realized that he would soon turn his attention to annihilating the evangelicals. John Eck was causing as many problems as possible, trying to use the Supper strife to turn the Protestants against each other, especially trying to alienate both Lutherans and Zwinglians from Bucer, because he feared Bucer's unity tactics and knew a divided Protestant world would be easier to defeat than a united one. He attacked the Regensburg Articles and worked to convince the imperial government that peace between Catholics and Protestants was impossible.

Bucer had his hands full with the Catholic Albert Pighius who was at Regensburg and was now trying to discredit Bucer. However, Pighius, to his dismay, could find nothing in Bucer's personal life to use against him. Nevertheless, Bucer spent much of his time in a written controversy with Pighius. By this time Calvin had returned to Geneva, Capito had died, Zell was feeling the effects

---

[120] Eells, p. 296.
[121] Eells, p. 297.
[122] Eells, p. 300.

of ageing, and Hegio was ill, and even Bucer was experiencing ill health. The workload at Strasbourg seemed oppressive, and with the failures in attempts to reach agreement with the Catholics, Bucer was ready for help. He called Paul Fagius, the young preacher from Isny and Peter Martyr (Vermigli) from Italy. These two younger, well-educated and committed ministers would work with Bucer in the last few years remaining to him in Strasbourg.[123] Fagius had earlier studied with Bucer at Strasbourg, and Peter Martyr did not require long to accept the doctrine of predestination and Bucer's spiritual interpretation of the Lord's Supper.

Hermann von Wied and the Köln Reformation

One of the most delightful experiences for Bucer was his friendship with Hermann von Wied, one of the seven electors of the emperor and Archbishop of Köln (Cologne). Bucer first met him at Haguenau, and in Hermann he found a man eager for reformation in his archdiocese. Hermann was not only concerned about corruption within the system, he was also open and eager to imbibe the theology of grace.

The situation in Köln was not as bleak as elsewhere as regards the degree of corruption in the church; however, professors who held tenaciously to the Catholic system staffed the university. Hermann von Wied invited Bucer to work with him and immediately incurred a reaction from the university scholars. There soon appeared a slanderous pamphlet against Bucer and the Archbishop, and the city council, seeking to avoid controversy, asked Bucer to leave. However, Bucer quickly wrote a defense of his actions to the university chancellor, won him, and the chancellor intervened on Bucer's behalf.[124]

The university theologians continued to threaten, even to the point of violence, and Hermann backed off from such a confrontation and asked Bucer to cease preaching for a while. Bucer did not, but rather he asked for political help from Philip of Hesse, the Elector of Saxony, and the Elector of Brandenburg. It was at

---

[123] Eells discusses these events pp. 317-320.
[124] Eells, p. 323.

this point that John Gropper, who had previously been in favor of reform, deserted the Reformation and turned against Bucer. Now, once Bucer's friend and supporter, he worked to overthrow the Reformation in Köln. Eells speculates that Gropper's change may have had to do with the possibility of an ecclesiastical appointment held out to him if he would defect to the Catholic cause.[125]

Bucer, however, was not about to back down. He saw the opportunity in Köln as perhaps the final one he would have to avoid war, for if Köln were to stand with the Reformation, it might provide enough strength to tip the balances in favor of the Protestants. Also, Hermann's influence was great, and if Köln were a Reformed city, the spread of the Reformation would be greatly facilitated. Bucer had every reason to stand his ground. He took his case to the people, and at that point Hermann set aside his timidity and gave Bucer his full backing. But the clergy was furious and openly rebellious. They condemned Bucer, yet in spite of their condemnation and the request of the city council for him to leave, Bucer continued to preach with significant results.

What was happening in Köln did not escape the notice of Protestant and Catholic leaders throughout central Europe, including the emperor. It was as though the whole struggle between these two camps was now focused in this one city.[126] And the battle for Köln drew champions from both sides. Catholic leaders could not afford to lose the city, and Bucer was determined to win it. Bucer used the printing presses extensively to reach the masses. Hermann called together the Landtag in an effort to reach three of the four classes represented in it: nobles, knights, and burghers. The other estate, the clergy, was beyond reach. The Archbishop claimed that he was following the rules of the "Regensburg Recess," a document authorized by the emperor when he dismissed the Diet which requested each estate to appoint representatives to confer on how to reform each archdiocese. Hermann refused to give in to the continual demands from the clergy to dismiss Bucer, and forged ahead. He realized that he would never be able to bring about reformation without Bucer; however, he was quite successful in

---

[125] Eells, p. 325.
[126] Eells, p. 327.

convincing the other three estates to commit to reform. The clergy responded by boycotting the Landtag.[127]

Bucer, sensing the significance of the battle for Köln, was now pulling out all the stops. He requested Melancthon to come to Köln and help him, and he did so.[128] Bucer answered the charges brought against him and requested a disputation at the university.[129] The request was refused. The university scholars published a pamphlet attacking the Reformation, and Melancthon replied with one of his own. Meanwhile Bucer was busy drawing up a code of ecclesiastical ordinances that would serve for a Reformed church in Köln. He was able to draw on his experience in bringing about reformed communities in several other cities, most importantly Strasbourg, to provide an excellent document. Melancthon read his ordinances and critiqued them, making several reasonable suggestions. By the time it was complete, it represented the best in Reformed thinking, and was published in August of 1543.[130] The document contained three hundred pages of text, including a small summation of systematic Reformed theology, emphasis on the Reformed society, teaching on marriage and the sacraments, and a liturgy patterned after Strasbourg.

Meanwhile the Schmalkalden League had won some victories, and Bucer wrote to Philip to request letters from him. He could once again envision the possibility of a reformation for the whole "German Nation."[131] The cause of Köln became now, certainly in Bucer's mind, the cause of the Reformation, and he saw himself on the front lines. The significance of what was happening in that which with he was directly involved as leader was quite apparent to him.

---

[127] Eells, pp. 327-328.

[128] Bucer's account of his efforts in Köln were published in a report entitled: Was in Namen des Heiligen Evangeli unsers Herren Jesu Christi jetzund zi Bonn jen Stifft Cöllen, gelehret unnd gepredigt würdt.

[129] Bucer, among other allegations, was charged with bigamy (He had been married twice, but the second time only after the death of his first wife in the plague.) He took the opportunity to write a lengthy defense of clerical marriage.

[130] Von Gottes Gnaden unser Hermanis Ertzbischoffs zü Cöln, unnd Churfürsten 2c einfaltigs bedenken, warauff ein Christliche....Reformation....anzurichten seye.

[131] Eells, p. 333.

At this point Bucer had the strong support of the Archbishop of the city, three estates of the Landtag, and a substantial number of townspeople. Gropper became the leader of the opposition and had the majority of the clergy behind him. Eells comments that if the reformation in Köln had been allowed to continue unhampered, it would have represented the greatest personal achievement for any Reformer in Germany.[132] The clergy realized it was isolated, and asked for time. They were simply waiting for help from the emperor.

Charles had been involved in a campaign against the Duke of Cleves who threatened some of his inheritance in the Low Countries when he received the plea for help from the Köln clergy. Of course, he was quite upset about the possibility of Köln joining the side of the Reformation, and thus he responded by sending in imperial troops to drive Bucer out of his house and threaten him with death. Charles personally demanded that Hermann dismiss Bucer and Melancthon, and Hermann yielded. Hermann probably understood that the emperor would not have dared make such demands on one of the electors who put him on the throne unless he had the military power to back up those demands and would be prepared to use it even against the Elector. It was with regret that Hermann dismissed the preachers. One can only wonder what would have happened had he resisted.

Bucer left with the highest regard for Hermann von Wied and made his way to Bonn where he worked to bring about Reformation in that city. Subsequently the emperor and church forced Hermann von Wied to step down as Archbishop of Köln, and the city remained firmly within Catholic control. The pope officially deposed him in 1546 and condemned his doctrines in the *Antididagma*, though Bucer vigorously defended him in a reply, *Constans Defensio.*[133] Although Bucer's intense efforts in Köln incurred the wrath of the emperor and the Catholic Church, he

---

[132] Eells, p. 334.

[133] Von Wied's work, expressing his endorsement of reformed ideas, is entitled *Pia Deliberatio.* Bucer's defense of him is in the Bodleian Library at Oxford, cf. Bodl MS Add C.97; cf. Hopf, "An English Version of Parts of Bucer's Reply to the Köln *Antididagma.* Cf. MacCulloch, p.p. 385, 393, 400.

regained much of the reputation he had lost with fellow Protestants who no longer saw him as a compromiser but a warrior for the truth.[134] Even his old enemy Bullinger praised him for his efforts. Still, it was little solace for Bucer who recognized that the last opportunity for a major alliance within the privileged classes of the Roman Church was now gone. Gropper and the moderate Catholics had now deserted him. He was depressed over the weakness of the concord among Protestants and their lack of discipline. He wondered if he suffered from the scourge of an angry God. He continued to work for the Kingdom of Heaven, but his work no longer made him happy.[135] In one real sense, the failure of the Reformation at Köln marked the high tide of the Reformation and the real beginning of the Catholic Counter-Reformation.[136]

Today the massive cathedral of Köln still towers over the city center. It escaped serious damage in World War II, while the rest of the city was flattened. The cathedral was still under construction during the days of Bucer and Hermann von Wied, but in use. Whether Bucer actually preached there or how much of his efforts in the city involved this particular church is uncertain, but whatever other buildings may have witnessed this significant chain of events between Bucer and the archbishop, if they still stood in the 1940's, were reduced to rubble by Allied bombing.

The St. Gall-Strasbourg Axis

One of the most significant contributions of Bucer's ongoing work to find unity was the alliance he forged with Grynaeus, the pastor of St. Gall. Grynaeus represented Swiss Protestants who were unwilling to accept the dictates of Zürich on the Lord's Supper, and agreed with Bucer that the communion was much more than representations but not the ubiquitous corporal presence of the body and blood of Christ as defined by Luther.

Simon Grynaeus developed the alliance in 1531 as a third element among Lutherans in the Schmalkalden League, and he

---

[134] Eells, p. 336.
[135] Eells, p. 337.
[136] Eells, p. 343.

obtained endorsement from French Protestant circles endorsed by Anne Boleyn. The alliance included reformed cities in the upper Rhineland and northern Switzerland and became an east-west chain across Europe that involved leading figures such as Bucer, Capito, John Sturm, and Joachim von Watt (Vadianus). It was Grynaeus, who had strong connections to Thomas Cranmer and who put Cranmer and Bucer in touch and helped to form their friendship and alliance.

It was the careful diplomatic work of Grynaeus and Bucer, with Bucer gradually becoming leader and spokesman, which laid the foundations to what became the Reformed faith. Without the powerful personality and influence of Calvin and his production of the *Institutes,* the Reformed faith, of course, could never have developed with the strength that characterized it. However, without the existing framework of cooperation and fundamental theological agreement forged by his predecessors, Calvin would have had no basis on which to build his work. The importance of this alliance, and of Bucer's untiring efforts in the cause of unity and understanding, cannot be overstated in regard to the formation of the Reformed Church and its defining characteristics.[137]

The Doctrine of Essentials

Associated with Bucer's efforts to bring about peace among Christians is the concept known as the doctrine of essentials. Bucer believed that in order to achieve the goal of harmony among the faithful, leaders must determine what is necessary to believe and thus to be bound on all Christians, and what can lie in the category of the *adiaphora,* or non-essentials. In the latter area Bucer argued that men should be tolerant and accepting of different convictions and not attempt to bind one's own views on others. Only then could peace and harmony exist among Christians. He tried to implement his philosophy of the doctrine of essentials both between Catholics and Protestants, and among differing factions of Protestants. He firmly believed that it was possible to reach a formula for peace

---

[137] Cf. Diarmaid MacCullouch, *Thomas Cranmer* (New Haven: Yale University Press, 1996), p. 174.

until, finally worn down by repeated failures; he began to see that it was impossible, particularly with the Catholics. Yet even in England in the last two years of his life, he worked tirelessly with Cranmer to set up an English church that avoided extremes and would allow all English Christians to feel comfortable.

Once again, Bucer was influenced and shaped in these views by Erasmus. He may well have been guided by principles that Erasmus set forth in a letter to the Czech scholar Jan Slechta in November 1519 that Bucer personally edited. Bucer added to his edition of the letter a title commending it as a guide to end religious strife.[138] It is entirely likely that these principles that Bucer so heartily endorsed in 1519 as an Erasmian remained with him to guide him through the perplexing wilderness of religious controversy that was his calling to endure. As a result, he gave to the Christian world a goal, a methodology, and an instrument that have been used repeatedly in subsequent Christian history to attempt to heal wounds and bring about peace among warring Christian factions. Unfortunately, the formula has met with as little success in later years as it did for Bucer in the sixteenth century, but the logic and validity of the concept still holds its appeal. The problem, of course, is reaching agreement on what are the essentials of the faith, and no one has yet come up with a recipe for solving that problem.[139]

Because of the significance of this letter, we include the text. Erasmus commented that many notions would be reconciled to the Roman church if people would hold to a few things in Holy Writ...

> Without which the system of our salvation cannot stand. For this a few truths are enough, and the multitude are more easily persuaded of their truth if they are few. As things are, we made six hundred articles out of one, some of them of such a kind that one can be ignorant of them, or convinced, without peril to one's religion. And such is the nature of mortal men

---

[138] Erasmus, *Letters,* tr. R.A.B. Mynors and D.F.S. Thomson (Toronto: University of Toronto Press, 1977), Vol. VII, n.p.120.

[139] One example of the attempt to implement the doctrine of essentials is to be found in early nineteenth century America in the movement initiated by Alexander Campbell called the Disciples of Christ. He and his colleagues insisted that in matters of faith there be unity, in matters of opinion liberty, and in all things love. It was but a restatement of Bucer's doctrine of essentials.

that we cling tooth and nail to what has once been laid down. Besides which the whole of the Christian philosophy lies in this, our understanding that all our hope is placed in God, who freely gives us all things through Jesus Christ his son, that we were redeemed by his death and engrafted through baptism with his body, that we might be dead to the desires of this world and live by his teaching and example, not merely harboring no evil but desiring well of all men; so that, if adversity befall, we may bear it bravely in hope of the future reward which beyond question awaits all good men at Christ's coming, and that we may ever advance from one virtue to another, yet in such a way that we claim nothing for ourselves, but ascribe any good we do to God.[140]

Erasmus included in the category of indifferent matters obscure questions about the nature of Christ or sacraments, vestments, festivals, the choice of bishops, holy days, and offices. The Erasmian influence on Bucer is obvious when he refuses to let the English practice of having bishops rather than elders or wearing vestments become matters of division, preferring to tolerate them rather than fracture the body of Christ over them. Bucer could consider it an obscure point how the true presence of Christ was present in the Lord's Supper, and he was always willing to word confessional statements in a sufficiently ambiguous way so that the way to unity was open.

And that would bring us to ask what to Bucer were the essentials of the faith; the non-negotiable items. By the decade of the 1530's, Bucer's theology had matured, but he had not changed the basic principles that had guided him since the time of his conversion. We may consider the following as essentials, and in view of the above comments about his role in establishing the Reformed faith, note that they have remained:

---

[140] Erasmus, *Letters,* Vol. VII, p. 126.

1. Belief in the Trinity, as defined by historic Christianity and stated in *The Apostles' Creed* and *Nicene Confession.*
2. Belief in other basic doctrines held by both Catholics and Protestants: virgin birth of Christ, heaven and hell, eternal judgment, etc.
3. Belief in the inspiration of Holy Scripture and that the canons of Old and New Testament served as the sole authority for the church, but always with a reverence for the traditions of the church beginning with the Fathers.
4. The centrality of the Holy Spirit in the church and in the lives of Christians.
5. The predestining grace of God (Although Bucer was willing to avoid teaching the doctrine in cases that it proved offensive and relegate it to commentaries, as in England).
6. The necessity of Christian sacraments and the grace they impart.
7. Justification by faith. (Although Bucer believed in "double justification," that is, that one's good works and godly life are a justification of his salvation and the presence of the Spirit in his life, i.e., Christian piety and holiness).
8. The Christian community, including the discipline necessary to make it effective (The power of the keys). This Bucer equated with the Kingdom of God, and he insisted that infants were a part, hence, infant baptism.
9. The necessity of teaching the word of God in an understandable manner.
10. The primacy of love in every relationship, including one's relationship to God, his relationship to the church, and in the home.[141]

---

[141] See the summary of Bucer's mature theology in appendix.

The Price of Peace

Martin Bucer was committed to Jesus Christ. His theology led him to believe that what happens in this life is the outworking of God's divine purpose. He believed he had been called to be a Christian and called to be a pastor for the flock of Christ. No one can doubt his convictions. However, the judgment of his peers in the sixteenth century and that of Christian scholars today is still divided. Bucer was condemned by Luther for being too Zwinglian, and condemned by Zwingli for being too Lutheran. Protestants condemned him for continuing dialogue with Catholics, and Catholics condemned him because he was a Protestant. The battle for the middle was difficult, because the extremes on both sides kept chipping away at it.

But then Bucer, as we have noted many times, was a former Erasmian, and Erasmus found out himself that the middle ground erodes away. It was Erasmus who styled himself, with reference to Papists versus Protestants, "a heretic to both camps." The question then as now is, do people who seek the middle compromise the truth? Erasmus and Bucer would not agree that they do; extremists always affirm so.

One can read literature today that reflects such a pejorative view of Bucer. Some very strong Calvinists think he sold out to Lutheran views, and some very strong Lutherans think he compromised with Zwingli. These people admire Bucer for his dedication and tenacity, but they hold him up as an example of what happens when one is willing to compromise the truth.

However, Bucer did not see himself in that posture, and the fierceness with which he stood for his convictions and his willingness to suffer for them, as we she see further, argues strongly against such a conclusion. Bucer sincerely believed in the Protestant cause and in the Evangelical/Reformed theology, as noted above. He denounced the papacy, clerical celibacy, concepts of salvation by works, sacramentally conveyed grace, superstitions, and all the other aspects of Catholic theology and practice that were objectionable to Protestants.

He did believe Christian pastors are under a mandate to endeavor to maintain the unity of the Spirit in the bond of peace,[142] and he took seriously Jesus' words in the Sermon on the Mount that those who are peacemakers are blessed and shall be called sons of God.[143] In order to do so, Bucer believed that pastors should distinguish between the essentials and the non-essentials (adiaphora) of the Christian faith, his "Doctrine of Essentials." It is evident that he followed this schema in the Supper controversy, as he believed that essentially both Luther and Zwingli were saying the same thing. What was essential to the Christian is that he discerns the Lord's body.

If organic unity could not be achieved, at least, there could be co-existence, and this policy he attempted to follow with Anabaptists and Catholics, but without success. The peacemaker is frequently doomed to failure because of extremists, human stubbornness and intransigence, but he has no course but to proceed. Bucer falls in that sparsely-populated and often lonely category of a leader, whether religious or secular, who has sought to achieve harmony in the midst of diversity while at the same time holding to values. Unfortunately, such people usually have few successes to show for their efforts, and they customarily win the opprobrium of opponents on both sides.

Ultimately, Bucer was a failure and bitterness of soul set in. He failed to win the Anabaptists, he failed to maintain peace in the Reformed camp due to the controversy over the Lord's Supper, and he failed to win support from even the moderate Catholics. He was finally driven out of Strasbourg, and the mass returned to most of its churches. Yet Bucer's methodology was always open discussion, disputation, writing, preaching, and dialogue. He probably possessed the best skills in defense of the Protestant cause of any of the leaders of the Reformation. In spite of all, he failed.

And yet he could not do otherwise. Thus Bucer's dilemma provides a question for every Christian leader today. What is the supreme good before God if a choice must be made between truth as we understand it and peace? To what extent should we pursue

---

[142] Ephesians 4:3
[143] Matthew 5:9.

peace? How do we find the balance between "Preach the word; be prepared in season and out of season; correct, rebuke and encourage – with great patience and careful instruction" and "… the wisdom from above is first pure, then peaceable, gentle, open to reason, full of mercy and good fruits, impartial and sincere. And a harvest of righteousness is sown in peace by those who make peace."[144]

[144] 2 Tim. 4:2-3, James 3:17-18. See also Gal. 1:8-9, Gal. 2:5, and Psalm 120, Jer. 8:15, Rom. 14:17 & 19, 1 Cor. 14:33, Gal. 5:22, and Heb. 12:14.

Chapter V

Bucer the Evangelical Diplomat

Bucer was unique in his position as mediator for peace among Christians of all camps, but he was also unique in his position as mediator between the evangelical church and political powers. No Reformation leader possessed the diplomatic acumen of Martin Bucer; no other leader even came close. He fearlessly and capably developed relationships with people in the highest positions, and proceeded confidently, assuming that God would use him to open the way for acceptance of truth. His ultimate failure to accomplish this goal led to a bitter and disappointing end, yet even in sickness and despair over exile, he continued to work tirelessly for acceptance of the Reformation community in England. His last and greatest work was written and dedicated personally to King Edward VI of England.

Philip of Hesse

One of the key men in the possible success of the evangelical cause was Philip, the Landgrave of Hesse whom Bucer met and befriended. Philip's political strength was so strong and so feared that he was a virtual bulwark against whom the emperor could not prevail, at least, not until Philip's own personal indiscretions led to his downfall and to his being forced to abandon leadership of the Protestant cause.

The paths of Martin Bucer and Philip of Hesse first crossed at the Second Diet of Speyer in 1529. It was that significant political event, as we have noted, that gave rise to the term "Protestant," when evangelical princes registered their protest to the imperial demands to cease appropriating ecclesiastical lands and to return them to the Roman Church. The demands of the emperor Charles for a statement of faith led to the Augsburg Confession of 1530, but aroused in Philip awareness that unless the evangelicals could unite, the emperor would employ a "divide and conquer" technique. That which stood in the way of unity proved, more than anything else, to be the controversy over the Lord's Supper. Unity was important to Bucer for theological reasons: Scripture commands that Christians preserve the unity of the Spirit for which Christ prayed.[145] But to Philip unity was vitally important for political considerations.

Philip accepted the doctrines of Martin Luther and very early lined up with the growing number of Lutheran princes. His position in Hesse soon proved strategic in the developing strategy of these princes to establish the evangelical church as a lasting reality in Germany. Not only was the location and position of the Landgrave of Hesse important, but Philip possessed personal characteristics of initiative, diplomacy, persuasion, and leadership that quickly distinguished him as a leader among the Protestant princes. Philip was keenly aware of the development of the Reformation in areas beyond Luther's direct influence, especially in Switzerland, and saw the distinct advantage to all evangelicals' presenting a united front.

After Marburg, Bucer wrote frequently to Philip, informing him of his every move and often asking his advice on matters. Martin Bucer and Philip of Hesse became intimate friends and colleagues, and Philip's involvement in Bucer's many and varied activities are evident from this point on. Philip often disagreed with Bucer, as he did when Bucer sought to develop a relationship with the king of France in order to encourage Reformation there. But through it all Philip remained a devoted friend and admirer of Martin Bucer, and Bucer respected the friendship and appreciated deeply the political influence that Philip lent to Reformation efforts.

Philip continued to work tirelessly for unity long after Marburg and the death of Zwingli. Of course, both he and Bucer had to deal with the intractable Heinrich Bullinger as Zwingli's successor in Zürich. Philip met Melancthon at Wittenberg in 1534 and agreed to a conference between Melancthon and Bucer, offering his castle at Kassel for a conference scheduled for Christmas 1534. Luther approved but sent Melancthon with strict instructions on how not to compromise the doctrine, and the Zwinglians were from the outset suspicious. By this time they came to regard Bucer as a traitor to their cause. The Kassel conference resulted in a formula based on Bucer's assumption that both sides misunderstood each other. The

---

[145] Ephesians 4:3, John 17:20-21.

Kassel formula was a restatement of Bucer's position, agreed to by Melancthon, that Christ is present by faith in the sacrament in a manner appropriate to the sacrament.

During 1538-1539 Bucer carried out a complete reorganization of the Hessian church under Philip's authority and guidance. One of the interesting aspects of Bucer's highly successful organization of the Reformed church as the established church of Hesse was the policy that developed toward the Jews. In Strasbourg the policy had been remarkably tolerant, and Jews were allowed to buy and sell. Philip preferred a similar tolerant policy in Hesse, but Bucer inexplicably opted for a harsher one. Bucer argued that Jews should be punished for their guilt in the crucifixion of Christ, and their restriction would enable the development of an unimpeded Christian community.[146] The threat that wealthy Jews would pose to Christian community may well lie at the root of both Bucer's and Luther's willingness to restrict them. One wonders why Strasbourg Jews fared so well unless Bucer believed the Reformation to be so well established there that they could be held in check.

Bucer's work with Philip in the restructuring of the Hessian church featured some of the enduring characteristics of the entire Reformed Church. For instance, Bucer introduced elders into the leadership of the church, a feature that has been continued generally in the Reformed tradition. He also introduced confirmation into Hessian churches, giving Bucer the title of "father of the evangelical confirmation." He developed a discipline ordinance book, and he revised his shorter catechism at the Kassel conference and applied it in Hesse. Through the implementation of discipline, catechism teaching leading to confirmation, and the guidance of the congregational elders, the morals and spiritual life in Hesse manifested remarkable growth and improvement. Although Bucer never held an official position in Hesse, Philip came to value his judgment more than that of anyone else. After 1538 Philip would consider Bucer to be one of his most trusted advisors.[147]

---

[146] Bucer published his views in a pamphlet: *Von der Juden,* 1539.

[147] Eells, pp. 240-241; Köhler: *W. Hessische Kirchenverfassung in Zeitalter der Reformation,* Giessen, 1894.

During the time of Bucer's work with Philip in restructuring the Hessian church, Bucer became concerned about how ecclesiastical property should be used. Who should own the property and how it should be used continued to be major concerns among both Catholics and Protestants. The immediate concern was the imminent death of the Duke of Albertine Saxony whose heir was a Protestant. The question arose as to what he should do about Catholic Church property in his domain. Philip turned to Bucer to organize a conference to deal with the matter, and Bucer went off to secure the approval of Luther and Melancthon at Wittenberg and that of Frederick, the Elector of Ernestine Saxony. This incident provides a good example of how Bucer comfortably moved between religious and political leaders, negotiating with both. The proposed conference occurred at Leipzig, January 2, 1539, and Bucer presented the proposal approved by both political and religious leaders that ecclesiastical property should be used for the support and training of ministers, and the relief of the poor. The property was to be considered as belonging to the true church and not to the emperor, but it would be administered by the local temporal power uniformly in all lands. The Leipzig conference led to the conference at Frankfurt to be discussed later. The calling of the Leipzig conference proved to be Philip's last truly successful contribution to the Protestant cause.

Philip, a good student of Scripture and a sincere and devoted leader of the Reformation found himself attracted to Margaret von der Sale, one of his sister's ladies in waiting. With no cause for divorce from his wife, and with Philip intent on marrying Margaret, Bucer found himself in a dilemma as to how he should advise his friend. He did not believe in divorce without scriptural cause, neither did he like the idea of bigamy. But he had earlier counseled Henry VIII of England that the best course of action was bigamy, for Bucer found a scriptural example for polygamy in that of David and Solomon, and Bucer saw it as a last resort effort to prevent immorality. Bucer actually hoped to forestall any marriage between Philip and Margaret until he had discussed the matter with Luther and Melancthon and all of them agreed on a course of action, and with that goal in mind, he agreed to meet with Philip. Philip, on the other hand, was as determined as Henry VIII to marry the woman of his dreams. He played on Bucer's sympathies and appealed to his ability to find solutions to problems. Philip had not yet revealed to Bucer the identity of the woman, nor, more importantly, the fact that he had already made plans with her family for a wedding. Philip wanted Bucer to give him written sanction to both the marriage and the open declaration of it. Bucer gave him written sanction to *secret* bigamy, which Philip interpreted as meaning, in time, public declaration. Bucer left to meet with the Elector John Frederick who wanted Philip to abandon his plans.[148]

At the same time Bucer continued to work with Philip to arrange an alliance of Protestant princes that could withstand the obvious intentions of the emperor Charles. He was still at work with Philip on a plan to settle the thorny issue of church property.[149] Philip deceived Bucer by requesting that he go with him to meet with the Schmalkalden League and present his plan for unity, but Bucer found that Philip kept changing the place where they were to meet until he finally met him at Rothenburg, not to find a meeting of the League, but rather to find out that he was invited to Philip's wedding.[150]

What followed seems from modern perspective to be a circus, but for those involved at the time, it must have been a horrific situation. Once news got out about Philip's marriage, all kinds of furor erupted. For one, Philip's sister was furious that such a thing had happened in her court, and Philip dispatched Bucer to try to calm her down. Now rumors reached all the way to Wittenberg, not only of Philip's bigamous marriage, but of immoral, drunken behavior of people in Marburg, and Melancthon wrote to Philip to suppress rumors and correct the immorality of his subjects. Philip wanted a conference of Hessian theologians and, of course, asked

---

[148] Eells, pp. 274ff for discussion of the problem of Philip's bigamy. Cf. Eells *The Attitude of Martin Bucer toward the Bigamy of Philip of Hesse,* AMS Press, 2000. Bucer wrote for Philip *Argumentum Buceri pro et contra* – both sides of the question of whether Philip should engage in bigamy.
[149] Bucer published *Von Kirchen Gütern* as a plan to settle the ecclesiastical property problem by peaceful means.
[150] Bucer still went to the Schmalkalden League meeting to try to negotiate a plan with the emperor and to present Protestant demands. By this time the ecclesiastical states feared the emperor more than the Protestants.

Bucer to arrange it. Bucer was trying diligently to keep the whole matter as secret as possible, but Philip wanted it out in the open. Bucer knew that Charles would use the fact of Philip's bigamy as a reason to demand that he abandon his support of the Protestant cause in order to receive imperial pardon, which is exactly what the emperor did. In the end, Philip was silenced and his capable leadership lost because of his lifestyle: both the fact of the marriage and the fact that Philip was unwilling to keep it secret.

The Emperor Charles V

Charles of Hapsburg came to the throne of the Holy Roman Empire in 1519 upon the death of his grandfather, the emperor Maximilian I. The election had been an interesting one. Because Maximilian married Mary, daughter and heiress of Charles the Bold, Duke of Burgundy, Maximilian came into possession of the Low Countries, including Holland and Belgium. He already held the vast Hapsburg domains, and he was the ruler of all the German Empire. He betrothed and married his son, Philip, to Joanna, daughter and heiress of Ferdinand and Isabella of Spain. Joanna brought with her a claim not only to Spain and Portugal, but to the vast new domains Spain acquired in the new world.

Philip died prematurely in 1516, leaving two sons. Joanna was insane and incapable of ruling, and thus the Hapsburg family looked to the young Charles, elder of the two brothers, as their hope for maintaining control of Germany. Of course, to Germany was now added the Low Countries and the impressive Spanish lands. The king of France, Francis I, looked in horror at the growing German threat, as did the young Henry VIII of England. Francis decided to make a serious attempt to block Charles in the upcoming election, and gained the support of three of the seven electors. Three supported Charles, and the Duke of Saxony, Frederick III, Luther's lord and protector, was the swingman.

Charles was elected in 1519, but his position was obviously shaky. Luther's religious revolt presented a threat to his power by adding further division to the German nobility and undermining his ability to exercise the kind of centralized authority present with his grandfather. Given the Hapsburg commitment to the Catholic faith, and the natural religious intensity of the Spanish, it is understandable that Charles was obsessed with the idea of exterminating Protestantism from Europe.

With Charles there never existed any remote willingness to consider the claims of the Evangelicals. He saw Luther and his colleagues as threats to his power, to the unity of the Empire, and to the very security and safety of its people, given the advancing threat of the Turks.

Charles first met Bucer at the Second Diet of Speyer in 1529, called in an effort to find some basis of settling the controversy. The Diet erupted into differences among Protestants over the Lord's Supper as well as into differences with Catholics. Bucer was disappointed in the outcome of the conference, although it did result in the Diet of Augsburg the next year, which gave Protestants an opportunity to state what they believed. Charles, naturally inimical to any Protestant, formed the impression of the loquacious Bucer that he was a "windbag."

The next time the two men physically met was at the Augsburg Diet. Initially, Strasbourg authorities considered the atmosphere at Augsburg too dangerous for Bucer, and they commissioned Matthew Pfarrer and Jacob Sturm to represent them. However, when these two arrived and saw so many theologians present, they sent word back to Strasbourg asking for Bucer and Capito to join them.[151]

Bucer found it imperative to present a united front to the emperor, and thus it was imperative that the Protestants reach agreement. The sticky problem remained the Lord's Supper, and with some softening of statements, Bucer managed to secure agreement. At least, Luther was convinced that Bucer and his party were sufficiently Christian so that he could enter into political alliance with them.[152] However, the emperor ignored the Augsburg Confession, promised another meeting, and then reneged.

Soon it was apparent to Bucer that the emperor could not be trusted. Charles feigned an interest in dialogue and a willingness to listen to the evangelicals, but in actuality he had no intention of

---

[151] Eells, p. 99.
[152] Eells, p. 101.

allowing any kind of accommodation to them. He would be satisfied only if the Protestants would recant and rejoin the Catholic camp. In that instance, Germany would again be united to stand against its enemies, the French and the Turks, in particular. If not, Charles intended the extermination of Protestants as his own "final solution."

The longer Bucer dealt with Charles, the more he became convinced that such was his agenda, but at the time, Bucer saw no other recourse than to try to schedule conferences with the hope that the Protestants could present their interpretations of the Christian faith and perhaps convince enough of the German princes to neutralize Charles. Ironically, dealing with Charles meant dealing with the pope and the Roman Church as well. If one were satisfied, so also would the other be satisfied. Bucer, as the undisputed diplomatic leader for the Protestant cause, held throughout the 1530's to the ever-diminishing hope of achieving accord with both Roman Church and emperor. For that reason, he was always willing to agree to the emperor's promise for yet another conference.

Bucer was increasingly aware of the emperor's duplicity, but he could not ignore the fact that the only opportunity for the Protestants lay in the Augsburg Confession, because Charles announced that he would not consider any other confession. With that in mind, Bucer arranged a meeting of the evangelicals in Schweinfurt in the spring of 1532. The city council of Strasbourg authorized Bucer to inform the pastors that they could endorse the Augsburg Confession. However, other cities were more reluctant to submit. For instance, Ulm would sign only after a certain section was reworded, and Augsburg would not sign. Much of the controversy boiled down to the question of whether an unbeliever who took communion was actually partaking of the true body and blood of Christ. Luther strongly asserted that he would; Zwingli that he would not. The Schweinfurt conference illustrated the damage that the controversy over the Lord's Supper had caused to the Protestants.[153]

Bucer never took his eye off Charles in the next few years, but he found himself immersed in a sea of activity that was far broader than political negotiation. Bucer's own personal passion for unity

---

[153] Eells, p. 141.

was augmented by the pressure he felt to achieve concord in order to stand against the alliance of pope and emperor and the threat that it presented to the Protestant cause. The thirties, then, was a period in which Bucer engaged in conference after conference to bring the Zwinglians and Lutherans together, earning for himself the reputation of being ready to compromise anything for the sake of agreement. This decade also found Bucer hard at work expanding the Reformation as far as possible, even beyond the borders of the German Empire. But the threat of imperial action always hung like an ominous cloud over his entire ministry.

After the refusal of the emperor to accept the Protestant demands at the Augsburg Diet, Protestant princes formed the Schmalkaldic League, a decision that would eventually lead to war. War stood in opposition to all the irenic Bucer believed in, and he labored as fast and as diligently as he could to avoid it. We have to see the thirties, then, as not only the most fruitful period of Bucer's life, but also the most frantic.

One of the thorniest issues that had to be confronted, if there could ever be a settlement with the imperial government, was that of church property. The Roman Church owned an enormous amount of real estate throughout Europe. Some have estimated that it approached half of all land. The old expression had it that the church never died; and thus, land that was bequeathed to the church remained from then on with the church. As princes became Protestant, vast amounts of land were secularized, especially the large monastic estates. The Roman Church was furious, for land meant wealth and power. In July of 1532 Bucer arranged a conference at Nürnberg that would protect the Protestants from prosecution for secularizing church property, and later in 1539 he organized, by the commission of his friend Philip of Hesse, a conference at Leipzig. The conference was occasioned by the death of the duke of Albertine Saxony and the succession of his son who was a Protestant.

Once again, nothing came from the conference unless it was a realization on the part of Protestant leaders that Germany was headed straight for a civil war, and that the only thing that would avoid it was some kind of compromise, which would have to involve addressing the question of church property.[154] Bucer was discovering how complicated and difficult imperial politics were, but there was no one else to do the job. Martin Bucer had been gifted with special diplomatic skills that the other Reformation leaders, great theologians, preachers, and writers though they were, simply lacked. Bucer realized that the progress of Protestantism in the decade since the Augsburg Diet would, at least, mean that the emperor needed the support of the evangelicals. And, not surprisingly, church and state combined and issued an invitation to meet with Protestants at Frankfurt in 1539. Bucer was commissioned by Strasbourg to represent them and sought to work the situation to the advantage of the Protestant cause. He held out for unconditional peace and an equal number of Protestant representatives in the imperial court as Catholics. Bucer was making high demands, but he had to pitch the demands high if he could attain any kind of compromise that would benefit the cause. The Catholic archbishop Lund refused, but did allow a suspension of prosecution against adherents of the Augsburg Confession for fifteen months or until a national diet would be held, providing that the Schmalkaldic League did not add any new members. The promise of an imperial diet to resolve the issues was one of the Church-Empire strategies that was held forth like the carrot on a stick before the Protestants. It is doubtful that the emperor ever planned such a definitive diet, but he was rather probably buying time. In the meantime, Protestants were expected to promise aid against the infidel Turk.

When agreement could not be reached because of demands and counter-demands, Bucer proposed to the Protestants taking a firm stand: the truce would not be restricted to adherents of the Augsburg Confession alone, the Schmalkaldic League would be permitted to take in new members, and all confiscated ecclesiastical property would be used only for the Christian ministry and schools. Melancthon and Luther agreed, but the body of Protestant princes lost their nerve finally agreeing to the emperor's demands on April 19, 1539. The princes lacked their boldest leader, as Philip was ill, and the new Duke of Saxony had not yet assumed his office.

---

[154] Eells, p. 247.

Another conference was scheduled for Nürnberg in August, and the Frankfurt Conference dismissed. When the ailing Duke of Albertine Saxony died, his son and successor could not join the Schmalkaldic League due to the signing of the emperor's demands. Their failure to act decisively as Bucer counseled meant that they had sold their aid against the Turks at a low price and weakened their bargaining position considerably.[155]

Bucer did not, indeed could not afford, to give up. He now enlisted Philip's help to garner enough support from the Protestant princes to force Charles to honor his word and convene the promised Diet at Nürnberg. He entered into negotiations, made demands and issued propaganda. He even published an anonymous tract designed to stir up popular demand for the meeting.[156] One of his strategies was to plan a trip to England to enlist the support of Henry VIII for the Protestant cause in Germany. He wrote to Thomas Cranmer to inform him of his need for support from the English monarch. By this point, imperial politics seems to have taken precedence even over the work of achieving religious unity. Bucer the diplomat overshadowed Bucer the theologian.

At this point the political efforts of Martin Bucer and the Protestant leaders received a severe set-back when the bigamy of Philip of Hesse became known. The Protestants lost their strongest prince, and the political advantage, which clearly was theirs in 1539, now was lost to the Church and imperial government. Still, Bucer did not abandon the cause. He worked for a national conference on religion that would achieve a political alliance, or vice-versa.[157] Once again, he issued a publication to garner support.[158] In this publication Bucer proposed a plan to settle the problem of ecclesiastical property by peaceful rather than forceful methods based on his successful policy in Strasbourg. Philip authorized Bucer to present the plan to the Schmalkaldic League, but nothing came of it other than to secure consent to a national conference, a conference that now seemed ever and always evaporative.

---

[155] Eells, pp. 250-251.
[156] Gotliche gesprech…vom Nürnbergischen fridestand.
[157] Eells, p. 264.
[158] Von kirchen gütern

The conferences at Haguenau and Worms were no more successful in settling the political differences over ecclesiastical property than they were in settling the theological ones that divided Catholics and Protestants.[159] By this point Bucer was attempting to forge some kind of workable coalition of moderate Protestants and moderate Catholics, as it was obvious that the radicals on both sides had given up on any possibility of accord. But the failure of the 1541 Regensburg Diet left Bucer with little hope.[160] In addition to facing an official conference of the Holy Roman Empire dominated by Catholics and presided over by a hostile emperor, Bucer was discouraged by Philip's immoral conduct, by the fact that Farel was wanting John Calvin to return to Geneva, by news of the plague advancing on Strasbourg, and the fact that Luther had denounced the proceedings at the earlier Worms conference. In spite of the fact that he found friendship and support in Cardinal Contarini, a man after Bucer's own heart, nothing came of the Ratisbon Conference.

However, Bucer had four more interactions with the emperor Charles V still ahead of him. Undoubtedly, the zenith of his efforts at reformation occurred in Köln, and in the context of the success with the cause there the German princes met in a Landtag on July 23, 1543. Bucer believed that victory at this point could mean "The reform of the entire German nation." He carefully prepared a policy statement that he hoped the Protestant states would adopt in order to make a united stand against the emperor.[161]

The emperor agreed to a diet at Speyer in 1544, but he was only stalling and buying time. He used the Diet to demand support in his campaign against the Turks. He made various promises to the Protestants, none of which he intended to keep, and used his contact with them to try to divide them against themselves. Bucer hoped

---

[159] See above discussion on these two conferences.

[160] See above discussion.

[161] Bucer's *Denkschrift* provided for restoration of ecclesiastical property by both sides to proper use, transfer of power from church officials to congregations, initiation of reform in the churches by the civil powers, Protestants agreeing on what were the essentials of the faith and demanding recognition from the emperor, the right of local congregations to choose their own officers, and other practical measures designed to achieve a working relationship between imperial government and evangelical churches.

that he would have an opportunity to meet with the Catholic leader Gropper, but Gropper left the conference. Gropper's loyalty to the Roman Church was overcoming his inclination for reform and moderation.

When Charles defeated the French in 1544, he could direct his attention to his problems within Germany. The success Bucer had with Hermann von Wied at Köln, while winning back approval for Bucer from Protestant leaders, drew down the wrath of Charles upon him and the whole evangelical cause. War was inevitable.

The final conference was a sham. On July 27, 1546, Regensburg hosted the second Colloquy of Ratisbon. The emperor continued his delaying tactics, and the Protestant leaders, one by one, finally gave up and went home. Bucer stayed until the last, until it was evident that no chance remained for any kind of settlement. The conflict moved finally from useless negotiations and the emperor's deceptive political strategies to violence in which the Protestant Schmalkaldic League was defeated militarily. The emperor responded by the Augsburg Interim in which he demanded the return of the mass and the Catholic clergy in Protestant areas, thus systematically destroying the evangelical community. He came short of annihilation of Protestants, obviously because he needed their help against the Turks. He settled on a compromise that even the usually compromising Bucer could not accept.

The council of Strasbourg was now under a new generation of men who had not been involved in the struggles to establish a reformed community and who were weary of war and conflict with the imperial government. The Interim caused them to decide to sacrifice Bucer for the cause of peace. It was indeed ironic that the apostle of peace became a scapegoat for a peace that he himself considered apostasy. Bucer left Strasbourg for exile and death in England.

The conflict between the German emperor Charles V of the house of Hapsburg and the preacher of Strasbourg, Martin Bucer, makes a fascinating study. Both men were well aware of the power wielded by the other. Both sought unity, and both had clearly-defined goals. Both believed God validated their positions. Neither Charles nor Bucer intended to yield to the other. Charles sought the unity of Germany in order to stand against the threat of the Turks, a threat that, to Charles, was of the gravest importance. Bucer sought to unify Germany under the banner of Christ, which he defined in terms of evangelical Christianity. Charles used the tools he had at his disposal: imperial power and political stratagems. Bucer used the printed word, the preached word, diplomacy, negotiations, councils, conferences and colloquies. Bucer traveled continually. He met and personally dealt with the great people of his day: princes, Catholic leaders of all factions, Protestant leaders, Anabaptists and Separatists, and nearly anyone who emerged as a leader of any kind in this great ideological contest.

In the contest between these two great leaders, the emperor and the preacher, who won? Bucer was forced out of Strasbourg and into exile. The Protestants were defeated and the Interim imposed. It would appear that Bucer lost. However, Bucer's work and influence became seed that continues to bear fruit, and the emperor finally abdicated in 1555 and sailed off to Spain to the monastery at Yuste. The Holy Roman Empire declined until Napoleon put it out of its misery in 1806. And the story has not yet ended.

Francis I of France

Martin Bucer was passionately concerned about the cause of Reformation everywhere, not just in Germany. Although his ministry was within the Empire and in German-speaking areas, he supported vigorously efforts in other countries. A good example of his ecumenical passion may be found in his work with France and its illustrious king, Francis I.

Normally we think of John Calvin's connection to France, for he was born at Noyon near Paris and educated at the University of Paris. His ministry was largely in Geneva, which was in the French-speaking region of Switzerland. However, Bucer's reputation spread into France, especially with his publication of his Commentary on the Psalms that proved very popular with French scholars. He was acquainted with Jacques LeFevre d'Etaples, Christian humanist professor of the University of Paris who sought to implement reform in an Erasmian style by inculcating Biblical principles in his students.

Bucer was drawn directly into French affairs when leaders of the Waldensian Church in south France, the areas of Provence and Dauphine, concerned about their own problems with spiritual and moral deterioration, sent representatives to John Oecolampadius in Basel for advice. Waldensians, some of whom still survive in France and North Italy today, were the result of the efforts of Peter Waldo of the twelfth century who had a vision of restoring spirituality and purity to the church by employing the example of the apostolic church and the best traditions of monasticism. The Waldensians developed their own liturgy, clergy, doctrines, and, thus, their own church, and for that reason were branded heretics by the Medieval Church. In spite of persecution, they had survived only to suffer more persecution later as a result of royal opposition to Reformed teaching in France.

The Waldensians wanted advice from Oecolampadius on how to purify their church, and Oecolampadius thought of Martin Bucer, who then worked with two of their leaders, Peter Mason and George Morel, and the two of them read the responses of Oecolampadius and Bucer at the synod meeting in Argrogne in September of 1532. These responses where then incorporated into their creed. Bucer's reputation spread as a result of his work with the Waldensians, and he came to be highly respected by Protestants throughout France. He began to develop connections in high places in France that eventually gained him the notice of King Francis. In particular Bucer came to know Henry Cop through his connection with John Sturm, and his correspondence with Cop put him in touch with the affairs of the court. That contact in turn led to his acquaintance with William du Bellay who was involved directly in court affairs. He informed Bucer that the king was greatly disturbed by the division within the church in France. Bucer and Melancthon, the two Reformers most committed to unity, could not envision a reunion in France, but nevertheless, collaborated on a statement of ways in which Catholics and Protestants could at least coexist. Their statement was conciliatory, so much so that other Protestants accused them of betraying the Protestant cause and recanting their beliefs, for they suggested a way in which the pope and the hierarchy could be retained and Catholic ceremonies continued, but in return for which Catholics would concede justification by faith.

Obviously, differences were minimized and language was, of necessity, ambiguous.[162]

They dispatched an embassy to France headed by a physician by the name of Ulrich Geiger with the statement from the Reformers. Whatever possibility of conciliation might have existed was precluded by the events of 1534 and the Protestant Day of the Placards that resulted in an angry King Francis driving all Protestants out of the country. Even then, Bucer continued to look for opportunities to encourage the Protestants in France and spread the message of grace there. He suffered much rebuke from his Protestant colleagues over his apparent "defection," but he defended himself by his comment: "Where there is pure teaching on justification, and faith in Christ, there is no peril which may not be easily suppressed."[163]

Francis continued to persecute Protestants in France after 1534, but he was cautious about overdoing it because he needed the support of German Protestants in his ongoing struggles against the Emperor Charles. He went so far as to request a visit from German Protestant theologians, preferably Melancthon. But Bucer knew that Luther would never allow Melancthon to reach any kind of accord with the papists, and would like to have gone himself. The other Protestant leaders were suspicious of either Melancthon or Bucer representing their interests in Paris lest they give away too much. Their position was that light and darkness have no fellowship and Christ has nothing to do with Belial. Bucer, they thought, would give away anything for the sake of unity. In the end neither Bucer nor Melancthon nor anyone else went to France, and the persecution of French Protestants continued. Still, Strasbourg bordered France, and Francis needed Bucer's help against Charles. Bucer, with his political acumen, knew the importance of his friendship to Francis, and continued to use it as a bargaining card to gain relief for persecuted French Huguenots. However, he never gained anything more than empty promises from Francis about permanent cessation of persecution. Still Bucer did not give up on France; still he tried to intercede whenever and wherever possible. And Strasbourg

---

[162] See Eells pp. 165-172.
[163] Eells, p. 169.

remained a city of refuge, as Geneva later would be, for persecuted French Protestants.[164]

Henry VIII of England

Bucer would live long enough to make a significant contribution to the formation of the Edwardian Reformation in England through his relationship both with the young king and especially with Archbishop Thomas Cranmer. However, long before his forced exile from Strasbourg took him to England to spend the remaining years of his life, he did have an opportunity to be involved in royal politics during the reign of Henry VIII.

So much of Henry's rule in England was dominated with "The King's Business," which, of course, resulted in the separation of the English Church from the Roman Catholics. At issue was the question of the legitimacy of Henry's marriage to Catherine of Aragon and the possibility of a divorce. For Henry, divorce from Catherine and marriage to Anne Boleyn meant the possibility of a male heir and the continuation of the Tudor line of kings, a matter of the utmost importance to Henry. Of course, his marriage to Catherine was arranged in order to solidify a treaty with Spain, and Henry had fallen in love with Anne, a lady of his court. Catherine originally was married to Henry's older brother, and Henry was destined for a career in the church. Actually, Henry was deeply committed to the Christian humanist reform program and was working closely with Thomas More. But the death of his brother necessitated his marriage to his brother's widow in order to keep the Spanish alliance alive. To marry one's sister-in-law required a papal dispensation, and now Henry sought another dispensation from another pope to annul that marriage.

Henry found a pretext in the Leviticus 18:16 passage that forbids "uncovering the nakedness of your brother's wife," setting aside the other passage in the law that required a brother to marry the widow so as to maintain the inheritance. Through the agency of Simon Grynaeus, Henry sought Bucer's advice and interpretation of the Leviticus passage. Of course, Henry wanted Bucer to validate the

---

[164] Eells, p. 172.

divorce, but Bucer, always able to see the long-term implications of an act, wanted time to consider it. Finally he wrote Grynaeus that Henry's marriage to Catherine was indeed a valid marriage and divorce would be inappropriate. Bucer's conclusion is interesting in view of the fact that he held rather lenient views on divorce, but never to the point of taking marriage lightly. In this case he felt Henry should honor his marriage commitment to Catherine, but, in view of his love for Anne and need for the male heir that Catherine obviously was not going to provide him, Bucer counseled bigamy. After all, King David had several wives, which the Lord had given him. Luther and Melancthon agreed with Bucer, but Oecolampadius and Zwingli disagreed. In the end they all sent separate opinions to the king via Grynaeus, including, in addition to the four named theologians, Capito, Hedio, and Zell. Although Bucer later withdrew his suggestion of bigamy, he won for himself the disapproval not only of King Henry but also of Zwingli and Oecolampadius.

However, Henry had aroused hope in the hearts of continental reformers by his courage in standing up to Rome. In particular, Simon Grynaeus was enthusiastic about the possibilities opened up by a Protestant, or at least, non-Catholic, king of England, and wrote to Bucer with the good news. Bucer took the initiative in opening a dialogue with Thomas Cranmer and wrote to him in 1531 to explore the possibilities of an alliance with Henry. Until Henry's death, Bucer remained the continental reformer most sympathetic with Henry's cause and continued to pursue an alliance with him when other reformers gave up. Grynaeus had forged a link between Strasbourg and England that would continue.[165]

The Politics of Reformation Theology

To the Christian living in the twenty-first century the interrelationship of politics and religion sounds very strange. To comprehend the complexities of sixteenth century church-state involvement requires disassociation with contemporary religious paradigms and accepting those of the Reformation era. Because the state had supported the Christian Church since the fourth century,

---

[165] MacCullouch, pp. 65-66.

those who sought reform in theology did not consider the idea of total separation. They saw their task as first to convince the theological leadership and then the prince. With the support of the prince, the church would then be reformed. Thus Luther worked first to gain the support of his colleagues at Wittenberg, then to spread the gospel of justification by faith by defending it in disputations at academic institutions such as Heidelberg, where Bucer heard him and was convinced. But Luther needed the support of the German princes, not only of his own Duke Frederick, but also of a majority of the nobility. Thus Luther addressed tracts to nobility and princes to gain their support for the Reformation.[166]

In Bucer's Strasbourg as well as in the Swiss areas where city councils rather than princes controlled communes, the theologians, after gaining support from a sufficient number of pastors, had to then acquire the backing of the city council.[167] When the councils officially declared for the Reformation, the theologians were free to organize the community according to their concept of the Biblical model. In a very real sense, all the theologians had to have political skills in order to navigate through the unstable, frequently changing, unpredictable waters of government.

Martin Bucer, as we have noted, was gifted perhaps more than any other of the Reformers in political abilities. He stood up to an emperor who tried in vain to ignore and demean him. He befriended, advised, relied on, and accomplished much with the capable Philip of Hesse. He had no problem meeting with papal representatives or ambassadors of foreign kings. Francis of France and Henry of England were well aware of the work of Martin Bucer. He moved freely and comfortably from conference to conference, negotiating, writing, offering proposals, lobbying for support, making compromises that he assumed would not deny essential truth when he deemed them necessary, and suffering abuse and criticism from friend and foe alike while he kept his eye on a well defined goal: the establishment of a Reformed church. Bucer knew when to

---

[166] E.g., *Address to the Christian Nobility* and *On the Liberty of a Christian Prince*.

[167] Thus Calvin was dependent on the city council of Geneva as Zwingli and Bullinger were dependent on the Zürich council.

back down and when to stand. He was willing to abandon the non-essentials, but never would he back away from the fundamental doctrine of justification by faith alone, congregational freedom, the right of clerical marriage, the authority of Scripture, and the concept of divine sovereignty. He chose his battles carefully and established priorities in even these essential matters. Bucer believed that once justification by faith could be affirmed, then the other essentials could be implemented.

Because he sincerely believed that unity must and could be achieved, he adamantly refused to divide over differences that he thought were not essential, and he constantly sought for a formula or way to achieve concord, as exemplified in the controversy over the Lord's Supper. Even when he saw the formula as no longer possible, he opted for a relationship of peaceful coexistence. And this program he had to sell not only to theologians but also to politicians, because without their support, it could never be accomplished.

As we have seen, the line between theological accord and political accord was often indistinguishable. To achieve success in one area would necessitate success in the other, and Bucer had often to proceed almost simultaneously in his dealings with theological groups and political leaders. Because no one else was able to operate with this kind of facility, although Melancthon certainly possessed great diplomatic skills, the leadership of the Reformation was forced to look to Bucer for political representation. Often they feared he would give away too much, and sometimes they disagreed with his formulas and conclusions, but they had no one to offer with better skills and with more opportunities for success and more contacts in the political arena than Bucer.

In the end Bucer failed to win the disputations. He failed to settle all the points of contention in the Protestant camp that he considered was producing an unnecessary division. He failed to reunite or gain acceptance from the moderate Catholics. He failed to set up permanent Reformed communities in many cities. Köln was eventually a failure, and he was ultimately driven out of Strasbourg. He failed to avert the bloody war over religion that he tried for so long and with so much effort to avoid.

However, his legacy is unique and remarkable. He stands forth as the greatest diplomat and the most courageous and capable advocate for Christian unity in the period. His dedication to and tireless efforts for the cause of evangelical Christianity, his intrepid negotiations, contacts in high places, and perseverance in the face of what would seem sure defeat, and his care and compassion for the people of Christ have provided a model for Christian leaders of all time.

And the legacy, as we shall see, is even greater. Bucer was, in a very real sense, the architect (from the human standpoint) of Reformed theology, for through his influence on John Calvin and Thomas Cranmer, the ideas and concepts he processed through the crucible of conflict and debate became the lynchpins of a movement that swept over the world and continues to gain importance and adherents even in the current day.

Chapter VI:

"The True Care of Souls:" Bucer the Pastor

Bucer's God-given gifts made him the consummate advocate for unity and evangelical diplomat, but Martin Bucer always saw himself essentially and primarily as a pastor, commissioned by God with the care and oversight of the precious souls of God's chosen people. Although Strasbourg was the focus of his efforts, he spent much time in other German cities laboring for the cause of the evangel, with a view ever to the blessing and benefit of the people.

What is true of Bucer as pastor is true of all the Reformers, but Bucer provided the most definitive picture of the role of the Reformed pastor with the publication in 1538 of his small book: *On the true Care of Souls and the right Pastoral Ministry and how the same is to be established and performed in the Church of Christ (Von der Waren Seelsorge...)*. It is written as a plea to the magistrates of Strasbourg to establish a truly Reformed church under a systematic, planned church leadership. The success of the Strasbourg plan, once implemented, became the model for other Reformed communities, including Calvin's Geneva.[168]

Bucer's pastoral perspective relates to his understanding of "double justification," which may have been a result of his studies of Erasmus and Thomas Aquinas. Bucer began to move the Reformed Church away from Luther's "law and gospel" to what Calvin would define as "gospel and law." Bucer understood and accepted Luther's concept of forensic justification, thus *sola fide,* but, based on James' comments on justification by works, insisted that a living faith would produce the fruit of good works. Thus the elect of God would manifest their salvation and identity with Christ by the kind of lives they lived. Godly lives needed to be nurtured by sound teaching in the context of a well-organized Christian community. It was the role and responsibility of the pastor to provide that leadership, with the support and backing of the civil

---

[168] William Pauck, *The Ministry in the Time of the Continental Reformation*, cited from "The Ministry in Historical Perspectives" in religion-online.org.

magistrates. "Bucer spoke of four marks of the church – biblical preaching, proper administration of the sacraments, ecclesial discipline, and the outpouring of charity. Bucer viewed charity as a necessary result of salvation by grace through faith, not a cause of salvation… It could be said that Bucer added gratitude to Luther's *sola gratia.* "[169]

Bucer's *duplex iustitia* may be discerned from these comments from *De Regno Christi:*

> For how can one acknowledge and adore Christ, God and Man, our only Savior, also as one's own Christ, Redeemer, King, and God, and not accept all his words and try to follow them wholeheartedly, just as they are, the words of eternal life? And is it not necessary for those to whom this has been given, that they receive and embrace the salvation which Christ the Lord offers in his gospel as well as in the sacraments and in all the precepts of his discipline, with as much more ardent a desire and greater a gratitude of spirit as the Creator excels every creature, as God excels men, and as the sure, eternal life and happiness excel a false, empty opinion and an imagined semblance of the good?[170]

Organization of the Reformed Community in Strasbourg

Once Bucer gained the support of the Strasbourg city council, he proceeded with his agenda to create a truly Reformed community. Bucer's efforts may be considered successful from the standpoint that he did create a Christian community that became the model for others.[171] Protestant pastors like John Calvin and John Knox who suffered opposition and persecution in their homelands flocked to Strasbourg, a genuine city of refuge in the thirties and forties, there

---

[169] Rebecca B. Pritchard, "Health, Education, and Welfare in the Protestant Reformation: Who Cared?" in *Luther Digest,* vol. V, 1997, p. 367.
[170] Martin Bucer, *De Regno Christi,* in Wilhelm Pauck, ed. *Melancthon and Bucer* (Philadelphia: Westminster Press, 1969), p. 385.
[171] See D.F. Wright, *Martin Bucer: Reforming Church and Community* (Cambridge at the University Press), 2002. Wright has assembled a collection of essays describing different aspects of Bucer's life and ministry with particular focus on his pastoral work in developing a Christian community at Strasbourg.

to become involved in the life of the community and to learn concepts that they could later take home and apply. Bucer's tolerant and irenic spirit drew several leaders who did not share his theological convictions, notably men like Hans Denck, Sebastian Franck and other Anabaptist leaders. However, Bucer received them with compassion and dignity that was unusual for his day.

Bucer went beyond Luther in his vision of the dimensions of the Christian community. To him the term, "Kingdom of God" included both church and state, and the restoration of the true Kingdom of God would then involve a reformation of both institutions simultaneously. The influences of Erasmus, Luther, and Thomas Aquinas all converged in Bucer's mind to create the concept, and Bucer focused much of his time, energy, and skills on the implementation of his goal, which he believed to be the plan and purpose of God.[172] Bucer conceived of the Reformation as a movement through which the Christianization of all human life would be accomplished, and the whole of society would be ordered according to the will of God.[173]

The outworking of Bucer's reform in Strasbourg, however, did not proceed according to a master plan that he devised early on, but rather he adapted, modified, and changed as he went to meet the exigencies of the moment, and the plan did not reach its final definition until the composition in England, at the end of his life, of his *De Regno Christi*. Although the Reformed community in Strasbourg was certainly realized, it was unfortunately of short duration, not outliving the emperor's Interim in 1548, although Strasbourg remained an essentially Protestant, open, refugee-welcoming city until the time of Louis XIV in the late seventeenth century.

Organization in Strasbourg: The Establishment of the Presbyterate

One of the features of the Reformed community in Strasbourg was the introduction of elders into church organization. The

---

[172] Wilhelm Pauck, *Melancthon and Bucer* (Philadelphia: The Westminster Press, 1969), p. 156.
[173] *Ibid.*

apostolic office of elders had been incorporated into the Catholic priesthood, but Luther had enunciated the doctrine of the priesthood of all believers. However, Luther carried out pastoral care and church discipline through the system of pastors with the help of the Visitation, which involved civil magistrates in the process. Bucer, of course, needed the help of the city council, but he was perhaps more careful to organize church matters as much as possible in the hands of its leaders. Bucer, therefore, restored the old office of presbyters, qualified men in the church who would work with the pastors to deal with matters of church discipline. Elders arose from the context of the congregation, but were aided by the additional office of *Kirchenpfleger,* or church wardens. Originally the *Kirchenpfleger* were appointed by the council for life terms and assumed similar roles as the elders, but provided a liaison with the city council.[174] Probably he formulated the concept of an eldership from his observation of the practice of the Bohemian Brethren who organized under a "bench" or college of elders.[175]

Calvin, during his stay in Strasbourg from 1538 to 1541 learned and then replicated in Geneva the forms he found in Bucer's Strasbourg. When thinking of the organization of a Reformed community, we think often of Calvin's four-fold offices in Geneva: pastors, elders, teachers, and deacons. But this arrangement was fully in place in Strasbourg, thanks to the work of Martin Bucer. Calvin merely implemented the arrangement quite successfully in Geneva.

When Bucer went to England in 1549, he encountered Cranmer's opinion, supported generally by the English, favoring episcopal government. Bucer certainly informed Cranmer of his preference for elders in the churches, but, in typical Bucer fashion, acquiesced to the organization of the English church under bishops.[176] In line with Bucer's strong convictions about binding only what is essential, he was willing to compromise on this point to

---

[174] Jean Rott, "The Strasbourg Kirchenpfleger and Parish Discipline: Theory and Practice," in Wright: *Martin Bucer: Reforming Church and Community*, p. 122; cf. BDS 7, pp. 244-5.

[175] Samuel Miller, "The Ruling Elder," in www.reformed.org/books.

[176] Basil Hall, "Bucer in England," in Wright: *Martin Bucer: Reforming Church and Community*, p. 155.

avoid unnecessary controversy. Certainly, he had enough opposition from the Catholics in England without exacerbating the situation by demanding that they change their form of church government. Would that some of the leaders of the churches in England and Scotland in later centuries had some of Bucer's spirit.

"The Power of the Keys:" Bucer's Concept of Church Discipline

Perhaps more than in any other area, Bucer's views on discipline changed during the years, always shaped by dialogue and confrontation with those who disagreed with him. Initially, Bucer reacted against the Catholic definition of the power of the keys that created a sacramental, penitential system based on private auricular confession of <u>all</u> of one's sins. Such a system Bucer defined as placing the Christian under "the yoke of the pope." In contrast, he defined "the yoke of Christ," Christian discipline designed to admonish Christians and gently lead to repentance those who had fallen into serious sins.

Again, Bucer's initial and lasting influence was from Erasmus who had assailed the Roman Church's system of penance and confession. Erasmus concluded from his study of Acts 19 that confession was *public* and *not compulsory.*[177] Bucer published his own views, quite similar to those of Erasmus, during his debate with Conrad Treger in 1524, and also in *Grund und Ursach.*[178] Soon after, he confronted the views and practices of the Anabaptists who demanded a strict separation of those they accepted as true Christians from the general body of professing Christians. Such views Bucer considered being extreme, yet their stress on the importance of discipline was not lost on Bucer.[179]

As Bucer began to organize his thoughts on the subject of Christian discipline, he looked, as was his usual policy, at the practice of the early church and the teaching of the church fathers. He considered that to some degree the primitive church's practices

---

[177] Erasmus, *Annotations on the New Testament, LB* 258C-D..
[178] For *Handel met Cunrat Treger,* see BDS Vol. II, pp. 38-173.
[179] Amy Nelson Burnett, *The Yoke of Christ: Martin Bucer and Christian Discipline* (Kirksville, MO: Sixteenth Century Journal Publishers, 1994), p.35.

were inspired to provide a norm for the conduct of Christians through the centuries, and the teaching of the fathers was also provided by God for the ongoing use of his church. He gleaned from these sources that confession of sin was public, and any private confession was for the purpose of receiving counsel, advice, or instruction, not for absolution of sin.[180]

During the 1520's, the time of Bucer's most focused efforts to bring about reconciliation with the Roman Church, he showed his willingness to alter his views. At the same time, he needed to reach accord with the Lutherans, whose views on discipline were closer to Rome's than his. Thus he admitted private confession and the role of the minister, agreeing that the bond between the visible and invisible church is significant, and that the inner workings of the Holy Spirit in a Christian would lead him/her to confess sins. His policy was becoming more specific as a result of each interchange.[181]

The first specific plan for church discipline was the one he drew up for the church in Ulm, drawing to some degree on a plan used in Memmingen in 1531 and the policy of John Oecolampadius in Basel. In the Ulm plan Bucer claimed that he was following a system of discipline ordained by Christ, instituted by the apostles, and practiced by the early church. The proposal called for those who sinned publicly against the Ten Commandments to be admonished repeatedly by one of the ministers, and, if he/she did not repent, to be admonished by two or three ministers, then banned and expelled from the congregation, and the sentence proclaimed from the pulpit. The purpose would be to bring the erring Christian to repentance, and when he was so moved to repent, he was to be readmitted to the church's fellowship.[182]

Bucer's definition of a Christian, and thus of one who would be subject to the discipline of the church, was broader than that of the Roman church or the Anabaptists. He believed that all those who professed to be Christians and did not contradict their profession by their deeds were to be regarded as part of the church and subject to

---

[180] Burnett, p. 41.
[181] Burnett, p. 54.
[182] Burnett, pp. 59-60.

discipline. It was not necessary that they come for communion in order to be considered Christians at all, for Bucer considered the one essential to be faith that "Christ is the unique savior of mankind, true God, true man, from whom we await all things."[183] He continued, "You should not think that ecclesiastical censure should only be exercised on those who accept all your doctrines and testify to this by receiving the sacraments, for you would exclude a great multitude from this fellowship of Christ whom he does not wish to be excluded, and you would deny this healing work of grace to those who especially need it and would neglect those whom you should especially watch over."[184]

When Bucer implemented his system of discipline at Strasbourg, it represented a total replacement of the Catholic system of penance. The elders in the churches exercised discipline in coordination with twenty-one Kirchenpfleger who were appointed by the Strasbourg city council.[185] Bucer continued to stress the importance of infant baptism, which he considered necessary in order that children be raised to recognize the disciplinary authority of the church.[186] Once more, the basic differences between Bucer and the Anabaptists in the definition of who was and who was not to be regarded as a Christian were manifested in the matter of who was subject to Christian baptism. Infant baptism for Bucer, as for all the Reformers, was tied to a broader concept of who belonged to the church. If infants were members, then they could be subjected to a pre-communion examination that Bucer considered essential for the purity of the visible church.[187]

---

[183] Bucer, E-II, 1359r Staatsarchiv Zürich, in Burnett, p. 64.

[184] *Ibid.*

[185] Burnett, p. 66.

[186] Burnett, p. 79.

[187] In the final charge to the young person prior to his/her admission to communion, the teacher would admonish the child to "be diligent in attending catechism, the sermons and the sacraments, confess your sins without ceasing to God your Lord, with particular examination of your conscience, and do the same thing in church as often as general confession is made, and also confess to all whom you have offended, above all your parents, godparents and teachers whenever they punish you for doing wrong, and all who teach you self-control, respectability and sanctity and punish you for your transgressions. Above all, beware that you do not scorn any kind of reproof from anyone, whoever he may

However, as the implementation of Bucer's program for church discipline continued in Strasbourg, he became increasingly discouraged over the possibility that the laity would not accept it, and thus he placed increasing responsibility for discipline, instruction, and admonition on the ministers and the lay elders.[188]

In 1538 Bucer published *Von der Wahren Seelsorge,* and in it he expressed his maturing thought on the subject of church discipline. He emphasized teaching and admonishing privately to arouse a person to true repentance, and he showed increased respect for the minister to administer the power of the keys. He also showed a greater emphasis on discipline of committed Christians, but he never moved to the separatist position of the Anabaptists.[189]

Yet Strasbourg pastors complained that they lacked sufficient support from the council to carry out the program of discipline, and they were largely ignored by the laity. They proposed that every parishioner, with his whole household, would enroll his name in the parish register, and that each individual would be required to make a yearly confession of faith that would consist of the chief articles of the Christian faith and the Ten Commandments. Also they proposed that the first confession made publicly by children between the ages of ten and twelve be repeated privately to pastors on a yearly basis, and that parishioners be required to seek out pastors before participating in the sacraments and ceremonies of the church.[190]

Bucer further defined his views when he helped to organize the Hessian church, which now included mandatory catechetical instruction for children and adolescents, and the provision of elders for each church. Also, the Hessian plan gave pastors the power to excommunicate, which Bucer tried to implement later in Strasbourg with limited success. He also included in the Hessian program a

---

be…Recognize the keys to the kingdom of heaven whenever someone reproves your sins and teaches you what is good, because although the ministers of the word are also the ministers of the keys, which is nothing other than the dispensing of the word and power of Christ, we are all members of one another and each person should always serve the others for edification in the Christian life." (in Burnett, p. 84.)

[188] Burnett, p. 86.

[189] Burnett, p. 92.

[190] Burnett, p. 102.

provision for the public confirmation ceremony he had labored to construct.[191]

By the late 1530's and into the 1540's, the composition of the Strasbourg city council was beginning to change and included more and more members who were less inclined to accept the authority of the pastors in matters of church discipline, fearing that they had exchanged the tyranny of Rome for that of the Protestant pastors. Additionally, the laity was increasingly indifferent to spiritual matters in general. The pastors complained that people were walking around and talking during services, and more children were out playing in the streets than attending catechism.[192] People were joining sects, staying with the Catholics, or showing no respect at all for religion. Bucer now increasingly attributed the growing failures in the progress of the Reformation and the victories of the imperial forces over the Protestant Schmalkalden League to God's punishment for the deplorable spiritual condition among the people.

The pastors drew up a proposal that was presented to the second Strasbourg synod in 1539 that included required catechism, confirmation, fraternal admonition, pastoral oversight, penitential discipline, and excommunication as a last resort after every other effort had failed.[193] But the council resisted by denying the pastors' request and limiting their authority to private admonition and instruction. Bucer was discouraged because the council-appointed Kirchenpfleger often could not be relied on, and he wanted to give more authority to the elders.[194] But the council continued to see Bucer's efforts as simply means to wrest their authority away from them.[195]

In her concluding comments, Amy Burnett writes: "The ultimate failure of Bucer's system was not due to any lack of effort on his part, but to the failure of the magistrates and the laity to see the difference between the papal yoke of the Catholics and the yoke of Christ as Bucer defined it."[196]

---

[191] Burnett, p. 119.
[192] Burnett, p. 175.
[193] BDS 6/II:195-199, in Burnett, p. 163.
[194] Burnett, p. 177, 180.
[195] Burnett, p. 206.
[196] Burnett p. 224.

The Christlichen Gemeinschaften: Beginning of Small Groups in Churches

As the Reformation progressed in Strasbourg, Bucer, as a concerned pastor, was deeply disturbed about the lack of personal commitment on the part of the citizens of the city to Christ and the Christian life. If the elect of God produce works indicating their salvation, if we are called to good works, if we have a grateful heart for the grace of salvation freely given to us in Christ, then our dedication to Christ and his service should be obvious. But it was not. The Kirchenpfleger system, although many of the wardens were committed, had ultimately failed.

This deplorable situation led Bucer to make a decision, which, although it did not lead to a solution in the context of his day, would have repercussions in the twenty-first century evangelical church. Bucer proposed, as his final attempt to bring order and discipline to the Christian community in Strasbourg, and for the first time in Christian history, creating small groups within the church. The concept of small groups is utilized by most large congregations today for exactly the same reason, to induce members to become more involved and more committed.

In the case of Strasbourg, Bucer sought to establish these groups, which he called *Christlichen Gemeinschaften,* or "Christian Associations" within the congregations as entirely voluntary in nature, composed of people who were willing to make a personal vow to live an exemplary life before the others, in hopes that their influence would spread.[197] Once again, the example Bucer followed was that of the early church and the days of the apostolic fathers, before the concept of true Christian community was corrupted by the medieval church. Part of the sense of urgency Bucer felt to organize these small groups derived from the ongoing presence of Anabaptists in Strasbourg and the horror of what Anabaptism

---

[197] Gottfriend Hammann, "Ecclesiological Motifs behind the Creation of the Christlichen Gemeinschaften," in Wright: *Martin Bucer: Reforming Church and Community*, p. 129ff; cf. BDS 17.

produced in Münster, but a greater motivation for Bucer was the Strasbourgers' own indifference to spiritual matters.[198]

The formation of the groups began with Bucer's preaching on the urgent need in these dangerous times to live as a true Christian community. Those who were moved by his sermon would then agree to meet at a suitable time and place. During the meeting the pastor would define the characteristics of this true Christian community, and the parishioners would be given an opportunity to ask questions and to express their views. Those who agreed to participate would then select two representatives, who with the pastor and the Kirchenpfleger would form a board for pastoral direction and disciplinary supervisions. The pastors would set the example by making their commitment, confessing their theology, and pledging their households. Then the chosen representatives and elders would make a similar commitment. The names of the elders would be entered in a register; then, the pastor, elders, and Kirchenpfleger summoned the members one by one or else visited them at their homes, interviewing each one and his family concerning doctrine, sacraments, Christian behavior, and repentance. If the member was ready to make a further commitment, he would do so by giving the right hand of fellowship with the pastor and representatives, and his name would be entered in a register as a member of the Christliche Gemeinschaft.[199]

Bucer hoped that these small groups, rather than divide the city into good and bad Christians, as his critics asserted, would actually promote unity and revitalize the Sunday Christian worship assemblies when all came together. The common meeting at the Lord's Table would be an expression of this internal unity.[200] Bucer, with his passion for the development of personal holiness, saw the small groups as a means of stimulating the whole parish to a better practice of the Christian life manifested in confession of one's own sinfulness, becoming truly one soul, one heart, and one body,

---

[198] Hammann lists Bucer's motives for the initiation of these groups as that of inner unity, "ecclesial places" (the model of the early church), holiness, and faithfulness.
[199] BDS 17, 184. 15-, 187.28, Hammann, pp. 139-40, Burnett, p. 186.
[200] Hammann, p. 141.

attending Sunday worship regularly, participating often in the Lord's Supper, sharing one's substance with others, having children baptized, watching over the nurture of the Christian household, accepting brotherly admonition, and, if necessary, even excommunication.

The council complained about the small groups, and the people complained about the pastors seeking to establish the control of the ban themselves. Bucer defended his program before the council in 1547, but the council members accused him of forming separatist church groups. Bucer replied that the groups were voluntary and always involved the participation of the council-appointed Kirchenpfleger.[201]   In October of 1547 the council received complaints from some parishioners who said they were pressured into joining a fellowship, whereupon the council told the pastors to suspend their practice, accusing them of setting themselves up as an independent authority and causing dissention in the city by refusing the sacraments to those who did not join. Bucer responded with an impassioned defense, claiming they were only carrying out God's word, that the situation in Strasbourg was deplorable, and that they did not pressure people to join. He further pointed out that the magistrates had done nothing to correct the spiritual problems in the city.[202]

Thus, the small groups were not successful in correcting the problems of lack of spiritual discipline; in fact they were a failure. Bucer had difficulty securing enough people to volunteer and to live up to their commitment, he did not have the full support of all the Strasbourg pastors, the city council was beginning to change in orientation and had become increasingly suspicious and hostile to Bucer's policies, and Charles was on the verge of the imposition of the Interim, drawing Bucer's attention away from the problem of discipline in the city.[203]   Nevertheless, the concept was born, to be

---

[201] Burnett, p. 191.

[202] BDS 303, 07:319-336; Burnett, p.193.

[203] Bucer originally did have the pastors' support, but the council refused to give official sanction, and several of the pastors withdrew including Zell, Hedio, and Steinlin. Paul Fagius, Lengin, Schnell, and Marbach continued to support Bucer. The insistence on the plan in the face of the council's unwillingness to authorize it contributed to their decision soon after to banish Bucer and Fagius from the city.

revived and put to good use in a later day. Once again, Bucer was ahead of his time. Once again, Bucer was contributing forms to the Protestant Reformation that would continue and become permanent institutions.

The Protestant Confirmation

A related institution, derived again from Bucer's impulse toward developing personal commitment and holiness in the flock over which Bucer served as a pastor, was the introduction of what would become known as the "Protestant confirmation." The Roman Church added confirmation as one of the seven sacraments, administered by a bishop to a baptized youth about the time of adolescence. Protestants generally eschewed the Catholic sacramental system, but Bucer was always willing to adapt anything useful from any source. His concern to develop a confessing church caused him to look again at the Catholic sacrament of penance and to design a Protestant counterpart. Bucer looked for ways to gain commitments from people that they would keep, and he believed that when a young person reached an age of responsibility, he/she should make a public profession of personal faith. In that way the young person would be encouraged to remember the occasion and to remain faithful to that confession, and also the congregation would identify young people whom they could encourage and nurture.[204]

His confirmation, like all that Bucer arranged, was a component of the well-structured Christian community. The confirmant, whether adolescent or adult, stood before the congregation and made an open profession of faith and commitment both to Christ and the church. The ceremony concluded by a prayer for the illumination of the confirmant, and then the officiating clergy laid his hands upon him/her. The clergyman announced that the confirmant was now accepted into the Christian community and granted access to the

---

[204] Amy Nelson Burnett, "Confirmation and Christian Fellowship: Martin Bucer on Commitment to the Church," *Church History,* vol. 64 #2 (June 1995), p. 203-4.

Lord's Table. He/she was exhorted to obey the gospel and to accept the discipline of the church.[205]

Once again, Bucer's actions were prompted by a challenge, and once again, that challenge came from the Anabaptists who criticized the Reformers for neglecting personal holiness and discipline in their zeal to present a doctrine of salvation by grace alone. Anabaptists, of course, removed infant baptism in favor of a voluntary baptism of a believer. At the time of Anabaptist baptism, the candidate would profess faith and pledge obedience to Christ and the church. Bucer could not disavow infant baptism, in which he believed with all his heart, but he could not ignore the merit of a public and voluntary profession of faith. Thus he drew up his confirmation ceremony first for Strasbourg in 1538 and then for Philip of Hesse in 1539. Many Lutheran churches accepted the practice, and Bucer thus earned the title "father of evangelical confirmation."[206]

The Development of a Liturgy

Central to any Reformed community was the public worship. Of course, the church was central in the lives of people in Medieval Europe as well, but church and worship took on a very different meaning in cities where the Reformation was adopted.

Certain practices that were considered as "superstitious" were omitted from the service, although Bucer, like Zell and Schwartz before him, had no problem with retaining features from the older

---

[205] Florence Couprie, "Eglise Reformee d'Auteuil – Martin Bucer, www.erf-auteuil.org/protestantisme/martin-bucer.

[206] Drawn up as a part of the Kassel Reformation, it was known as "Kasseler Kirchenordnung." The age of confirmation originally seems to be twelve, but later was raised from fourteen to seventeen. Cf. John M. Brenner, *A Brief Study of Confirmation: Historical Development, Theological Considerations, and Practical Implications;* Ronald K. Heins, *The Age of Communion and Confirmation in Light of Recent Trends in Lutheranism;* and *Confirmation: History, Doctrine, and Practice,* ed. Kenig Burbaker Cully (Greenwich, CT: The Seabury Press, 1962). For the term "father of evangelical confirmation," see Amy Nelson Burnett, "Martin Bucer and the Anabaptist Context of Evangelical Confirmation," *The Mennonite Quarterly Review,* vol. LXVIII, #1 (January 1994), p. 122.

rite as long as they were biblical and not misleading. Of primary importance was the removal of offensive elements of Roman Catholicism. The mass was abolished, the organs removed, the altar replaced often with a table containing an open Bible, the altar rail was totally removed, and invocation of saints disappeared, as did statuary and incense burning. Bucer also abolished the practice of making the sign of the cross. Worship became much simpler, and the sermon became a focal point of the service. Hymns were derived from Scripture, especially the Psalms, and sung in the vernacular. However, many of the elements of Catholic worship remained because they were considered biblical and not misleading the people into superstition. Protestants made a conscientious effort to create a God-centered worship in which He alone received all the glory.

There is no question that the essential pattern of worship found in Medieval Catholicism that found its origins in the early church became a model for the Reformers. They had no intention of throwing out all Christian liturgical traditions and starting afresh. If one compares the liturgies of the leading Reformers, he would observe more similarities than differences; yet, there were some points that Bucer strongly believed needed to be emphasized at Strasbourg, points that carried directly into Calvin's worship at Geneva and rather indirectly into Anglican worship under the organization of Thomas Cranmer.

The beginning of liturgical reform in Strasbourg occurred under the city's original reformer, Mathew Zell, who changed the mass into German. The first radical change in the liturgy occurred under Zell's assistant Diebold Schwartz (Theobald Niger). On February 16, 1524 Schwartz read his German mass in a chapel at the cathedral. Although he deliberately kept as much of the old as possible, it breathed an evangelical spirit.[207]

When Bucer assumed leadership of Strasbourg, he continued the tradition already in place, but he deepened the meaning, for Bucer saw an organic connection between liturgy, theology, the operation

---

[207] G.J. Van de Poll, *Martin Bucer's Liturgical Ideas: The Strasbourg Reformer and His Connection with the Liturgies of the Sixteenth Century* (Assen, Netherlands: Koninklijke Van Gorcurn and Company, N.V., 1954), p. 12.

of the Holy Spirit, and the Christian life. The doctrine of freedom in Christ through God's grace meant that the preaching of the word should be central in the service. In that regard, Bucer placed a great emphasis on the public reading of scripture, especially the Psalms, which he believed should be read through entirely over a given period of time.[208] Bucer's belief in the centrality of the Holy Spirit led him to embrace the concept that unless the Holy Spirit illuminated the heart, the service was meaningless. God indeed speaks through the external word, but without the internal word, the illumination of the revelation by the Holy Spirit in the heart, nothing is effected.[209]

Elements of the liturgy expressed ideas of brotherly love and the Christian community. Thus worship and liturgy did not exist in isolation but in living relationship to the whole of Christianity, but worship and liturgy represented the focal point of it all. Bucer probably emphasized love even over faith, for the community of love marks the life and works of the church. Bucer took the Pauline figure of the church as a body quite literally and thus stressed the interdependence of the members on one another. In Bucer's distinction between the visible and the invisible church, the common love of Christians for one another becomes a vital characteristic.[210]

Thus Bucer spoke of four principles that would govern the public worship: first, that the Word would go forth through the clear and plain declarations of Holy Scripture, to which the church makes response in prayer and praise; second, that precedence is given not to the physical and structural aspects of worship, but rather to the activity of the Holy Spirit who impresses the external Word on human hearts and makes it the living Word of God, calling us to repentance, impelling us to prayer, assuring our hearts, and providing us with spiritual gifts that we may serve our neighbors in love; third, Christian liberty allowing people to pray and praise without restraint, and enabling freedom on the selection of the acts of worship (except for the sermon which would always be necessary); and fourth, because the church is a community of love,

---

[208] Van de Poll, p. 20.
[209] Van de Poll, p. 23.
[210] Van de Poll, p. 58.

the activity of the Spirit through prayer, praise, and preaching would inspire the members to serve one another and lead them in love to the worship, being freed from the bondage of believing they had to attain salvation by works.[211]

In 1524, the same year Schwartz initiated his evangelical liturgy at Strasbourg, Bucer wrote in his *Grund und Ursach* a proposal for worship that was essentially implemented and characterized worship in Strasbourg between 1526 and 1539 when further revisions were made:

> When the congregation comes together on Sunday, the minister (Diener) admonishes them to make confession of their sins and to pray for pardon; and he confesses to God on behalf of the whole congregation, prays for pardon, and proclaims the remission of sins to those that believe. Then the whole congregation sings several short psalms or hymns of praise, after which the minister makes a brief prayer and reads to the congregation a passage from the writings of the Apostles, expounding the same as briefly as possible. Thereupon the congregation sings again: the Ten Commandments or something else. The priest (Priester) then proclaims the Gospel and delivers the sermon proper. After this the congregation sings the Articles of our Faith. The priest then offers a prayer for the civil authority, in which he prays for an increase of faith and love, and grace to keep the remembrance of Christ's death with profit.
>
> Then he admonishes those who wish to observe the Lord's Supper with him, that they would do so in remembrance of Christ, to die to their sins, bear their cross willingly, and love their neighbor truly, being strengthened in faith, which must then come to pass when we consider with believing hearts what unlimited grace and goodness Christ hath shown us, in that He offered His body and blood to the Father on our behalf. After the exhortation he proclaims the Gospel of the Lord's Supper, as the three evangelists, Matthew, Mark, and Luke, have described it, together with Paul in 1 Cor. 11. Then the priest divides the bread and cup of the Lord amongst them, and also

---

[211] Ideas developed in *Grund und Ursach.*

partakes of it himself. Presently the congregation sings another hymn of praise. After that the minister closes the Supper with a short prayer, blesses the people, and bids them go in the peace of the Lord. This is the manner and custom with which we now celebrate Christ's Supper on Sundays only.[212]

The revisions of the liturgy in 1537 resulted in a somewhat more lengthy and complex service, but the essential structure remained unchanged. It is important to note that it is this latter liturgical arrangement that Calvin would have learned during his years in Strasbourg, 1538 to 1541, and that Calvin virtually replicated it in Geneva with only minor adaptations and alterations. Bucer also had considerable influence on the development of liturgy in England, as we shall note later. In one true sense, Bucer shaped the nature of Reformed worship throughout Europe.

Then how would we find an order of worship if we were to attend a service at St. Thomas Church in Strasbourg during the time of Bucer's pastorate? Given variations that we would expect, as not every service was identical, a typical service would proceed as follows:

The Liturgy of the Word
Confession of sins
Scriptural words of pardon (1 Tim. 1:1)
Absolution
Psalm, hymn, or *kryies* and *Gloria in excelsis*
Collect for Illumination
Metrical Psalm
Lection (Gospel)
Sermon

---

[212] Bucer, *Grund und Ursach ausz gotlicher schrift der newerungen an dem nachtmal des Herren.* BDS, Kb2, vol. 1, p. 246. A more complete discussion of the various Strasbourg liturgies may be found in William D. Maxwell, *An Outline of Christian Worship: Its Developments and Forms* (London: Oxford University Press, 1963), pp. 87-111, and Bard Thompson, *Liturgies of the Western Church* (New York: World Publishing Company, 1961), pp. 159-181.

The Liturgy of the Upper Room
Collection of alms
Preparation of elements while Apostles' Creed sung
Intercessions and Consecration Prayer
Lord's Prayer
Words of Institution
Fraction
Delivery
Communion, while psalm or hymn sung
Post-communion collect
Aaronic Blessing
Dismissal

Externally one of Bucer's contributions to Protestant liturgy would be an emphasis on weekly communion. Calvin accepted Bucer's stress on weekly communion, but failed to gain the support of the Geneva city council in implementing it, and thus the Calvinistic tradition does not usually incorporate a weekly observance, although many conservative Presbyterian churches have recently implemented weekly communion. His communion service, the liturgy of the Upper Room, strongly resembles that of the other Reformers, all of whom held the highest reverence for this observance of the sacrament.

However, by 1539 only the cathedral observed communion weekly, the parish churches moving to monthly communion. The reason for the change was not reconsideration by Bucer, but probably a reluctance of the people. Popular resistance may well have also influenced the decision in Geneva. In any instance, Bucer blended the two aspects of worship: word and sacrament in a way that was unique and different from Zwingli or Luther's liturgies.

Another feature of worship that would be discernible to a worshipper in the sixteenth century was the emphasis on music. Bucer, like Luther, was a musician who appreciated music, but Bucer introduced the singing of Psalms into public worship, and encouraged the writing of hymns.[213] He himself published a songbook in 1541 so that all the Strasbourg parishes would have the same hymns.[214]

Another aspect of worship stressed at Strasbourg was the centrality of the sermon in German with a deliberate attempt to explain the Word in terms that the laity could comprehend. Of course, as we noted, Bucer believed that only the Holy Spirit could provide genuine understanding, but the pastor must labor to be clear in what he said.

Finally, one would be impressed with the beginning of each service involving a confession of sins, followed by an assurance of pardon and the Confiteor, words of comfort taken from a familiar Scripture passage, frequently 1 Tim. 1:15-17,[215] followed by the words "Let everyone, with St. Paul, truly acknowledge this in his heart and believe in Christ. Thus in his name, I proclaim unto you the forgiveness of all your sins, and declare you to be loosed of them on earth, that you may be loosed of them also in heaven, in eternity. Amen."

Of greater importance were the underlying assumptions that governed Bucer's arrangement of the liturgy. By his arrangement of confession and assurance at the beginning of the worship, the Protestant doctrine of justification by faith alone and the gratitude that should fill the heart were rooted in the worshippers.[216] His emphasis on confession and discipline and the stress placed on clear and simple proclamation of the word both manifest Bucer's concept

---

[213] For a discussion of Bucer and the Psalms, see Gerald Hobbs, "Martin Bucer and the Englishing of the Psalms in the Service of Early English Protestant Piety" in Wright.

[214] Jack Kinneer, 'The Liturgy of the Word at Strasbourg" www.wso.net/echohills/Worship/Word.htm., p. 3. One hymn used at Strasbourg in Bucer's time is "I Greet Thee Who My Sure Redeemer Art," often sung to the same tune.

[215] [15]Here is a trustworthy saying that deserves full acceptance: Christ Jesus came into the world to save sinners--of whom I am the worst. [16]But for that very reason I was shown mercy so that in me, the worst of sinners, Christ Jesus might display his unlimited patience as an example for those who would believe on him and receive eternal life. [17]Now to the King eternal, immortal, invisible, the only God, be honor and glory for ever and ever. Amen.

[216] Kinneer, p.2.

of the congregation as a community and the primacy of engendering love and purity of life among the members. His pneuomatology, his firm belief that the word of the Holy Spirit is involved at every juncture of the Christian's life, his assumption of divine election, and the role of the pastor as a true shepherd of the flock undergirded all that was done. The service, although it retained much of the form of the Medieval rites, was nevertheless, due to these presuppositions, a living experience for the believer in Strasbourg, and the worship came to have a power and appeal that propelled it into both the Genevan and Anglican churches, and thus became the model and the spiritual essence of Reformed and Anglican worship.[217]

Wandering through the streets of old Strasbourg today is a wonderful journey back to the Reformation. St. Thomas, St. Peter the Younger where Wolfgang Capito was pastor, St. Peter the Elder, and St. Auriole still stand and are still Protestant churches, although only St. Thomas has had a continual history of Protestantism since the Reformation. When Louis XIV conquered Strasbourg in the seventeenth century, he restored Catholic worship in all the churches except St. Thomas, and only through the influence of one Protestant noble, Marshal Maurice of Saxony, who served in the army of Louis' successor, his great-grandson, Louis XV, was St. Thomas allowed to continue as a Reformed church. A monument in the apse, erected by Louis XV, commemorates "Maurice of Saxony, Duke of Courland and Semigall, Marshal of France, ever victorious." Since that time, obviously, Protestant worship has been restored in a number of the key churches of Bucer's day, although some of them,

---

[217] In addition to the scholars already cited, see Joshua Clark, www.chasinghats.org/people/martin_bucer_the_reformations_own_chesterton; Mark Moore, http://courses.indwes.edu/REL435H_reform.htm; "The Church – Worship: The Heavenly Pattern", http://www.michianacovenant.org/sermons/church11.html; D.K. Deddens, http://spindleworks.com/library/deddens/missing.htm; Sherman Isbell, "The Singing of Psalms: Part XIV, http://members.aol.com/RSISBELL/psalms14.html, 1996; Dennis Royall, "The Genevan Tunes: An Introduction," http://spindleworks.com/library/royall/genevan.htm, all of whom have some interesting observations to make on the importance of Bucer's liturgical work.

like St. Peter the Younger, have both Catholic and Protestant congregations.

St. Auriole today is connected to a Protestant school and is accessible only through the school building; however, St. Thomas is open regularly to visitors and the attendants have been quite helpful every time I have gone there. There is a medallion of Bucer hanging on the wall of the nave, on the right as one faces the altar. The pulpit where Bucer preached is still there. In the Strasbourg cathedral I could only visualize, with some sense of amusement, the wooden pulpit that was constructed on the floor to circumvent the Catholic refusal to open the pulpit to Protestant preaching and from which Zell and Bucer preached. The area of Jacob Sturm's academy still houses a Protestant center, and one can still visit the church where Calvin preached to French refugees during his three-year tenure in Strasbourg. Near St. Auriole is a street with a sign that reads "Rue Martin Bucer." One wonders how many people in Strasbourg today stop to consider the importance of the preacher after whom that street was named.

Bucer's Views on Marriage and Divorce

In discussing Bucer's role as pastor in Strasbourg, we need to consider his understanding and teaching on the subject of marriage for two reasons. First, as leading pastor of the city, his doctrines on the subject would have been highly important to the people living there; and second, because his views on the subject were remarkably different not only from those of the Roman Church, but also from those of his fellow Reformers.

As the sacramental system of the Roman Church developed, marriage was designated one of the seven, and so was the sacrament of Holy Orders. Marriage as defined by the Church was for life and divorce was never an option. To be sure, the wealthy and the nobles could obtain a papal dispensation, usually for financial consideration, that would allow for an annulment of marriage. Of course, there had to be some justification for declaring that the marriage was sinful from the beginning and thus no marriage at all. The church considered to be possible grounds of annulment cases involving impediments such as disabilities or impotence, unbelief, a preexisting marital obligation, or a vow of chastity.[218]   With divorce not allowed, for most people those who were so inclined engaged in extra-marital affairs.   Taking a mistress or mistresses was not an unusual practice for the upper classes. Bucer was appalled by the fact that the Church's views on marriage facilitated brothels.

Holy Orders, developing out of the rise of the hierarchy and monasticism in the early days of the church, was defined by the Church as requiring celibacy. Vows involved poverty, chastity, and obedience, and the Roman Church has consistently enforced clerical celibacy to this day.[219]

Bucer came to believe that required celibacy among the clergy was a dangerous and unscriptural practice, probably as a result of his careful study of the many Erasmian texts that exposed, often with high satire, the corruption of the clergy. As an Erasmian, Bucer was beginning to sense the concept of Christian freedom, and the doctrine of justification by faith alone that he imbibed from Luther gave him the theological basis for Christian freedom. Bucer was also influenced by the views of Jacob Wimpheling in his early studies at Schlettstadt.[220] Increasingly, humanists were questioning the rule of celibacy and concerned about its role in contributing to an immoral life style among the clergy.

The fact that God created marriage, that God saw that man needed a helper and gave him woman, and the fact that Scriptures speak of marriage as a holy institution led Bucer to reject the doctrine of enforced celibacy on anyone.[221] He noticed especially the two texts of Scripture that teach that marriage is for all unless they have a special gift from God that allows them to be unmarried,

---

[218] H. J. Selderhuis, *Marriage and Divorce in the Thought of Martin Bucer,"* tr. John Vriend and Lyle Bierma, in *Sixteenth Century Essays and Studies,* XLVIII (Kirksville, Mo: Thomas Jefferson University Press at Truman State University, 1999), p. 24.

[219] The Eastern Church allows for the secular clergy (church pastors) to be married but prohibits the marriage of monks and nuns.

[220] Selderhuis, p. 24.

[221] See Heb. 13:4: "Marriage should be honored by all" (NIV).

obviously a control over sexual passion. Otherwise, as Paul taught, it is better to marry than to burn.[222]

Another major factor in Bucer's arrival at his marriage and divorce doctrine arises from his passionate concern for the happiness and well-being of his flock. Understanding Bucer always requires that we confront his great pastoral concern, for all his ideas were filtered through it. He could not comprehend that God, whose great love was poured out on his people in his choice of them before time began, in the death of Christ for them at the cross, and in the Holy Spirit's regeneration of them, would consign these same people to a life of despair and joylessness by denying them a lawful expression of love and intimacy in this life. He deplored people finding an outlet for sexual passion in illegitimate ways, such as by taking mistresses. Thus he came to believe that the doctrine of enforced clerical celibacy was dangerous to the moral fiber of the clergy by driving them to illicit sexual activity or into loneliness and despair if they tried to abide by the Church's requirement. How could they be a faithful pastor if they were unhappy? How could they counsel married people when they did not understand what it meant to be married themselves? How could they fulfill the Biblical requirements of a pastor who demonstrates his ability to shepherd God's flock by first doing so in his family?[223] In short, he thought the rule of required clerical celibacy was unscriptural and laid an impossibly heaven burden on people.

---

[222] 1 Cor. 7:9. The text of the two relevant passages is as follows: (1 Cor. 7) "I wish that all men were as I am [unmarried]. But each man has his own gift from God; one has this gift, another has that" and (Matt. 19:8-12) "Jesus replied, 'Moses permitted you to divorce your wives because your hearts were hard. But it was not this way from the beginning. I tell you that anyone who divorces his wife, except for marital unfaithfulness, and marries another woman commits adultery.' The disciples said to him, 'If this is the situation between a husband and wife, it is better not to marry.' Jesus replied, 'Not everyone can accept this word, but only those to whom it has been given. For some are eunuchs because they were born that way; others were made that way by men; and others have renounced marriage because of the kingdom of heaven. The one who can accept this should accept it.'" (NIV)

[223] 1 Tim. 3:4-5: "⁴He must manage his own family well and see that his children obey him with proper respect. (If anyone does not know how to manage his own family, how can he take care of God's church?)" (NIV, see also Titus 1:6.)

The depth of Bucer's convictions on the right of the clergy to marry cannot be overstated. He came to believe that it was evil and wrong to require celibacy, and he demonstrated his convictions by his open marriage to Elizabeth which, in turn, resulted in his excommunication.[224] Throughout his career he labored to establish clerical marriage, except for those who had the God-given gift of celibacy, as a privilege and even obligation of pastors. For those with the gift, the unusually strong, celibacy could be an acceptable life style, but for everyone else, marriage was the God-ordained arrangement.

Another factor in Bucer's thinking arises from the fact that the Roman Church had come to view the state of marriage entirely in reference to procreation. Bucer saw from Scripture a much deeper and more extensive concept that involved companionship, the pleasures of sexual intimacy, and partnership in life's labors and joys. Bucer came to see the institution of forced celibacy as abusive of women, that women were, in fact, being victimized by canon law.[225] Gratian, Medieval author of the Church's Canon Law, allowed for wife beating or imprisonment, and Bucer reacted by speaking of the "poor oppressed wives."[226]

In this regard, again it was Erasmus who exercised a great influence on the formation of Bucer's thinking. Erasmus had been bold enough to call into question the sacramental idea of marriage and the concept defined by canon law that marriage was only for procreation that resulted in arranged marriages for children. Erasmus introduced the notion that marriages had to do with love and mutual devotion: "I do not call a real marriage one that is established by laws but one that has been cemented by feelings of sincere affection between persons of the same moral quality."[227] Although Erasmus did not deny clerical celibacy, he certainly advocated a far different and much broader concept of marriage.

---

[224] Luther, of course, joyfully entered into marriage with Katherine von Bora, but Zwingli, on theother hand, kept his marriage secret for some time.

[225] Seldenhuis, p. 30.

[226] Seldenhuis, p. 30; cf. Bucer, EE 41a, 42a.

[227] Erasmus, LB 5.620F cited in Seldenhuis, p. 38.

As far as reasons for divorce were concerned, Erasmus advocated that "except for the cause of adultery" was meant to be illustrative of reasons rather than definitive. The Roman Church found his views on marriage unorthodox, and his works were later placed on the Index of forbidden books by Pope Paul IV. However, these views provided Bucer with a hermeneutical principle that would guide his entire pastoral ministry.[228]

Emboldened by Erasmus' view of marriage for love and his disdain of clerical celibacy as contributing to lax morals and by Luther's emphasis on Christian freedom, Martin Bucer married Elizabeth Silbereisen. When he came to Strasbourg, he did so as an excommunicated, married monk. The bishop wanted to bring him before the episcopal court for trial, but to do so; the bishop had to persuade the Strasbourg city council to suspend the protection they had granted Martin as the son of Strasbourg citizens. The council decided to give Bucer the opportunity to defend himself, and thus Bucer drew up a defense, his *Verantworten*, which was read in his presence before the council.

In the *Verantworten* Bucer discussed his views of monastic vows, marriage, and, especially, his own marriage, using only Scripture as his basis for reasoning. He claimed that the Christian had the right to choose the style of living that best enabled him to live a godly life. He argued that human vows invented by men are not binding, especially if they constitute a hindrance to godly living, and that celibacy could and should be followed only by those who possess the special gift to do so. If a person were to vow perpetual chastity while lacking such a gift, the outcome, Bucer argued, would be the opposite of what was intended by that vow, and he cited the sexual conduct of people living in monasteries as proof. Then, using himself as an example of one who sought marriage in order to live a godly life, he wrote, "God has joined us together; he has helped us, and it is not true that one has craftily persuaded the other to take this step."[229] Bucer's defense seemed adequate to the council, and they decided to protect him, opening the way for his highly effective ministry in Strasbourg.

---

[228] Seldenhius, pp. 42-43.
[229] Bucer, BD 51.175 cited in Seldenhuis, p. 61.

Bucer continued to develop and teach his broader views on the subject of marriage and divorce, views that were often quite controversial and provocative, in his commentaries on Matthew, John, and the Psalms. Bucer further clarified his views on marriage during the years he traveled about spreading the Reformation.[230] In his Eighteen Articles of church doctrine that he drew up for cities such as Memmingen and Ulm, he included his laws on marriage (*Ehegericht*). When these views were read earlier before the Augsburg Diet in 1530, Erasmus reacted by distancing himself from the Reformers, as he could not endorse breaking monastic view of celibacy because he asserted such a practice would introduce all kinds of evil and licentious behavior that the church had never known before.[231] Bucer responded, in his typical lengthy and verbose style, by answering Erasmus' concerns that the Reformers were only satisfying carnal lusts by writing, "If we had only been interested in carnal love and riches, we would have gained both one and the other much, much more readily had we remained in the Catholic Church.....the church would not have restricted us to just one woman, nor to always the same one, nor would we now have been bound to our present limited financial means, for this church, after all, allows every man to grab as much of much of these things as he can get a hold of."[232]

After Bucer inaugurated the Reformation in Ulm, he and Pastor Martin Frecht became good friends and worked together closely. Several cases of divorce arose in Ulm, forcing Bucer to come to terms with that thorny issue. Frecht frequently sought Bucer's advice, and once write to him complaining of the inflexibility of divorce laws by stating, "You after all are accustomed to be somewhat more flexible in the confirmation of marriages."[233] When the Ulm marriage court could not handle cases, they consulted Bucer. For the meeting of the court on October 27, 1533, Bucer

---

[230] Ironically, it was the fact that Bucer turned into the itinerant missionary for the Reformation that prevented him from completing his intended purpose of writing commentaries on all the books of the Bible. The above cited commentaries plus the commentary on Romans came to constitute the bulk of his exegetical works.
[231] Erasmus, LB 10:1573A-1587D.
[232] Bucer, BOL 1:183, in Seldenhuis, p. 81.
[233] Seldenhuis, p. 94.

wrote a lengthy treatise arguing that every case should be examined on its own merits, and policies should be pursued, even if perceived more liberal and less rigorous, that would prevent rather than foster licentiousness.[234] He taught that the civil authority should be like a father to the Christian family, guiding and nurturing it in godly ways. Although the Ulm mayor and council did not officially accept Bucer's views on divorce, they promised to consult Bucer on matters and placed the marriage court under civil authority. When Bucer moved on to Augsburg, he succeeded in having the marriage court there transferred to the civil authorities, and used his views in Ulm as codified in *Von der Ehe und Ehescheidung* as a suggestion for Augsburg.

Bucer's own marriage to Elizabeth Silbereisen was as joyous a union as that of Martin Luther and Katherine von Bora. However, Elizabeth was faced with ill health since the days of the convent, and her frequent pregnancies left her increasingly weak until, on November sixteenth, 1542, during an outbreak of the plague in Strasbourg, she died. Bucer was away on a preaching trip at the time, returning to Strasbourg to witness the death of his wife and three of his children at the same time.

Despite the fact that the Bucers were always struggling financially, never able to recover Elizabeth's inheritance that had been appropriated by the convent, in spite of her ongoing ill health and the eventual loss of five of their children, Martin and Elizabeth had twenty years of a happy marriage, and Elizabeth bore Martin thirteen children. Their home was always open to refugees who had been driven out of their cities by persecution. We know of two Italian, four French, and two German refugees. Bucer had nothing but praise for his wife. On her death bed, Elizabeth urged Wibrandis Rosenblatt, widow of three Reformed pastors, Ludwig Keller, John Oecolampadius, and Wolfgang Capito, to marry Martin. Capito had died only the night before.[235] Wibrandis married Capito as a result of Bucer's mediation after Oecolampadius' death. Capito's own wife had died six months earlier. Thus Martin

---

[234] Bucer, *Von der Ehe und Ehescheidung aus göttichem und keyserlickem rechtenn;* Seldenhuis, p. 97.
[235] Keller (Cellarius) died in 1526 and Oecolampadius in 1531.

Bucer and Wibrandis Rosenblatt entered into marriage "for the furtherance of the glory of God." Wibrandis brought to the marriage a girl by Keller, another girl by Oecolampadius, and a boy and two girls by Capito. The Catholic Church now opposed Bucer on the grounds of violating Scripture by having two wives. However, Wibrandis proved a very supportive wife, although Bucer never ceased to miss Elizabeth. He would write of Wibrandis in his will in 1548 of his "dear, faithful wife W.R. and the dear children we have on both sides."[236]

In the development of Bucer's thoughts on marriage and divorce, common sense and the benefit of people were always considered even when his conclusions appeared outrageous to many people. For instance, on two occasions he advised bigamy, to Philip of Hesse and to King Henry VIII, to avoid divorce and to allow for these men to marry the women they loved. He did, however, denounce consanguinity, and he denounced the idea that marriage is made by virtue of intercourse and/or a church pronouncement; rather, love and commitment between two parties are the essence of a marriage. When love and commitment exist, we may conclude that God has joined the two together. The church ceremony only confirms the action of God.[237]

On the matter of divorce, Bucer was considered "the radical libertarian among divorce reformers in the sixteenth century."[238] He saw canonical law forbidding divorce as forcing couples to live in impossible situations where there was no love between them. Although Bucer believed that marriage was meant to be indissoluble, that divorce was contrary to nature, and that couples should always try to reunite, he did admit to divorce as a last resort. If no love was left and quarrelling was incessant, then the marriage that was based on mutual love and helpfulness no longer existed.[239]

In such cases, anything and everything that threatened or destroyed this personal relationship became possible grounds for divorce. By exalting marriage to a level higher than just sexuality,

---

[236] Seldenhuis, p. 126.
[237] Bucer, EE 29b in Seldenhius p. 230.
[238] Seldenhus, p. 257.
[239] Seldenhuis, pp. 258-259.

Bucer automatically expanded the divorce possibilities. But divorce for Bucer became then an intermediate step to remarriage, rather than the situation of concubinage that resulted from the restrictions of canonical law. In this regard Bucer could cite Erasmus and his comments on 1 Corinthians 7.[240] The Old Testament allowed a bill of divorce to protect wives and to serve as a certificate of innocence. Jesus' teaching was against the abuses of this provision, not to rescind it entirely. The bill of divorce would give wives the right of remarriage, not remove them from it. If a husband fails to honor the covenant of marriage, his wife should not be victimized by his infidelity. Bucer argued that the government should allow divorce where a Christian married to a non-Christian was forced to live a secular life style. In this case it would be for the good of the Christian community. Bucer was carefully searching Scripture to find norms for a reformation of public life and the life of the church. These norms were not to be construed as universal law, but as guidance for each case, which should be considered separately.[241]

Bucer considered that the primary grounds for divorce lay in the lack of love and goodwill, but he admitted causes such as adultery when it becomes public, desertion, banishment, impotence, or leprosy. Any of these causes not only allowed divorce but allowed the divorced partner to remarry. He believed there should be penalties for the guilty party, but penalties not so severe that people would shrink from divorce and continue to live in impossible situations.[242] He allowed remarriage even for the guilty party, for divorce terminated the marriage, and both partners have the option of entering a new marriage, for forbidding remarriage would force one to sin, unless he were to be totally isolated from all society.[243] Bucer's views actually divided the Reformed community. Even his protégé, John Calvin, disagreed with his liberal views on divorce and remarriage. Probably his marriage views had a greater impact on the English than on the continental Reformation in the long run,

---

[240] Bucer, BDS 17:375 in Seldenhuis, p. 264.
[241] Seldenhius, p.272.
[242] Seldenhuis, pp. 287ff.
[243] Bucer, Ev. 151 B, BDS 17:521, 540, in Seldenhuis p. 319ff.

but they have great relevance to the church of today and the question of how it will handle these marital situations.

We may state with certainty that the Reformation generally brought a radically different view of marriage to Christianity, and certainly, from the perspective of the Reformers, a more Biblical view. The family rather than the monastery became central to the Christian community. While all Reformers endorsed clerical marriage and the importance of the family, no Reformer did more the liberate women, to exalt the joy of the married life, to bring about reason to the sticky issue of divorce, and to promote the concept of the primacy of love in every relationship, than did Martin Bucer.

The Organization and Offices of the Church

Fundamental to the creation of a Reformed Christian community would be the concept and formation of the ecclesiastical offices. When Bucer repudiated the mass, he swept away the rationale for the entire official structure of the Roman Church. The new concept of offices would be based on the underlying presuppositions of the Reformation: that Scripture alone was authoritative, that every Christian is a priest, that the sacrifice of Christ on the cross alone is sufficient for the payment of sin and the salvation of the elect, and that the Christian community exists to further the Kingdom in bringing glory to God and blessing the lives of his people. Love rather than fear, confidence and assurance rather than uncertainty provided the foundation of leadership in the Reformed community. In all things the Holy Spirit guided the work of the church and the lives of its people, but always parallel with the Word. Bucer's practical applications in this case, as in all that he did, reflected his underlying beliefs and passions.

Thus we can see the obvious implications that guided Bucer in forming his church offices in such statements of his as "But as Christ says, 'Anyone who believes in me has eternal life," and "We however, teach according to Scripture, that man and woman, young and old, may have equal access to all good works, and point to the only brotherly love, a master in all good works, which unites all things." Similarly Bucer wrote, "Good works are not the church, altar, mass, monastic discipline and the like, but rather to take care of the good and needs of our neighbors."[244] Christ alone is Lord; he is the true Prophet, Priest, and King. It is his kingdom, and "he rules in the hearts of the elect, justifying and redeeming them."[245] In view of these principles, the mass and Roman sacramental and hierarchal system became mechanical and impersonal, *ex opera operato*. The Roman view of the power of the keys took on a new meaning to Bucer. Rather than the tyranny and power of a priesthood over the lives of people, it represented the opportunity and need to minister to and nurture the flock of God. Rather than trusting in confession of sin to a priest, in essence trusting in a work that a person had done that would supposedly result in forgiveness of sins, Bucer believed that true evangelical repentance was the gift of the Holy Spirit that would bring joy to a life. Bucer's concept of leadership erased qualitative distinctions between clergy and laity, resulting in his views on clerical marriage and denial of clerical immunity to civil authority. The Protestant clergy was taking on an entirely new form.[246]

Because of Bucer's belief that the development of the church rested on the personal work of the Holy Spirit, he believed that ultimately all who serve in the church are called by Christ to do so. However, the congregation had the right to select its officers, a right that was denied by Rome.[247] Pastors and elders, under the guidance of the Spirit, would then exercise the power of the keys in a Biblical sense, to admit to the fellowship of the church those who professed faith in the gospel and manifested the fruit of regeneration, to teach and govern them to live to the glory of God, to cast out those who refuse to live according to the laws of God, to readmit to the church those who were penitent, and to appoint ministers of the church. Bucer identified four offices: doctors or teachers, pastors, governors or elders, and deacons.[248]

---

[244] Bucer, *Acta Bern* 40, BDS 1:193) in Spijker, p. 21.

[245] Bucer, *Ev.* 1527 45v.

[246] Spijker, p. 23.

[247] Spijker, p. 103.

[248] Bucer, *Ev.* 386; Spijker, p. 133.

Each one holding office in the church was to see himself called by Christ and accountable to Christ in the exercise of his office in the building up of a true Christian community. Bucer visualized the invisible, mystical body of Christ which Christ rules directly through his appointed ministers, in distinction to the Roman structure, which Bucer viewed as a perversion.[249] Through the provision of gifts, Christ endows the leaders of the church with what they need to exercise their offices, not necessarily in a miraculous way, but in an effective, spiritual manner through the indwelling Spirit. Bucer wrote: "The church will never lack the possibility to live a happy life...If only we had an eye for all the things the Lord works in his own, then everything would be for us an absolute miracle."[250] Obviously, Bucer's concept of calling is inherent in his concept of church offices and gifts.

The most important office bearer in the church to Bucer was the minister of the Word, whom Christ calls and empowers to equip the saints. They are instruments of God who cannot do anything of themselves "unless God uses them as the carpenter his plane and the blacksmith his hammer, i.e., puts his word in their mouths, impels them to speak, and then gives his hearers the ability to recognize, accept, and believe this Word of life."[251]

The power of the keys to bind and loose is then exercised in three ways: the church preaches the gospel, excommunicates the disobedient in cases of public sin, but unbinds when there is repentance, and then readmits to the sacraments when repentance is demonstrated.[252]

Beyond the preaching of the word, Bucer saw Christ as exercising his ministry externally through deacons who would take offerings given by Christians and distribute to all the needy of the church community. Thus the church's care of people consisted essentially of two kinds [253] of ministries: the ministry of pastoral care and the ministry of mercy.

---

[249] Spijker, p. 133, 140.
[250] Bucer, *Rom.* 539.
[251] Bucer, *BDS* 5:299; Spijker, p. 148.
[252] Spijker, p. 149.
[253] Spijker, p. 174.

Elders were involved in overseeing the totality of the church's work. As we noticed earlier, Bucer was the first of the reformers to restore the ancient office of elder, providing John Calvin with a model that he would use in Geneva, and from there the presbytery would spread throughout the Reformed Church and even be accepted into many modern denominations. When the church selected elders, they would give themselves to prayer that the will of the Lord would be done. The church would then pay special attention to the indications given by the Spirit as to whom to select. Bucer again did not intend a miraculous sign, but rather signs within the character of a person as to the extent of the qualifying work done by the Spirit in that individual. The election itself would be done by the minister and the other elders, but with the consent of the entire congregation. The elders were then installed in a ceremony befitting of the seriousness of the occasion and the holiness of the office, with an offering, the celebration of the Lord's Supper, prayer, and the laying on of hands.[254] Bucer then distinguished between ruling elders and teaching elders, a distinction that Calvin would maintain in Geneva. He also allowed for the office of bishop as leading elder, the chief presbyter among the other presbyters. Although the concept was not developed to any extent on the continent, it explains why Bucer did not have a problem with the continuance of the episcopate in England.

All the offices of the church exercised their calling on the presumption of divine predestination: that through their ministry God would call his elect and preserve them to eternal life, using the ministry of the church to teach and equip them for Christian living. However, Bucer's view of election did not mean that he neglected the commission to preach the gospel to all creation, for God would call his elect from those who heard the word, creating faith and repentance in their hearts, and the non-elect would continually reject the gospel. The ministers of the church would then see their responsibility before Christ to bring estranged sheep back to him, to bring to repentance those in the church who have committed serious

---

[254] Bucer, *BDS,* 135; Spijker, p. 177.

sins, to strengthen the weak, and to keep the healthy from straying.[255]

When Bucer established the community in Ulm, he suggested to the city council that they form a committee of the most learned and able ministers to examine candidates and to act as a body to supervise the churches, providing assistance and calling a council, if necessary. He arranged for twice-yearly synods and for ministers and church wardens from the magistry once a year to conduct a church visitation in the churches of the surrounding area, giving the churches direction in the context of Christian community. The Ulm council followed word for word what Bucer suggested. Bucer returned to Strasbourg to set up a similar pattern as he had established in Ulm, dividing Strasbourg into seven parishes and creating a committee of twenty-one parish wardens, the Kirchenpfleger. Every three months preachers' meetings were held to discuss the things the pastors should concentrate on to build up the church, to exercise oversight over doctrine, and to examine candidates for the ministry. In this council of preachers, Bucer was president, and others included Kaspar Hedio, Peter Martyr, Mathew Zell, M.M. Steinlin, and John Lenglin.[256]

Bucer's organization of the church in Strasbourg became, as would be expected, far more complex than in Ulm or any other city where he labored. Strasbourg was his home pastorate, and he spent much more time connected to this city than any other single location. It was also larger and had more churches than many of the other cities where he labored. But there is another factor. Bucer's contact with Anabaptists impressed him with their devotion, although he was later repulsed by their doctrines and hypocrisy and backed the council's decision to expel them from Strasbourg. However, their initial emphasis on piety was not lost on Bucer. When he came in contact with the Moravian Brethren, who manifested a much more consistent display of godly living, Bucer was all the more committed to sanctification. Thus, he developed his doctrine of double justification, that those truly justified by faith will justify their faith in good works and pious living. Bucer was driven

---

[255] Spijker, p. 180.
[256] Spijker, p. 202.

to organize Strasbourg into workable smaller units, as we have seen earlier, with subdivision of parishes, assignment of wardens, and later the attempt to enroll people in small groups in which they would be accountable to one another.

The plan ultimately failed for two reasons: first, the people were unwilling to make such a commitment, and second, the composition of the city council changed with a new generation that lacked the appreciation for the work of Bucer and the other preachers that the earlier members had. When the emperor imposed the Interim, this council was willing to dismiss Bucer from the city and force his eventual exile in England.

Even though Bucer's concepts developed and became admittedly more complex, he always based his view of the church and its offices on the assumption of Christology, pneumatology, and ecclesiology. The church was to him a living organism, a covenant community ruled by Christ and empowered and directed by the Holy Spirit. The Spirit directed the church as a whole, not just the clergy, as Rome insinuated. Thus the division between clergy and laity was essentially removed with Bucer. The priesthood of all believers took on greater dimension under his tutelage. The differences that exist among Christians are simply a matter of the differences in gifts of the Spirit. Ministers arose from the congregation, responsible to the congregation, to serve the congregation. Rather than believe in apostolic succession, Bucer believed that the Spirit and the Word would ensure a reliable succession of truth.[257] Bucer's concepts of ministry he took directly from Scripture, keeping a view of the totality of the Word of God. He conceived of these offices in reference to redemptive history, and thus they were always interpreted and implemented in accordance with theology. Not only was his understanding of Scripture historical and redemptive, but it was always ethical, with the goal of the offices always to build up the church and encourage its members to live holy and godly lives.[258]

Spijker concludes his study of the ecclesiastical offices of Bucer with these words: "The revised interest in the thought world of the man whom Capito called the bishop of Strasbourg' is most

---

[257] Spijker, p. 467.
[258] Spijker, p. 475.

gratifying – not the least because, as long as the pilgrimage of the church continues, his views on the ministry of the church will remain relevant."[259]

The Educational Impulse

Leaders of the Protestant Reformation were traditionally committed to education, believing that God calls the whole person to himself, and that God sovereignly rules over all creation. All truth is God's truth, and people should be taught as much as possible the wide scope of learning, including the sciences, law, and letters. In some sense, the educational impulse among the Reformers was the result of Renaissance thinking that emphasized the whole man and the entire scope of knowledge. Reformers adapted this concept and made the Bible the centerpiece, much as Erasmus would advocate.

Luther established schools and stressed education in eastern Germany, and Bucer would do the same for the central and west part. In Strasbourg Bucer wanted an academy with faculty of the highest ability. He chose John Sturm in 1536 as the rector, and when Calvin came to Strasbourg in 1538, he was admitted and distinguished himself as a teacher. Sturm had been an evangelical leader in Paris who had corresponded with Bucer for some time. He first came to Strasbourg from Louvain in 1528, but only in 1536 did Bucer persuade him to stay in Strasbourg where he taught dialectic and rhetoric.

Bucer set aside the cathedral in 1534 for a theological school, then after the death of the pastor of St. William's, moved the school to that location where it developed into the academy, and, in 1621, after his lifetime, into the University of Strasbourg.

Bucer provided scholarships for poor students, using funds confiscated from the convent of St. Mark. His goal was to make Strasbourg a center of theological instruction for all of upper Germany, but instruction in the broader sense that would show the interrelation of theology to all disciplines. In time merchants who believed in the purposes of the school came to underwrite scholarships for indigent students. Bucer took a personal interest in

---

[259] Spijker, p. 476.

each student and gave attention to building a good faculty. Although he made some poor choices, for the most part, the academy gained a reputation for excellent teachers.

Sturm was officially appointed professor in 1537, gained the approval of the school board, and set forth his concept of a unified school system in terms both of purpose and methodology. The system divided education into three categories: Kindergarten where children under six were taught the alphabet, the Gymnasium that was a nine-year course for boys over six, and the Hochschule, a five-year study for those who had finished the Gymnasium. In the Hochschule students could pursue a variety of disciplines including theology, languages, and letters. In both the upper schools classes were offered in such specific areas as theology, law, medicine, mathematics, philosophy, poetry and elocution.

In spite of the fact that the educational system was, at best, poorly funded and never very well organized in Bucer's day, the discipline was strict and the curriculum rigorous, the school had an excellent reputation for academic excellence and high quality teachers, and attracted many students. John Sturm remained rector until 1581.[260]

Bucer the Itinerant: Spread of Reformation

Bucer spent much of his time outside Strasbourg organizing Reformed communities, preaching evangelistic meetings, organizing and attending conferences to promote unity, or negotiating with political or ecclesiastical leaders. He did so with the permission of the Strasbourg city council, and he could afford to leave because Strasbourg developed several capable pastors like Zell, Fagius, and Capito who could carry on in Bucer's absence. Yet it was during these times that opponents of Reformation thought and theology capitalized on Bucer's absence to spread their doctrines, often effectively, as in the case of Capito and Anabaptist ideas. Also, Bucer's absence from his family was detrimental; as such absence always is in the case of dedicated church leaders who find themselves often away from home. Yet the fruits of his labors

---

[260] Eells, pp. 225-228.

outside Strasbourg were considerable in terms of the spread of Reformation theology and the organization of viable Reformed communities.

The Ulm Reformation

One of the cities reformed by Bucer's preaching was the beautiful German town of Ulm situated on the Danube River. Ulm remained one of the more committed and steadfast of the cities that were the fruits of the labor of Martin Bucer. Once again, the catalyst for Bucer's greatest accomplishments lay in challenge and adversity. It was out of the desperate need to find some kind of harmony between Zwingli and Luther in the great controversy over the Lord's Supper that the Ulm reformation developed.

In March 1531, several preachers met at Memmingen to discuss a letter that Bucer had drafted representing his formula for unity. Ambrose Blaurer read the letter, and it met with the approval of the preachers. By this time Protestants in cities throughout the southern and western parts of Germany were awakened by the crisis over the Supper and the need for harmony. The reasonable solution to the crisis appeared to them to be the establishment of solid, well-organized Reformed communities in their cities, and they began to seek help from the one person who could do so, namely Martin Bucer. By this time, Bucer was away from Strasbourg for much of the time organizing churches and Reformed communities. His expertise in this field was being widely recognized and his services sought, from pastors as well as communities.[261] Thus Ulm Protestants asked Bucer to come to their city and bring about Reformation. They also included in their invitation John Oecolampadius and Ambrose Blaurer.

Bucer left for Ulm on May 21, 1531. While there he preached to the people and wrote up ordinances for the organization of the community that incorporated not only his views, but also those of leading Protestant theologians. The work was done quickly, for by

---

[261] Bucer not only organized Reformed communities and churches while on these forays away from Strasbourg, he also preached evangelistic crusades, attended public conferences, and met in private sessions with church and political leaders.

the middle of June 1531, he had Eighteen Articles ready for presentation to the Ulm city council, which were subsequently adopted. In implementing his organization of the community, the Catholic altars and organs were removed, mass was abolished and the liturgy Bucer had composed for Strasbourg was modified for Ulm; all holidays except Sunday were abolished, and he set up a Board of Eight to administer discipline. He also provided a synod of pastors and an assembly of lay representatives that met twice a year. On June 16 1531, a Protestant service was conducted for the first time in the Ulm Cathedral. On August 6 the new ordinances were officially accepted, and Bucer made Ulm the center of his operations as he reached out to further the Reformed cause in a wider and wider circle of cities. These cities included Memmingen, Augsburg, Biberach, Esslingen, Kempter, and Reutlingen. Bucer's work caused him to be highly respected for his judgment, energy, imagination, capabilities, and faithfulness.[262]

During the years of the ongoing Supper-controversy, Ulm stood consistently with Bucer. He went there in 1534 to gather support for a pre-conference meeting of preachers in Schaffhausen, leading to a general conference scheduled for Constance. Ulm, along with seven other cities, sent representatives to Schaffhausen, although the conference was not successful. After Bucer left to attend a conference at Kassel, the preachers, including Martin Frecht of Ulm, remained behind to discuss a number of theological topics. Bucer later wrote to Martin Frecht to explain the formula for unity that he drew up at Kassel. The close relationship between Bucer and Ulm continued. By this time Ambrose Blaurer, who leaned in his interpretation toward Zwingli, was beginning to move away from Bucer, failing to attend the conferences, and letting his disapproval be known. His sister, Bucer's good friend, Margaret Blaurer, called Bucer, "a fanatic for unity."[263] Bucer's later reputation as a compromiser caused Martin Frecht to pull back on one occasion from supporting him, showing that Bucer was not invincible nor was Ulm completely dependent on Bucer. Although Bucer's efforts for the formula for unity hurt him in the short run, he finally regained

---

[262] Eells, pp. 119-121.
[263] Eells, p. 179.

the respect of Protestant pastors by his firm stand against the efforts of the emperor to restore the mass and impose the Interim.

The Augsburg Reformation

Shortly after his highly successful efforts in Ulm, Bucer carried the Reformation to the city of Isny, aided by two younger colleagues, one of whom was Paul Fagius who would bind himself to Bucer the rest of Bucer's life. However, much of this time "on the road" was spent in the larger city of Augsburg.

Augsburg had early put in with Luther's Reformation, but Bucer had stationed Wolfgang Musculus and Boniface Wolfhard, two young men whom he personally trained, in Augsburg, and they moved the church there more in the direction of a Reformed as opposed to a Lutheran orientation. Under the strong influence of Bucer, Musculus and Wolfhard met with success in presenting Bucer's peace policy. Wolfhard later adopted Anabaptist concepts and turned against Bucer, but Augsburg remained, for the most part, loyal to the cause.

The Köln Reformation

As we have noticed, Bucer met with amazing success in working with the Archbishop of Köln, Hermann von Wied. Von Wied was delighted to have Bucer and other Reformed pastors help him to inaugurate a Reformed community in this great city, but the success in Köln actually led to Bucer's ultimate failure, for it drew down the wrath of the emperor Charles upon him. As the archbishop was one of the seven electors of the emperor, in effect a member of the board of directors that employed the emperor and to which he was accountable; Charles could ill afford to have one of the electors to be a Protestant. When Charles became aware of the success Bucer was having in Köln, he determined to end Reformation efforts there with military force and to return the mass via the Interim.[264]

Bucer worked assiduously as well in other cities such as Bonn, Isny, Constance, and Nürnberg to bring about reformation. He was

---

[264] See the earlier discussion of this topic in the preceding chapter.

the incessant itinerant during the thirties and forties, working to organize Reformed communities, to reconcile differences among Protestants, especially over the Lord's Supper, and with Catholics if possible, trying to instill practices of church discipline that would ensure godly behavior, appearing in debates to defend his position, and meeting with both ecclesiastical and civil leaders. Bucer exhausted himself and his physical resources and neglected his family in the passionate cause of the Kingdom. In the end, he met with, what he considered dismal failure, overcome by imperial and Catholic opposition united against him, and the lack of firm commitment among Protestants. Bucer despaired of this world by the time the decade of the forties drew to its end and sadly took his refuge in England. But to the end, ill, growing older, still meeting with opposition, Bucer never flagged or faltered. He continued to write, teach, debate, plan and expend unbelievable effort for the cause to which he committed his life. Only from the perspective of contemporary times may we see the true fruit of his labor.

Influence on Calvin

Before following Bucer on his final journey, we need to stop to consider what Bucer meant to and how he influenced the life and thought of his younger protégé, John Calvin. Calvin was born in Noyon, France, in 1509, the son of a notary who held the account for the cathedral. He entered the University of Paris in pursuit of a degree in theology, and like so many who later become Reformers, Calvin was committed to humanistic studies, and as such his first published work was a commentary on Seneca's *De Clementia.*

Little is known about Calvin's conversion, in distinction from Luther and even Bucer. Calvin alludes to it in a comment about how when he had but begun to have a better understanding, several fellow students came to him for teaching. Some speculation exists that Calvin was converted by Bucer because there is mention of a young man from Noyon who studied in Strasbourg in 1528. This speculation is based on a letter from Bucer to Farel that a youth of Noyon, who had been expelled from Orleans, was learning languages at Strasbourg. Bucer had an intense interest in helping to spread the Reformation into French-speaking lands, and customarily welcomed French exiles. Although Calvin studied at Orleans, there is no indication that he was cast out of the city, and the general expulsion of Protestants from France which brought Calvin to Basel did not occur until 1534.[265]

Calvin later did write to Bucer in a rather familiar tone indicating that he shared Bucer's theological views, and he came to Strasbourg to see Bucer in 1536, but Bucer was out of town and said that he was disappointed that he had missed him. Bucer expressed delight over his recently published first edition of the *Institutes of the Christian Religion*.[266] The first extant letter of Bucer to Calvin is dated December 1, 1536, in which Bucer showed respect for the young theologian by expressing his high expectations for him and his sincere desire to meet him in order to discuss the "entire administration of the teaching of Christ." It is interesting that a significant part of Bucer's last letter to Calvin dealt with issues of the doctrine and discipline of the church. As Spijker says, "Bucer and Calvin were theologians of the church. Their work was placed in service of the church, which is the dominion of Christ."[267]

Calvin was expelled from the University of Paris after he helped rector Nicolas Cop write an address that was very Protestant and offensive to the Catholic administration, and he left France when Francis I drove out all Protestants after the infamous "Day of the Placards." Calvin took refuge in the Protestant city of Basel where he worked on the *Institutes*, probably with help from Johann Froben. In 1536, after secretly visiting some Protestants still in France, he was returning via Geneva when William Farel induced him to stay in the city and help him with the Reformation there. Calvin was loath to do so, but convinced by Farel that God would curse him if he did not, he remained, and the two of them tried for two years to bring about a Reformed community.

But John Calvin was yet young and inexperienced, and the strict policies of the preachers aroused the opposition of the "libertine" party who, in turn, gained influence over the city council and had the preachers expelled. By this time Bucer was well aware of

---

[265] Eells, p. 229.
[266] Calvin, *Opera* Xb, 22,n.1; Eells, p. 230.
[267] Spijker, pp. 32-33; cf. CO Xb cols. 67-68.

Calvin's potential for becoming a great leader in the Reformation, and he urged him to take refuge in Strasbourg. Calvin accepted and remained there for three years, which were probably the three happiest years of his life.

There he accepted a position on the faculty of the academy that Bucer founded, which was headed by John Sturm, and distinguished himself with his scholarship and ability to teach. Bucer also arranged for him to preach for a small congregation of French-speaking refugees. He also arranged a marriage for him with Idelette de Bure, who, unfortunately, died prematurely as did their small daughter. Calvin never remarried.

During the time Calvin was in Strasbourg, he worked closely with Bucer, often traveling with him to many of his conferences. Bucer deliberately tutored him not only in theology, but in the practical outworking of that theology in the organization of a Reformed community, and Calvin learned well. Although much of what Calvin believed, understood, and became eventually was the result of Bucer's influence on him, it cannot be said that Calvin gullibly accepted everything from Bucer or that he did not think for himself, for he sometimes strongly disagreed with his mentor. And although the primary relationship of these two men was that of teacher to pupil, in Bucer's later years, the influence sometimes went from the younger to the older man.

If we look for specific examples of Bucer's influence on Calvin, it may be found in a number of areas. Doctrinally, Calvin readily accepted Bucer's view of the centrality of the work of the Holy Spirit in the life of both the individual Christian and the church. Everything was seen, for both men, in light of the Spirit's operation.[268]

Calvin accepted Bucer's definition of the spiritual presence in the Lord's Supper, the middle view that Bucer worked out in his intense study as he attempted to find a solution for the controversy that divided Lutherans and Zwinglians. As a result, this

---

[268] For a thorough discussion of Bucer's pneomatology, see W.P. Stephens, *The Holy Spirit in the Theology of Martin Bucer* (Cambridge: At the University Presss, 1970); also Willem van't Spijker, "Bucer's Influence on Calvin: Church and Community" in Wright: *Martin Bucer: Reforming Church and Community.*

interpretation was passed on, through Calvin, to become the traditional concept of the Reformed community and of the modern evangelical world for the most part. Calvin accepted from Bucer the importance of weekly observance of the Lord's Supper, but both men were thwarted from full implementation of their convictions. Calvin wrote, "Indeed this custom that enjoins that men should communicate only once a year[269] is certainly an invention of the devil. The Lord's Supper should be celebrated in the Christian congregation once a week at the very least."[270]

Both men also founded their theology on the firm belief in God's predestining his elect people to eternal life. Of course, all of the leaders of the Reformation, except the radical groups, such as Anabaptists, looked to God's invisible church made up of his elect as opposed to the Roman Catholic view of the church's identity being established through its visible manifestation. While we cannot say that Calvin learned his view of predestination from Bucer, we may be sure that Bucer reinforced and clarified it for Calvin.

Both men accepted the idea of incorporation into Christ through the work of the Spirit and expressed in the Lord's Supper. Whereas later Reformed scholars would place a greater emphasis on the *ordo salutis,* the order of divine decrees that result in salvation, Bucer and Calvin stressed the personal process of God bringing us into communion with the Son.[271] The point is not a difference of theology but of approach.

In regard to church offices, Bucer's defining of the four offices of elder, pastor, teacher, and deacon were accepted by Calvin when he organized the church in Geneva, and, of course, have come down to us today in Reformed and evangelical circles. Even the tripartite work of Christ as prophet, priest, and king, so often associated with Calvin, was elucidated by Bucer. Truly, Calvin was an excellent pupil and Bucer a remarkable mentor.

Additionally, Calvin accepted Bucer's views of the vital importance of church discipline, and he observed carefully the structure and operation of the community in Strasbourg, which he

---

[269] As stipulated by the Roman Church at the Fourth Lateran Council of 1215.
[270] Cited in Maxwell, p. 117.
[271] Spijker, p. 34.

then replicated in Geneva. Ironically, Calvin's Geneva succeeded where Bucer's Strasbourg failed.

In regard to liturgy, Calvin copied almost verbatim the Strasbourg rites. His changes were very few, some of them demanded by the city council who wanted a more simplified service. Calvin added "a long and tiresome paraphrase of the Lord's Supper" to the Strasbourg rite,[272] but, as a comparison of the order of worship in the two cities will show, Calvin's was essentially the same. Like Bucer, he appreciated the importance of integrating the liturgy of the word with the liturgy of the upper room.

Finally, the concept of vocation, of divine calling to a line of work as well as to salvation in Christ, a concept that came to characterize the Reformed community as the "Protestant work ethic" and is associated so strongly with Calvin, was a concept that Bucer firmly held and taught in Strasbourg.[273]

Calvin and Bucer enjoyed an interesting and intimate relationship. They held deep mutual respect for each other, but were open enough in their friendship to speak of one another honestly, even critically at times. Calvin once wrote to Bullinger, "I will not proclaim at this moment the rare and manifold virtues which this man [Bucer] possesses. Let me just say that I would do a great deal of injustice to the church of God if I were to hate or despise him. I will remain silent as to how he made himself serviceable to me personally."[274]

In another letter Calvin wrote, "That most excellent servant of Christ, Martin Bucer, employing a kind of remonstrance and protestation like that to which Farel had recourse before drew me back to a new post."[275] Calvin refers to Bucer's insistence that he remain committed to the call of God in Geneva, for Bucer referred in a letter to Calvin about Jonah trying to avoid God's call, and went on to warn, "Don't think that you can leave the ministry even for a short time without offending God, if another ministry is offered to

---

[272] Maxwell, p. 115.
[273] Spijker, p. 43.
[274] Calvin, *CO XII,* col. 729, in Spijker p. 32.
[275] William J. Bouwsma, *John Calvin* (New York: Oxford University Press, 1988), p. 21.

you."[276] Farel and Bucer both knew very well that Calvin could be moved to action best by appealing to the danger of offending God by refusing to heed his call.

Calvin did return to Geneva, taking with him Bucer's promise to follow him and personally help him to establish a reformed community there pattered on that of Strasbourg. However, Bucer's pressing commitments in the need to work through the maze of threats to the German Reformation both from internal disunity and external threats from Catholics and the emperor prevented him from honoring his promise to Calvin. However, Calvin would write to his mentor six weeks after he returned in 1541, "Until I shall have confessed that I can bear no more, do not doubt that I am performing faithfully what I have promised you. And if in any way I do not match your expectation, you know that I am under your power. Admonish, chastise, do all those things that a father may do to his son."[277]

Calvin often admitted the debt he held to Bucer, "I have particularly copied Bucer, that man of holy memory, outstanding doctor in the church of God, whom I judge to have pursued a line of work in this field which is beyond reproach."[278] He paid tribute to Bucer's "profound learning, abundant knowledge, keenness of intellect, wide reading, and many other varied excellencies in which he is surpassed by hardly anyone. No one in our time has been more precise or diligent in interpreting scripture than he."[279] On his deathbed Calvin admitted that much of his order of worship was borrowed from Bucer.[280]

When Bucer died in 1551, Calvin, who had not seen him since he left for England in 1549, wrote to Viret, "The grief I have felt at the death of Bucer increases my anxiety and fear."[281] Yet Calvin disagreed with Bucer on his views concerning marriage and divorce, and he felt that he often compromised truth in his obsession with attaining unity and pleasing all parties, and he often stretched the

---

[276] Bouwsma, pp. 21-22.
[277] Cited in Bouwsma, p. 24.
[278] Calvin, prefect to his commentary on the synoptic gospels, in Bouwsma, p. 22.
[279] *Ibid.*
[280] *Ibid.*
[281] *Ibid.*

interpretations of these parties beyond what they really believed to create the illusion that they were in essential agreement. He disagreed with some of his administrative decisions and his excessive wordiness, but he freely admitted that Bucer's intentions were always good.[282]

On the other hand, Bucer dearly loved Calvin, but was often concerned about his anger and impatience. Calvin was clearly not suited for the diplomatic role given to Bucer, nor was Calvin willing to press into new theological territory, as did Bucer in the interpretation of the Lord's Supper and his marriage doctrine. In short, Calvin was not original, although that fact does not take away from the man's genius. Calvin was a second generation reformer who benefited from the pioneering work of the first generation. Taking what he had learned, analyzing and systematizing it, Calvin was able to produce the *Institutes,* the single most influential book of the Reformation. Bucer, given his verbosity and inability to systematize succinctly, would never have been able to accomplish such a task. A comparison of these two men reflects the wisdom of God in granting the gifts that he did to the men he chose, and placing them in the sequence that he did.

Influence on Cranmer

Whereas Bucer had many years to mentor and shape John Calvin, he had only two years to work with Thomas Cranmer in England. However, there exists an obvious difference between Calvin and Cranmer. The latter was older and already an established and respected theologian. Cranmer had gained the divorce Henry VIII sought from Katherine of Aragon to wed Anne Boleyn, he had authored early editions of *The Book of Common Prayer,* had written the *Ten Articles* which revealed, even during the reign of Henry, his truly Reformed heart. However, Henry forced him to rescind the decidedly Protestant *Ten Articles* for his *Six Articles* that validated the essential Catholic nature of the Church of England. As far as Henry was concerned, with the exception of the

---

[282] He criticized his verbosity in *Commentarius in harmonium evangelicam,* ep. And *Comm. Rom.,* ep. XXI, 8; Cited in Bouwsma, p. 25.

dismantling of the monasteries and setting up an English Bible, downplaying Purgatory and indulgences, the church simply changed heads. But Cranmer was willing to bide his time until Henry's death and the accession of his son Edward, a true Protestant, under whom he could effect a genuinely Protestant church in England. Two years after Henry's death Bucer arrived in England in answer to Cranmer's invitation.

As noted earlier, Bucer first wrote to Cranmer in 1531 to explore the possibilities of some kind of alliance with Henry VIII. Prior to his move to England, Bucer carried on correspondence with Cranmer, especially in his attempt to forge a grand alliance of evangelicals led by Cranmer and Bucer that would include, in addition to these two, John Sturm, Wolfgang Capito, Simon Grynaeus, Joachim von Watt, and Heinrich Bullinger. Bucer had confidence in Cranmer and believed that England would join in the continental wide evangelical alliance.[283]

Cranmer always considered Bucer as one of his "secret and special friends" in whom he was willing to confide, as he wrote to him in a letter.[284] The relations were always friendly. When the Supper controversy arose, Bucer wrote to Cranmer in 1547 and commented on his interpretation of the Eucharist, as Cranmer had requested.[285] Bucer's influence in shaping Cranmer's concepts of the Lord's Supper, moving him away from Lutheran consubstantiation, is perhaps the single most important effect on the English Reformation that Bucer would have. Cranmer wrote to Stephen Gardiner, arch-enemy of any attempt to reform England, in 1551 that Bucer "denieth utterly that Christ is really and substantially present in the bread, either by conversion or inclusion, but in the ministration he affirmeth Christ to be present...so do I also."[286]

We shall consider Bucer's work in England in greater detail in the following chapter, but for now it is appropriate to notice that his influence on Cranmer was extensive. The two men respected each

---

[283] MacCulluch, pp. 174-175.
[284] MacCullouch, p. 2.
[285] MacCullouch, p. 381.
[286] MacCullouch, p. 390.

other, and rather than a father-son relationship such as Bucer sustained to Calvin, Bucer and Cranmer worked together as two colleagues who were willing to learn from each other. Bucer's influence on Cranmer's interpretation is the most obvious contribution, as a study of the *Thirty-Nine Articles* will show. Of course, the confession in place at the time of Edward was the *Forty-Two Articles* which bore the stamp of Bucer in spirit as well as doctrine.

Bucer had a great influence on the 1552 edition of the *Book of Common Prayer*, and was virtually the author of the English ordinal. Perhaps most significant was the concept of Christian community which he detailed to King Edward VI in his *De Regno Christi*, which, even if not fully implemented, has certainly shaped the thinking of the English nation through the years.

Additionally, Bucer strengthened Cranmer's belief in predestination, which he already held, and Cranmer adopted Bucer's phraseology on the work of the Holy Spirit.[287] He helped Cranmer change his views on the wedding rite from the old Sarum concept that it was for procreation and the avoidance of sin to place first priority on loving, cherishing, and enjoying one another. Cranmer, like Bucer, a happily married man, was quite willing to accept this new definition.[288]

The Effect of the Pastoral Impulse in Bucer

Above all, Martin Bucer was a Christian pastor who cared for the souls of the people of God. These were God's elect; they were the Lord's sheep, who deserved the tender care of the shepherds whom he had appointed on earth to care for them. Bucer took the charge quite seriously. As he was called to Strasbourg, the Christians of Strasbourg were always his greatest concern, the people nearest to his heart. All that he did, every program he organized, manifested his concern for their welfare.

It was this pastoral impulse that motivated his program of discipline, his program of education, his small groups, and his

---

[287] MacCulloch, pp. 428, 416.
[288] MacCulloch, p. 421.

division of offices both in the local church and the cooperative efforts of the pastors of the entire city. Behind the liturgy was his passionate desire that the people would worship God in an understanding way, knowing what they were doing and the meaning of the acts of worship.

All that Bucer did, he did as a pastor. In Strasbourg as the leading pastor, he felt keenly the responsibility to organize and oversee the Reformed community; in cities to which he was called as advisor, he felt the responsibility to set up an arrangement that would function there to the glory of God and the benefit of the people under pastors he often installed. Bucer was a man who acted always on the basis of his fundamental convictions and presuppositions. For him, love of neighbor was foremost, as he set forth in his earliest work, *Das Ym Selbs*. With the view of love of the Christian community under girding all else, Bucer was guided by his belief in the elective grace of God, which has determined who the people of God's church are, rather than human pronouncement from ecclesiastical authority. And the third consideration of Bucer in his pastoral policy was the centrality of the Holy Spirit. We should view these concepts as transparencies, each overlaying the other, and forming the filter through which Bucer saw everything, and through which he formed his policies and acted. Though he may be accused of equivocation and vacillation in his ongoing search for the formula of unity, he could never be accused of flagging in his zeal and determination to implement a true Christian community that would reflect these basic concepts.

With the emperor's Interim and Bucer's exile from Strasbourg, it would seem that all his life's work was in vain. As we shall see in the following chapter, Bucer simply moved his sphere of operations to England and continued his work, benefiting from all he had learned in his lifetime, although weakened by age, illness, and living in a foreign country with people who spoke a language he did not understand. However, again we point to the fact that Bucer's influence on Calvin was significant, and the Reformed communities and concepts of pastoral ministry that Bucer developed in Strasbourg were not only implemented in Geneva but spread all over the world as a result of those who came under Calvin's influence. One can read Richard Baxter's *The Reformed Pastor*, which continues to be a guidebook to evangelical pastors throughout the world today and compare it with the principles embraced by Bucer and see the similarities. The Christian historian can reach no other conclusion than that God raised up Martin Bucer for a work which had far greater and more long-lasting consequences than what he accomplished in Strasbourg and its locale during his lifetime.

But the final chapter of Bucer's life was to be lived out in a far-distant strange land. He had only two years in England, but he made every minute count, and he left his imprint on the Church of England that was in the process of development at this critical time.

Resume of Christian Doctrine:
The Maturation of Bucer's Theology

In 1547 an anonymous book appeared advocating rebellion against the emperor and the Interim. The emperor thought the Strasbourg pastors had something to do with it and accused them of following the rebellious doctrines of the Münster Anabaptists. He met with John Sturm and others from Strasbourg at Köln on September 10 and refused to allow Protestantism to continue as the established religion of Strasbourg and entrusted the bishop with administering the Interim. He also demanded that the Strasbourg authorities punish the authors of the seditious document. Sturm assured the emperor that these documents were confiscated in the house of the printer, but after lengthy deliberations with the bishop and the emperor, Sturm had to return with the news that Bucer and Fagius were to be dismissed from the city. The bishop was to receive the cathedral, St. Peter the Old, St. Peter the Young, and All Saints. Protestant services could continue in the other parishes of the city.[289] When the more determined Protestants of Strasbourg resisted and spoke of gaining help from the Swiss and the French, the emperor threatened a military attack on the city. The pastors

---

[289] Bucer, *Resumé of Christian Doctrine (Resumé de la Doctrine Chretiènne)* tr. François Wendel, (Universitaires de France, 1951), p8.

continued to try to garner resistance and to raise the courage of the people, and tension grew between the city council and the pastors.[290]

Bucer presented a lecture on the third of June that would serve as a confession of faith for the community and a summation of the essential points of his doctrine. He sought to set to rest ideas that they were at all connected to the spirit of Münster. The lectures, endorsed by the other pastors, provide us with an understanding of the nature of Bucer's theology at this point. Following is an exposition of the main points Bucer makes in his summary:

1. **The foundation of all doctrine** is nothing except what is expressly taught in Holy Scripture or what can be deduced by a true and certain conclusion.

2. **One should teach,** based on the divine Scriptures with the aid of the Holy Spirit, a true and living knowledge of the eternal God, and the unity of his divine essence and Trinity. He should also teach our Lord Jesus Christ as true God and true son, who possesses entirely and immutably the two natures in his person. He died for our sins and rose anew for our justification, was raised to the right hand of God the Father, to be Prince and Savior and to give the elect of God repentance and remission of sins.

3. **The knowledge of man created in the image of God.** We are fallen through the transgression of Adam resulting in a horrible perversion of our nature and the loss of the divine nature, becoming thus the enemies of God.

4. **True contrition** comes through the knowledge of God and of ourselves, of the divine grandeur in which we were created and of where we have now fallen. We repent of unbelief and ignorance of divine things, of our opposition to the good will of God, of our bad thoughts, words, and deeds of which we are guilty, of the perversion of our nature since

---

[290] At this time the pastors included, other than Bucer who was the acknowledged head pastor, his secretary Conrad Hubert, Caspar Hedio of the cathedral, John Marbach of St. Nicholas, Thiébaut Schwartz of Old St. Peter's, Paul Fagius of New St. Peter's, John Lenglin of St. William, Conrad Schell of St. Thomas, and John Steinlein of St. Aurelia.

Adam, of acting freely and without restraint but always contrary to the divine law.

5. **Redemption and justification.** We cannot be saved from hereditary perdition unless God Almighty takes pity on us. He has chosen us to this effect before the foundation of the world, by pure and free mercy and uniquely for the love of his beloved Son, and without being incited by any good work on our part which has either preceded or followed our new birth. Grace and redemption are in Christ; the Holy Spirit gives us true faith and includes us in Christ in such a way that we can have a firm confidence in his grace and in Christ's redemption. God our Father has pardoned us for the love of his beloved Son in consideration of his sufferings and his death and no longer imputes sin. He treats us eternally as children and heirs. Through his word and the Holy Spirit, in the midst of his assembly, he renews us to his image in wisdom, holiness, and divine righteousness. He will do toward us everything for our salvation in this life, and afterwards we have access to him in eternal life.

6. **The true faith** consists of faith of the holy gospel and in our Lord Jesus Christ. By this faith we are justified before God from all our sins in view of life eternal, regenerated like children and heirs of God, without any merit of our works.

7. **Confidence in God, hope of eternal life, love of God and of our neighbor.** The Spirit produces in us a profound love of God, confession, joy, sanctification, and courageous acceptance of suffering and even death that we may have to experience for his sake. The Spirit incites us to obey all his commandments. He causes to be born in us a true, faithful, active love for all men, whether their attitude toward us is good or bad. This love fulfills the divine law and leads us to learn, do, suffer, or shun according to what is necessary for the temporal and eternal salvation of our neighbor.

8. **Mortification of the old Adam, virtue and the new life** are worked by the same Spirit of divine sonship through the same faith, enabling us to endure with good will what our Lord uses to discipline us in the way of the maladies of the body. We freely put on the Lord Jesus Christ, the new man

created in the image of God in righteousness and true holiness and devote ourselves to every good work. Those who do not evidence true faith, zeal, and good works are not Christians and do not belong to him, and are not members. Those who are able to boast have a dead, not a true, faith.

9. **Weakness and failures of our righteousness.** We were created in Christ for good works, but the flesh lives on and exerts power in us so we never possess faith, hope, love, or any good work perfectly so that Almighty God is obligated to us according to his good law. We continue to commit numerous sins and failures to keep God's commandments, which is why all saints preceding us continued to pray to God for forgiveness of sins. That is why they considered all their good works nothing but dirt and remained fixed on Christ. All consolation and hope for their salvation they set absolutely and uniquely in our Lord Jesus Christ who alone is reconciliation of their sins and has become for us wisdom, righteousness, sanctification, and redemption.

10. **Reward for good works.** We teach that the Lord will reward all good works, puny and weak though they be. We need to confess continually while we do good works that we are only useless and insufficient servants who really only deserve heavy punishments and no rewards. Any reward from the Lord is not because of righteousness but free grace, and for the love of his beloved Son in whom he has chosen us before the foundation of the world and created us for good works. As St. Bernard writes, if we consider all our righteousness in the light of the truth, it appears as filthy rags. God recompenses us for more than our works deserve. Although it is certainly true that our faith and good works require our free will, it is, however, God who produces in us a good will and incites us to it by the Holy Spirit, all of which is the result of his grace alone.

11. **The Christian Church** consists of all who have true faith and are regenerated in Christ and have faith that justifies. They are the members of the body of Christ. Christ builds them up, fortifies them, makes them progress in this faith, this confidence, this hope, this love and this holiness by his

constant teaching and discipline, all their lives. This he does among all his members without exception. He assembles them and connects them to himself, he incites them to assemble when they are able and instruct themselves, guide, console, advise reciprocally in the same spirit, by the word of God and the holy sacraments, by prayer and discipline of the Lord. He uses ministers whom he designates to be pastors, teachers, overseers, ministers, and dispensers of his mysteries. They ought to watch the flock and tend them.

12. **Nomination of ministers.** They should be chosen from the midst of all the community; examined, ordained, consecrated, and installed in his name with solemn prayer and imposition of hands. Their doctrine and conduct should be irreproachable. Ministers should be selected who appear most capable to exercise the ministry by their knowledge of spiritual things, good will, and zeal to edify the community. They should be people in whom Christians can have confidence.

13. **Bishops and elders.** There are two distinct degrees in each ministry: the bishop is responsible for teaching, for dispensing the sacraments, for Christian discipline, and for the care of souls; the elders aid the bishop and tend the lambs of Christ, helping the poor.

14. **All must receive authority from the Lord.**

15. **All should be baptized with water in the name of the Father, Son, and Holy Spirit** in front of the entire church, all converted to the Lord by the preaching of the gospel, and sufficiently instructed in the faith by the catechism. They must confess their faith before the community of Christ, renouncing Satan and the world, submissive to the obedience of Christ and the discipline of the church. Also infants of believers should be baptized. Young and old are to be instructed all their lives as true disciples of the Lord, in obedience to his commandments by preaching and catechism.

16. **Baptism.** When administered and received according to the order of the Lord is truly, in both adults and young infants, a baptism of the new birth of the Holy Spirit. Those baptized

are cleansed from all their sins, buried in the death of our Lord Jesus Christ, incorporated and clothed for the death of sins and for a new and pious life in view of the glorious resurrection. Through Christ they become children and heirs of God. All those who do not reject, by sinning intentionally thereafter, this grace communicated in baptism, receive certainly this inheritance in its entirety and take possession of it. For all their sins are pardoned and remitted in holy baptism, and that which indwells in them of original sin is not imputed to damnation, but held by this grace; they do not let free course to evil. The ability to struggle against indwelling sin with energy is given to them and the ability to arise each day to obtain equally by their prayers pardon from all their actual sin.....

17. **Confirmation.** Those who receive baptism in their infancy should be instructed in the Christian faith through the means of catechism, so that the ministers...are able to confess the communicant before the community of God. They should be confirmed following prayer by the whole community, and, following the example of the Lord, by the imposition of hands and by the Holy Spirit, in order to persevere in the faith and Christian life.

18. **Holy Communion** should be celebrated as the Lord himself did, and as he commanded us, "Do this in memory of me," and "Know what I am about to do." We should not add anything to the commandment of the Lord or take away, but honor it, not as it pleases us, but as he prescribed it....We should prepare for the Lord's Supper with great seriousness and true devotion, by intelligible teaching taken from prophets, apostles, and evangelists. Ministers should lift them [the congregation] to recognition of God and the communion and blessed life with our Lord Jesus Christ. Since the Lord requires that they do not present themselves with empty hands before him in assembly, they should bring gifts for the poor, as did the early church. The minister must declare the power of the Almighty Lord God in the assembly with prayers, supplications, and intercessions of the whole assembly. The minister should glorify His remembrance,

announce what He has done, and exhort the congregation to receive the sacrament with devotion. Then he should distribute and present the two elements....

19. **We believe and teach, regarding the substance of the holy sacrament of the body and blood of the Lord,** that we have the right to believe and think about this matter that which the Lord himself and the holy apostle testified, to know that the bread that we break (that is to say, that we consecrate, distribute, and eat according to the Lord's ordinance) is the communion of the body of Christ which he has given for us, and the cup, the communion of his blood that he has shed for us. This communion is such that it unites us more and more to his body, blood, and bones, that we always dwell more and live more in him and he in us, that we form in him one body and one bread. We thus confess with the holy bishop and martyr Irenaeus and with all the ancient church apostles and fathers, that there are two things in the holy sacrament: a terrestrial element, the bread and the wine, that remain unchanged in their nature and their substance....and a celestial element, the true body and the true blood of Christ, our Lord, true God and true man. He does not leave heaven, and he is not mixed naturally with the bread and wine, nor locally included in them, but he offers himself there to us, in a celestial manner, as nourishment and sustenance for eternal life and in order to give us assurance of the glorious resurrection. We need to hold to this simple confession and conform to the Scriptures and leave to the Lord other trifling questions and keep ourselves with care from all unreasonable disputes that alienate the body and even fill it with grief, which the true Christian faith does not allow, which true faith leads only to love.

20. **Penitential discipline.** As sin continues throughout our lives to reside in our flesh, where we find nothing good, and which overtakes us frequently so that we daily commit sin in ignorance or weakness, we teach that God, in his goodness, has prescribed and commanded the remedy of penitence. People need to give heed to brothers and pastors who exhort them to amend themselves from besetting sins, secretly if the

sins are secret, and publicly if they are public....If he refuses to listen to the community of Christ, he must be considered as a heathen and publican, according to the commandment of the Lord, excommunicated, until he gives proof of a true desire of divine grace. He is not to be bad leaven in the whole community....

21. **Holy marriage.** The teaching of the word of God should apply also to marriage. It is necessary to instruct the population of the sanctity of this state and union ordained and blessed by God, to whom all the Lord does not assign a different calling. The Lord joins, and they become one. The husband is the head and savior for his wife, the wife the aid and body for her husband. The Lord confirms and sanctifies it in the midst of the community of God, by word and by prayer, and the Lord maintains it, by God's grace, in a most elevated love and indissoluble communion all their lives, until he separates them by death. But if a divorce occurs, conforming to the word of the Lord where one encounters it, one always will observe the word of the Lord, the attitude of the first and true apostolic church, and also the Christian ordinance of the pious emperor.

22. **Daily meetings.** The Holy Spirit has ordained, for holy ministries and ecclesiastical ceremonies when there have been questions, daily meetings, designed for those who have leisure for them by particular grace and blessings. In the course of these meetings they should give a lecture by the assistance of the holy books of the Bible in an intelligible language and extract from their meaning exhortations to piety, to say together prayers, and to sing psalms and songs of praise. Meetings are to be scheduled each day at a convenient hour and often enough that they will be considered useful for building up the piety of the different communities.

23. **Christian festivals.** Since apostolic times Christian communities have celebrated the first day of the week on which Christ, our beloved Lord, was resurrected....We should consecrate the day and celebrate it to the Lord with spontaneous piety and with as much zeal as was prescribed

to the ancients for sanctification of the Sabbath. The faithful, and all those who live with them, should abstain from all work on this day, and from all temporal matters, so that they can put them off and attend assiduously to the assemblies of God, to hear there the reading and preaching of the divine word, to pray and to give thanks with the community, to bring alms for the poor and to receive the holy sacraments. The whole day should be devoted to exercise of piety, as the Lord required in the holy prophets. In the same way the other festivals that have been prescribed should be celebrated, in order to meditate on the great deeds of the Lord that he accomplished for our redemption and for our eternal salvation, and in order to give thanks to God. Such festivals would include those of the incarnation, birth, and ascension of Christ, etc.

24. **The commemoration of saints** who lived near the time of Christ taught about in Scripture and from other sources, should set forth to the community the grace of God the Father, theirs as well as ours, conferred on them, and give thanks to God and rejoice with them, as members of the same body, in order that we also may have a greater confidence in the grace of God and encourage one another to imitate their faith.

25. **The young Christian.** In times of discipline, he should be consoled and implored to live a life of piety, and to pray earnestly. His practice of piety should not be by constraint or hypocritically, not to acquire any merit before God or pay the debt for our sins, but by true repentance and regret for sins and a profound desire for grace and help from God.

26. **Visiting the sick.** Ministers of the church should visit, at an opportune time, according to the ancient customs and conduct of the apostles, people whom the Lord tests by sickness, and console them, exhorting them to be strong, to the degree that they are able, by the word of God, prayer, the consolation of absolution, and communion. Unction is questionable, and [in apostolic times] was a sign accompanied by a miracle.

27. **The deceased.** We need to recognize those held by the community to conform to doctrine and religious ceremonies in the true communion of Christ, in accord with all true Christians and the true churches of Christ.

28. **The civil authority.** It is a holy and divine function, invested with a legitimate role... [Christians] should contribute most of all to what makes the community of God comfortable, and that leads people to pious and holy lives. All men should be subject to the authority that God instituted and live according to their laws, pay taxes, and do what they are required to do.[291]

Bucer commented that these principles expressed the gospel and doctrine that he taught and preached for twenty-eight years, all coming from the divine scriptures, and from the doctrine and practice of the ancient and true apostolic church. He stated that those who have faith would recognize and bear witness to the fact that it is the only gospel and doctrine of Christ. He pointed out that what he taught differed radically at many points from what was taught at Münster, and he pointed out also the misrepresentations of the anonymous author who denounced him, answering his charges in considerable detail. He closed with encouragement to trust God, and he signed it along with the preachers and pastors of the Church of Strasbourg. It is dated 2 July 1548.

---

[291] Bucer, *Resumé of Christian Doctrine*, in Wendel (my translation from the French in the text). See original in BDS Vol. I, pp. 78-147.

Chapter VII:

Bucer Again in Exile (England)

The Augsburg Interim

With his influence in the ascendancy, but by no means triumphant, the emperor Charles V summoned the Diet of Augsburg in the spring of 1548 to try to achieve some kind of reconciliation between the warring parties. Now that Philip of Hesse was silenced because of the loss of his influence as a result of his bigamy, and with military victory over the Schmalkalden League, the Catholics dominated the Diet. But Charles was in no position to destroy his opposition; he chose rather to disarm it.[292] He considered that the endorsement of the proceedings by Martin Bucer, the great advocate of reconciliation, would be of tremendous value, and thus, through the Elector of Brandenburg, he summoned Bucer to the Diet.

Bucer made his will and secretly set out for Augsburg with the emperor's dubious promise of protection. When Bucer arrived, he was secluded while the Catholics attempted to gain his stamp of approval on their proposal. Bucer was certainly willing to accept formulas that permitted unity in matters where truth could not be compromised, but when it came to surrendering the doctrine of justification by faith and others that undermined and contradicted all that evangelicals stood for, Bucer resisted firmly. It was at this point that he regained the respect and influence he had in the Protestant community over those who had to this point believed that he was ready to surrender truth in order to achieve unity.

The Catholics, especially Granvelle, were furious that Bucer would not acquiesce and secured an order for his arrest, but Bucer quietly slipped away and escaped from Augsburg on April 20, 1548, becoming now a bitter opponent of the imposed decree resulting from the diet, known as the Augsburg Interim. He returned to Strasbourg to do all in his power to prevent the adoption of the

---

[292] Eells, p. 393.

Interim which would restore the mass and unravel the Reformed community, and he succeeded for a year.[293]

During that time the change in the composition and disposition of the Strasbourg city council became apparent, and he sensed support eroding. He lacked the full support of all the pastors, and the citizens of the city were increasingly indifferent to the structure of the Reformed community. Even though the council did petition the emperor not to impose the Interim and to allow them to abide by the provisions of the Augsburg Confession, under the threat of force, they capitulated. Although the council still permitted some churches to continue evangelical worship while the Interim was to be imposed in others, Bucer refused to agree. In the struggle between the ultra-Protestant party and the Catholic bishops, Bucer became the scapegoat.[294] On March 1, 1549, the city council voted for Bucer and Paul Fagius to leave the city. Bucer accepted graciously, saying he would rather remain and hoped to return, if it were God's will. On March 3 he gathered up his possessions, accepted a yearly pension from the council, and delivered his farewell sermon with no bitterness or attack on the council. He then delivered his last lecture on Saturday March 23, and on April 6 left the city of Strasbourg forever. He left as he entered, a fugitive.[295]

Bucer's Call to England

Bucer received an invitation from Calvin to join him in Geneva and one from Myconius to Basel. Melancthon invite him to come to his house, and he was invited to teach at the University of Copenhagen. But the most insistent and prevailing invitation came from his old admirer, Archbishop Thomas Cranmer in England. In a letter from Cranmer dated October 2, 1548, Cranmer wrote to Bucer:

> The grace and peace of God in Christ. I have read your letter to John Hales, in which you recall to mind the most miserable condition of Germany, and wrote that you can scarcely preside

---

[293] Eells, pp. 394-395.
[294] Eells, p. 399.
[295] Eells, p. 400.

any longer in the ministry of the word in your city. With groanings therefore have I exclaimed with the prophet, "Show forth thy marvelous loving-kindness, O thou that savest them that trust in thee from those that rise up against thy right hand." Nor do I doubt but that God will hear this and the similar groanings of the godly: and will both preserve and defend the true doctrine, which has hitherto been sincerely propagated in your churches, against the rages of the devil and the world. Meanwhile those who by the tempestuous fury of the waves are unable to sail out into the deep must flee to the harbor. For you, therefore, my Bucer, by far the safest harbor will be our kingdom, in which by the blessing of God, the seeds of true doctrine have already happily begun to be sown. Come therefore to us; and become a laborer with us in the lord's harvest. You will be of no less benefit to the universal Church of God when you are with us, than if you retained your former post. In addition, you will be better able to heal the wounds of your afflicted country in your absence, than you are now able do to do while present. Laying aside all delay, come to us as soon as possible.[296]

Peter Martyr had already taken up residence at Oxford, and was quite concerned about Bucer's safety, especially after Bucer had virtually been held prisoner at Augsburg by the Elector of Brandenburg. He expressed his concern in a letter to Bucer dated December 26, 1548, and when Bucer agreed to come, Martyr replied grimly in a letter of January 22, 1549:

I would advise you, since you now see the case to be hopeless, not to delay too long, nor to wait till the last moment. If you do, I fear that the means to escape will slip away from you. You know what I mean. The antichrists are thirsting. I tell you, thirsting for your blood and for the blood of all men like you: and so take care, if you love Christ's church, to withdraw yourself before that time....You and Paul Fagius, who have been invited, ought to come hither; how welcome and

---

[296] Cited in C. H. Smyth, *Cranmer and the Reformation under Edward VI* (Cambridge: at the University Press, 1926), p. 157.

acceptable you will be, there is no need for me to write to you: for besides that he [Cranmer] is ardently longing for you both, you are greatly needed in the universities; and when you are here, I do not doubt that it will be very easy to provide for the three others whom you mention, and they will soon be invited, I am confident....Only look to it that you escape thence in safety. Greater perils await you than you are aware of..."[297]

Bucer made the decision to accept Cranmer's offer. He knew no English, and he would be far away from home. But he loved the English people and had long held a passion for the possibility of seeing a genuine Reformed community on the island. He had tried to open negotiations with King Henry VIII, but now with young Edward VI on the throne, a lad who, although he never was in good health, yet was genuinely committed to the evangelical cause, Bucer believed it was God's will for him to take up his exile in England.

Persistent Resistance

However, not everyone shared Peter Martyr's enthusiasm about Bucer's arrival in England, and Bucer would find that he could not escape opposition by escaping there; it would follow him. John Hooper was leader of the Zürich party, and he was greatly concerned that Bucer would influence Cranmer to accept his view of the Lord's Supper, which he certainly did. To Zwinglians, Bucer's interpretation smacked of Lutheranism. Burcher, in informing Bullinger of the decision of Martin Bucer and Paul Fagius to go to England, wrote sarcastically, "The Lord preserve England from both of them!"[298]

The Zürich party was strong in England, led by John Hooper, who worked tirelessly to prevent Bucer from spreading his ideas. Hooper kept in close contact with the Zwinglians in Switzerland, and when he reported that Bucer's influence was strong at Lambeth Palace, headquarters of the Archbishop, Burcher wrote again to

---

[297] Cited in Smyth, pp. 158-159.
[298] Smyth, p. 159.

Bullinger, "I pray that they may not pervert him or make him worse."[299] Bucer was not at all inclined to create turmoil, but to try to unify the evangelical community in England. However, although he did not publicly stress his middle position, he certainly was responsible for Cranmer's coming to adopt it, and thus the Church of England stood squarely with Calvin's Geneva and the developing Reformed Faith on this matter.

The other group that did not welcome Bucer in England was the Catholic constituency, which still remained quite strong even under Edward. Opposition to Bucer and the theology he represented had been centered in Bishop Stephen Gardiner, whom Bucer once believed was on his side, but found out that he was wrong. Their primary disagreement was over the doctrines of God's sovereignty and the celibacy of the clergy, and especially of justification by faith. The two men carried on a lengthy written debate, although they met only once, at the disputation at Regensburg.[300] Bucer came to blame Gardiner for sabotaging his negotiations with King Henry VIII, for he believed that, had Gardiner truly accepted the doctrine of justification, he could have convinced the king.[301] Rather than working together, as Bucer had once thought possible, the two became bitter enemies. Bucer questioned Gardiner's sincerity, and Gardiner questioned the sincerity of the whole Protestant movement and came to regard Bucer as a major threat to the English government.[302]

The controversy with Gardiner raged before Bucer arrived in England, but while he was at Cambridge, Bucer engaged in a disputation with three Catholic theologians: Sedgwick, Perne, and Young on the matter of justification by faith. Young was the most assertive, and accused Bucer of teaching serious error. Bucer replied from the university pulpit, and the matter became so heated that the school required a written statement from each on his views. Bucer requested a public disputation, and invited as many as objected to his teaching to come and meet with him on September 9,

---

[299] Smyth, p. 161.
[300] Hopf, p. 7.
[301] Hopf, p. 171.
[302] Hopf, p. 172.

1549. Only Young showed up, no judges presided, and no official report ensued. Young seems to be the only serious threat to Bucer while at Cambridge. Bucer's friend and personal secretary, Conrad Hubert, disgusted by Young's attacks and his methods of doing so, referred to him as *fungus*, rather than *iungus*.[303]

Cambridge Professor

As soon as Bucer and Fagius arrived in England, on April 25, Cranmer installed them at Lambeth Palace and arranged for them to become professors at Cambridge University, with their lectures slated to begin with the opening of the fall term. Bucer's plans seemed to be unlimited: he would work with King Edward to bring about a Reformed community, he would work with Thomas Cranmer in revising *The Book of Common Prayer,* he would produce a commentary on Paul's letter to the Ephesians, and he would translate the Bible into Latin from the original texts and then into English, presumably with someone's help. He actually did accomplish several of these tasks in the two years he was in England, although several would remain unfinished.

As soon as they arrived on May 5, 1549, they were given an audience with King Edward VI. Cranmer arranged the meeting, and it seems that a bond of mutual admiration and respect was formed between the aging Bucer and the teen-aged monarch. Bucer wrote, "We were taken to the king's palace, where immediately after dinner we were granted an audience with his majesty. I cannot express how kindly he and the Lord Protector and other nobles received us, and how delighted he was at our arrival: at which indeed we were overjoyed beyond measure."[304] While they were at Lambeth Palace, they met Roger Ascham, who asked Bucer to write a letter to Princess Elizabeth on his behalf and came to forge a strong friendship with Bucer.

During the summer, Fagius and Bucer took up residence at Croydon Palace, where they were to work on the Bible translation. It seems that Fagius was also preparing his lectures on the book of

---

[303] Smyth, pp. 164, 165.
[304] Smyth, p. 160.

Isaiah for Cambridge. They returned to Lambeth on August 28, and both Fagius and Bucer fell ill of a fever. Although Bucer was severely weakened by his illness, he did recover; however, Fagius grew worse, and on November 5, he died at Cambridge in Bucer's arms. Bucer never recovered from Fagius' death.[305] Soon after Cambridge University appointed Martin Bucer Regius Professor of Divinity and elected him Doctor of Divinity by acclamation. His introductory speech reflected his sadness of heart:

> For what else could have moved them to such great benevolence and beneficence toward me, I say, an old man, sick, useless, foreign, and so scantily furnished in every way, but that they esteem me, far above what I have ever deserved, because for some years the Lord has deigned to use me, although unworthy, in the ministry of the Gospel?....For my years forbid me, especially with my body now so broken by ill health, to hope that I may anywhere discharge my ministry in the Church of Christ more commendably or more fruitfully by the evidence of this rank and dignity…"[306]

A nearly contemporary account of Bucer's arrival and the death of Fagius is given by Thomas Fuller in his church history of Britain:

> Martin Bucer, and Paulus Fagius living formerly at Strasburg, at the instance of Arch bishop Cranmer, were sent for by King Edward to become Professors in Cambridge. My Authour, a German, living then hard by, makes them to depart thence, *Magistratus Argentinensis voluntate et consensu,* whom the Jesuite Parsons will have both banished by that State. If so, the disgrace is none at all, to be exiled for no other guilt then preaching the Gospel, opposing the *Augustine Confession,* which that Emperial City embraced. Besides, the greater providence, if when commanded from one place, instantly called to another. Over they come into England, and last year were fixed at Cambridge, where Bucer was made Professor of Divinity, Fagius of Hebrew. The former had the ordinary

---

[305] Smyth, p. 161.
[306] Smyth, p. 162.

stipend of his place tripled unto him, as well it night, considering his worth, being of so much merit; his need, having wife and children; and his condition, coming hither a forrainer, fecht from a far Country. So it was ordered, that Fagius should in Hebrew read the Evangelical Prophet Isaiah, and Bucer in Greek the Prophetical Evangelist St. John. But alas! The change of air, and diet, so wrought on their temper, that both fell sick together. Bucer hardly recovered; but Fagius, that flourishing beech (nature not agreeing with his transplanting) withered away in the flower of his Age (as scarce fourty five) and was buried in the Church of St. Michael.[307]

Bucer continued to miss Strasbourg and cling to the hope that he might return, and he wrote repeatedly to his flock in Germany, but never with any response. He wrote despairingly to the pastors of Strasbourg:

When I took leave of you, no one uttered a word I reply, the French pastor alone excepted. Yet I labored among you with all fidelity, and there are few of you to whom I have not endeavored also to make myself useful in my private capacity. If you knew what I have suffered since I left you (Bucer complained of the cold climate, the different diet, and his inability to speak the language; the king did arrange to have a huge, German stove sent to him), you would, I am sure, be moved with compassion for me.[308]

With the death of Fagius and his own illness, Bucer grew increasingly despondent and depressed. John à Lasco endorsed the Zürich position on the Lord's Supper, and Peter Martyr was increasingly inclined to do so. Bucer was disappointed by the lack of progress in the Reformation in England, despite the fact that

---

[307] Thomas Fuller, *The Church History of Britain from the Birth of Jesus Christ until the Year 1648* (London: Printed for John Williams at the Sign of the Crown in St. Paul's Church-yard, 1655), p. 128.
[308] Eells, p. 406.

Cranmer assured him that progress was being made slowly.[309] Bucer simply felt that the English Reformers were overly cautious. He wrote back to Strasbourg:

> I gather that some concessions have been made both to a respect for antiquity, and to the infirmity of the present age; such as, for instance, the vestments (Bucer did not approve of the colorful vestments, but was willing to tolerate them for the sake of unity) commonly used in the sacrament of the Eucharist, and the use of candles; so also in regard to the commemoration of the dead, and the use of chrism...They affirm that there is no superstition in these things, and that they are only to be retained for a time, lest the people, not yet thoroughly instructed in Christ, should by too extensive innovations be frightened away from Christ's religion, and that rather they may be won over."[310]

He also wrote to Farel that none of the exiles were given the opportunity to advise English leaders, "although we have not ceased to lobby our Patron (Cranmer) face to face and in writing about a true and firmly grounded restoration of the kingdom of Christ."[311] He wrote to Calvin that the he believed that Geneva alone represented the only reliable confidential counselors he had in the world.[312] He lamented to Calvin in another letter, after telling Calvin how Hooper had falsely accused him of teaching Luther's doctrine of the ubiquity of Christ's body, and that Bullinger was writing to England:

> To know how I have carried myself...as though it were right that Satan should be excited against me here...As though it were not enough for me at my age to be in exile from my country, cast out from my beloved Church, from my Academy, from the State (in which I have labored somewhat by the grace of the Lord); excluded from my sweetest friends and brethren; living in a nation, humane and friendly, I allow,

---

[309] MacCulloch, p. 410.
[310] MacCulloch, pp. 410-411.
[311] MacCulloch, p. 470.
[312] *Ibid.*

but of whose language I am ignorant, to whose diet I am altogether unaccustomed, to whose manners I am unhabituated, in which I have no certain prospect of doing anything worth my labor.[313]

But there were positive achievements for Bucer. He and Cranmer did complete a commentary on the first eight chapters of Matthew, and Bucer's influence, as we noted earlier, was felt not only in Cranmer's understanding of the Lord's Supper, but in the 1552 edition of *Book of Common Prayer*. That influence was especially manifested through Bucer's *Censura,* his critique of the 1549 edition that Cranmer requested him to write. Half of his suggested fifty-eight changes were adopted, and the English ordinal, was essentially his creation. Bucer formed a friendship in a circle of English Reformers who came to respect him highly and on whom he had considerable influence. These included Matthew Parker, who spoke at his funeral; Nicholas Ridley; Roger Ascham; John Hales; Sir Thomas Smith; John Cheke; Edwin Sandys; John Bradford, who was Bucer's pupil; Edmund Grindel, bishop of London; the famous historian John Sleidan; and Bishop Goodrich of Ely.

He formed a close friendship with the Duchess of Suffolk who took an instant liking to him and supported him in every way and tried to make his life in exile more comfortable. She gave him a cow and a calf, which the Catholics claimed were two devils who taught him what to lecture at Cambridge. Bucer only laughed at that idea and said that animals would be fine teachers because they didn't know the languages he knew: Latin, Greek, Hebrew, and German.[314] She took a house at Cambridge and invited Bucer frequently to be her guest.[315] She later purchased most of his books.[316] She also sent her two sons to Cambridge so that they could study under Bucer.[317]

---

[313] Hall, in Wright, ,p. 152.
[314] Hopf, p. 23.
[315] Smyth, p. 169.
[316] Eells, p. 413.
[317] Hopf, p. 22.

Bucer had considerable influence on the development of the English Bible through Miles Coverdale, who read his works. Coverdale was particularly impressed with Bucer's commentary on the Psalms, and he used Bucer's commentary on Matthew to provide notes for his *Matthew's Bible*. Coverdale met Bucer in later years and held a high admiration for him. In designing worship services, because the Psalter was so important, Coverdale used Bucer's Latin Psalter, which he translated into English, selecting certain parts of it that he considered appropriate.[318]

The Commentary on the Psalms became, perhaps, Bucer's most influential work on English scholars. It was carefully produced, for Bucer was well-trained in the Hebrew language and made copious use of the Targums, particularly some of the most reputable Medieval Jewish scholars. He took a passage, examined the possible interpretations from the Rabbinic scholars, and then compared them with the Vulgate, Septuagint, Jerome, Augustine, and other church fathers, and of Thomas Aquinas. He then gave his own interpretation, but always with deep respect for the above mentioned theologians. He referred as well to Roman and Greek classical scholars, and subjected the work to several further editions. Calvin praised the work highly,[319] and the Scottish reformer Alexander Celsius referred to Bucer's commentary in his own. John Boys, Dean of Canterbury, used it in his *Exposition*, and Thomas Holland, one of the translators of the King James Bible possessed a copy of Bucer's commentary.[320] Originally it was published under the pseudonym of Aretius Felinus, for which Bucer received strident criticism of cowardice. Bucer directed the work to Protestants in France, hoping to encourage the Reformation there, and feared that his true identity would call forth attention and opposition from both Catholics and Lutherans. However, the *Commentary on the Psalms* by Martin Bucer became one of the most useful and influential reference books of the Reformation.[321]

---

[318] Hopf, pp. 206-207.
[319] Hopf, p. 213.
[320] Hopf, p. 217.
[321] Hopf, p. 211.

The question of Bucer's influence on the rising Puritan movement is debatable. Puritans could not agree with his accommodation to vestments, his view on "sports," or his endorsement of the episcopal tradition. They did, however, appreciate his concept of Christian piety and unwavering commitment to basic theological principles of salvation by grace. Later Puritans tended to claim that Bucer was really on their side and only misunderstood.[322]

Finally, he had a great influence on his students at Cambridge as he lectured forcefully on the need to take seriously the Christian life. Of course, not all students at Cambridge appreciated Dr. Bucer's lectures. One of them, Thomas Horton, wrote that "Doctor Bucer cries incessantly now in daily lectures, now in frequent sermons, that we should practice penitence, discard the depraved customs of hypocritical religion, correct the abuses of feasts, be more frequent in having and hearing sermons, constrain ourselves to some sort of discipline."[323]

Mrs. Cranmer and Mrs. Bucer got on well, for both were educated women and committed to the evangelical cause. Wibrandis had been married to three pervious husbands, all of whom were pastors, including Oecolampadius and Capito, and Mrs. Cranmer was a native German. They are said to have had many enjoyable sessions together.[324]

Some of Bucer's most significant works were done in these brief two years, included in the *Scripta Anglica*. These include his masterpiece, *De Regno Christi*, the *Censura, Formula Vivendi Prescripta Familiae Suae, De Ordinatione Legitima*, and *De Vi et Usu Sacri Ministerii*. His sermons on Ephesians, unfortunately were never completed. Although he had earlier written his commentary on Ephesians, his views had matured considerably since then.[325]

---

[322] Hopf, p. 137.

[323] Hall, in Wright, p. 148.

[324] MacCulloch, p. 481.

[325] *De Regno Christi: On the Kingdom of Christ ,Censura,* his critique of the 1549 edition of the *Book of Common Prayer; Formula Vivendi Prescripta Familiae Suae,* the only description Bucer gives us of his own personal family life; *De Ordinatione Legitima, On Restoring Lawful Ordination,* and *De Vi et Usu Sacri Ministerii, On the Significance and Practice of the Sacred Ministry.*

In his *Formula Vivendi Prescripta Familiae Suae* he speaks of his own family life. Bucer was a good father and a faithful husband, and his home was indeed a model for the Christian community. Before each meal he read a passage from the Bible and made comments. His home, which included a large family, was always open to guests: refugees, scholars, statesmen, and others. All were welcome. However, as he was away frequently, Elizabeth managed the home well. She was no scholar or intellectual genius, but a good mother and housekeeper, and she also took care of the finances of the household.[326] Even the Catholics spoke well of her. On her death bed, she urged Martin to marry Wibrandis Capito. When they suffered the loss of many of their children, Elizabeth accepted it as the loving scourging of their heavenly father.[327] Bucer never mentioned his children in his letters, and it was thus up to Elizabeth to fill that void. She accepted the fact that her husband was a public man, and she had duties to fulfill at home. She truly complemented her husband who, although he dearly loved his family, found that the demands of his work prevented him from spending the time with his family that he probably would have wished to do.

The *Censura*, his critique of *The Book of Common Prayer* provided Thomas Cranmer with helpful suggestions most of which he incorporated into the 1552 edition. Bucer commented that he generally found little fault with the 1549 edition, only a few points that needed attention. But he did emphasize that everything that is said in the assembly should be fully understood, citing 1 Corinthians 14 as a basis. The ministers should speak with reverence and a clear and expressive voice and speech where everyone present can hear.[328] Bucer expressed gratitude that the Reformation was underway in England and that the doctrine of justification by faith was being taught. However, he was discouraged by the condition of the universities, which should have been the starting point for the Reformation and by now should be sending forth ministers: "It is

---

[326] Eells, p. 415.

[327] Eells, p. 417.

[328] E.C. Whitaker, *Martin Bucer and the Book of Common Prayer* Mayhew-McCrummin, Great Wakering: The Alcuin Club, 1974), p. 14.

from these colleges that the swarms of faithful ministers ought to have been sent forth from time to time" he later wrote to Calvin.[329]

He complained of abuses in rites and ceremonies, unscrupulous ministers who despoiled churches, pluralism (the practice of a minister holding more than one office), and unqualified clergy. He believed that by correcting abuses in the universities and ministry, other problems, such as the inattention of people during the worship, would be eliminated.[330]

The *Censura* and *The Book of Common Prayer*

When Bucer arrived in England, Cranmer asked him to read through his recent edition of *The Book of Common Prayer* and suggest possible revisions. Bucer did so, and published his findings in his *Censura,* a list of suggestions, most of which Cranmer adopted in his 1552 edition.

Bucer said that he actually found nothing unscriptural in Cranmer's 1549 edition, but he did have a few suggestions. For Bucer, who lacked the ability to express anything in succinct and brief terms, the *Censura* became a rather detailed analysis of the functioning of the church. However, his comments are worthy of our examination here for two reasons: first, their incorporation into Cranmer's 1552 edition, and, second, because, like the *De Regno Christi* analyzed below, these suggestions represent Bucer's mature theological concepts.

In the *Censura* he deals with a number of issues, all relating to the church; whereas in *De Regno Christi* he is concerned primarily about the state and what it can do to establish and regulate a true Christian community. His chapter headings reveal these ecclesiastical topics: (1) the Order of Prayers said Daily in Churches, (2) the Order of Holy Communion, (3) Baptism, Catechism, and Confirmation (4) Solemnization of Matrimony, (5) Visitation of the Sick, (6) Burial of the Dead, (7) Purification of

---

[329] Bucer, to Calvin, *Original Letters,* Vol. II, p. 546, cited in Constantin Hopf, *The English Reformation* (Oxford: Basil Blackwell, 1956), p. 104.
[330] Hopf, p. 104.

Women after Childbirth, and (8) Public Supplication for the Forgiveness of Sins.

In all that he suggests to Cranmer there are two guiding principles, which Bucer had embraced throughout his ministry, but only continued to stress and emphasize as he reached this point of theological culmination: first, that the welfare of the Christian flock be first priority in what the church and its ministry does, and, second, relating to it, that the ministers speak clearly and understandably. He was also very concerned that all vestiges of "superstition" imposed by the anti-Christ be removed, and that Scripture alone be the basis for all that was done and said in the church by the Christian ministry. These points he repeatedly stressed as he discussed the details of each of his topics. In his words: "It is our business to detect all the superstition of the Roman Anti-Christ and to restore the simplicity of Christ and the apostles and the early churches."[331] Again Bucer stated: "It will be agreed that nothing should be introduced or performed in the churches of Christ for which no probable reason can be given from the word of God."[332]

His views on the Lord's Supper remained the same from the days of his search for the middle ground between Zwinglianism and Lutheranism, but their articulation at this point in his life is interesting and important. Again, he stressed his strong conviction that communion be observed every Lord's Day: "For if it is right to celebrate the Lord's Supper on every Lord's Day, then equally it is right that every single Christian should communicate on that day, and not defer their communion to the solitary occasion of the Lord's Nativity."[333]

Bucer wanted to remove any vestiges of transubstantiation, but his definition gave little encouragement to the English Zwinglians like John Hooper and John à Lasco. Bucer believed that the early fathers saw the bread and wine of the communion as "trans-elemented" rather than transubstantiated. He explained:

> We do not receive all of this [confirmation of the new covenant and of the whole spirit of Christ] for the first time

---

[331] Bucer, *Censura,* cited from Whitaker, p. 34.
[332] *Censura,* in Whitaker, p. 44.
[333] *Ibid.*

now in this sacrament, for in baptism also the Lord Christ gives his whole self to us and incorporates us in himself [a major theological concept for Bucer] and confirms to us the pledge of eternal salvation...we receive him again and again in this Holy Communion of his table so that we may abide and live in him more fully and have him abiding and living in us and may delight more fully in him who satisfies and justifies us...For let it be far from us to say that he commanded us to receive from him at his supper merely bread and wine, and to eat and drink them, and not also those things which he offers at the same time, his body and blood. The same language is commanded to us also by the Apostle, who says that the bread is a communion of the body and the cup over which we give thanks is a communion of the blood of the Lord. Nor is this inconsistent with any other passage of Holy Scripture, nor does it detract in any way from the character of Christ as the only master of our salvation, as retaining a truly human body, or as reigning in celestial glory after having left this world.[334]

In regard to baptism, Bucer held to the same principles. He urged that baptism be administered on feast days in the presence of the whole church so that as many as possible of the members would recall the baptism of their members and the covenant undertaken on that occasion.[335] The members should be present on the occasion of the baptism of an infant "to pray for the child thus born in the church to everlasting life....the infant becomes a member of each one of them, each one receives him as a member of himself and binds himself to him in the presence of the Lord to all the bodily and spiritual obligations."[336] Bucer says that the minister must faithfully communicate to the congregation the meaning of baptism, which is best performed after the sermon and before communion. Parents desiring to have their children baptized should let their intention be known to the minister. He comments that children of Christians are holy and thus rightfully should be included in the fellowship of the

---

[334] *Censura,* in Whitaker, pp. 64-66, 68.
[335] *Censura,* in Whitaker, p. 82.
[336] *Censura,* Whitaker, p. 82.

church and sanctified by baptism.[337]   He was concerned that the people understand that baptism and communion are outward signs, and that they discern the true meaning, in distinction from the way the Roman Anti-Christs have turned the sacred rites of worship into abominable spectacles.[338] He wanted it understood that there was no magic in the water itself:

> If baptism is the sacrament of the washing away of sin, it is because the Lord gained it for us not only by his baptism in Jordan but also and much more by the baptism of the cross. And finally, although water is used in baptism to confer the washing away of sins, yet this effect is not the work of the water but of the Lord Christ. We must pay great respect to the early churches and most holy Fathers.[339]

Bucer allowed the sign of the cross to be made on the forehead and breast of the person to be baptized, for it was used by churches in very ancient times, but its use was acceptable only with very strict understanding of its meaning, untainted by any mixture of superstition or "servitude of an element of causal adherence to common custom."[340] He urged pastors to avoid theatrical diversions, superstitions or magic in their remarks, and preferred the greatest simplicity and accuracy in these sacramental mysteries.   He suggested this prayer:

> O God, grant that this child, thy creature, may so receive the merit and power of the cross of the Son of God that he may never be ashamed of it, so that he may always be crucified to the world and the world to him.   Beneath this sign may he fight manfully against sin, the world, and Satan, and continue thy faithful soldier and servant unto his life's end. Amen.[341]

He believed that adults who are baptized should be catechized and then questioned regarding their faith, and that sick infants should be

---

[337] *Ibid.* p. 86.

[338] *Ibid.,* p. 88.

[339] *Ibid.,* p. 90.

[340] *Ibid.*

[341] *Ibid.,* p. 92; cf. David Wight, "Infant Baptism and the Christian Community," in *Reforming Church and Community,* pp. 94-106.

baptized in private without delay. He rejected the whole idea of baptism for the dead and the consecration of the water itself.[342]

As to the meaning of sacraments, both baptism and the Lord's Supper, Bucer commented:

> Our sacraments exist in their use; they are actions, by which the Lord gives the remission of sins and the communion of himself to his people, not to water, not to bread and wine: and these gifts are made when these signs are set out and received in conjunction with his word and in obedience to his commands....Our religion is turned upside down when we tolerate rites received from the ancients which are not consistent with the word of God but which rather give service to Satan, confirming in the minds of too many people things which are manifest superstitions and plainly magical notions.[343]

In regard to confirmation, he taught that children should be confirmed if they can recite the articles of the faith, the Lord's Prayer, and the Ten Commandments, and make appropriate replies to questions from the shorter catechism.[344] They should make a confession of faith that is accompanied by signs of conduct and manner of life that would proceed from a heart that truly believes the gospel and from the teaching of the Holy Spirit.[345] They should carefully learn the catechism, attend the sacred assemblies studiously, and show themselves obedient to parents, teachers, and all in authority over them.[346]

With reference to marriage, Bucer urged that the ceremony be performed in the clear light of day and before the whole church. He felt it unworthy of a Christian to want to live openly with a wife and not consent to receive confirmation from the church.[347] He insisted that divorce be allowed, no matter how we depreciate or deplore it, and that inquiry into whether or not divorce is lawful is

---

[342] *Ibid.*, p. 94.
[343] *Ibid.*, p. 98.
[344] *Ibid.*, p. 100.
[345] *Ibid.*, p. 102.
[346] Ibid.
[347] *Ibid.*, pp. 114,116.

preposterous. He particularly opposed clandestine engagements between older men and young girls, in which the girls were lured by false promises of marriage.[348] Bucer again showed his concern for the rights of women. He taught that marriage involved great danger and required the most acute deliberation and best advice. Marriages should be made first and foremost for the mutual help of each other, and then for procreation and as a remedy against the sin of fornication.[349]

In his admonition at the end of the book, Bucer explained the reason why some of the old ceremonies have been abolished and some retained; for some ceremonies are unworthy of Christians, and others are made unworthy by their abuse in the Roman Church. He listed a number of specific examples including the abuse of bells, festivals, traces of idolatry and the mass, the movements of vessels, vestments (which he allowed but preferred to be abolished), crossings, and lights. He encouraged works of brotherly kindness, such as visiting the sick, and he stressed faithful observation of the Lord's Day and other holy days. Every sign of false cults and of the mass should be abolished, and extravagant, harmful, and profane games and merriment avoided. He wanted to see an end to ungodly strolling around and chattering during worship services in the churches, "the whole infantile uproar," and urged people to listen to sacred prayers with the greatest attention and to reply to the minister not only "Amen" but also other things said to ministers, including reciting together with the minister both confession of sins and the prayer before the reception of the sacraments.[350] He again stressed the importance of the Lord's Supper every Sunday,

> Because the Lord commanded the use of this sacrament to his disciples as a ceremony involving a solemn memorial of himself to be celebrated among us, which certainly lays upon us the obligation of celebrating it on every Lord's Day...it appears that the early churches accepted from a sure tradition of the apostles that they should provide the sacred supper on

---

[348] *Ibid.*, p. 118.
[349] *Ibid.*, p. 120.
[350] *Ibid.*, pp. 136-144, passim.

every Lord's Day and festival, and indeed whenever the whole church was gathered together.[351]

He urged that suitable ministers be cultivated for the churches through the necessary repair to the schools and universities, and he made a lengthy and impassioned plea for the equipping of these well-trained pastors and teachers. They should be men who devoted themselves to much study and whose life could stand under scrutiny, including inquiry among his neighbors as to his burning zeal for their salvation. They should be subjected to a careful examination on each point of doctrine, and it should be ascertained that they are not pursuing the ministry for wrong reasons.[352]

He concludes with these words to Archbishop Cranmer:

> May your most reverend Paternity be pleased to accept and consider all these things in such a way that you will pardon me if in any point of what I have written I seem perhaps to have you beyond my duty. May our Lord Jesus Christ, in whom we live and move and have our being, be present in his Spirit to your most reverend Paternity, so that you may ever give every possible benefit to his churches and live in perfect happiness in this world and in the world to come. Amen. The fifth of January in the year of our Lord 1551. At Cambridge. To your most reverend Paternity, your most humble bondsman in the Lord, Martin Bucer.[353]

The *Censura,* along with all of Bucer's works in England and some of his continental works, were published in 1577 in Basel by Conrad Hubert. His is the only printed edition of the *Censura,* although a copy in Bucer's own notoriously poor handwriting exists in Cambridge. A copy done by his amanuensis in beautiful script and signed personally by Bucer is in Oxford.[354]

---

[351] *Ibid.,* p. 146.
[352] *Ibid.,* pp. 150-170, passim.
[353] *Ibid.,* p. 172.
[354] Whitaker, p.2; Whitaker adds that Hubert mistakenly considered that the *De Ordinatione Legitima* was an appendix to the *Censura,* when, in fact, it was probably written on the continent because he refers to "our church," a term he applied to St. Thomas, pp. 4-5.

De Regno Christi: Blueprint for a Christian Community

The most complete and mature statement of Bucer's views on the Christian community is contained in his best-known work, *De Regno Christi,* written at the urging of a friend who believed that Bucer was qualified to suggest to King Edward an outline for turning England into a truly Christian country. Bucer was also anxious to express his gratitude to the king for allowing him refuge in England. The work was hastily done, and in typical Bucer style, was long and wordy. It was presented to Edward as a "new year's gift" from the old German reformer. Due to Edward's brief tenure as king and the accession of Mary in 1553, Bucer's plan that England would become a "Christian commonwealth," a *respublica christiania,* was never actualized, although Queen Elizabeth, who remembered Bucer when she was yet princess and re-consecrated his remains, may well have utilized some of Bucer's concepts in her government. Those friends of Bucer who survived the Marian persecution: Matthew Parker, Edwin Sandys, John Jewel, and especially Edmund Grindel, recognized Bucer's influence on Elizabeth's program.[355]

On October 21, 1550, Bucer sent a completed copy to his friend and admirer, the humanist John Cheke, who was the tutor of the king. The methodology he proposed was a series of laws that the king would enact. These laws were based on his experiences in Strasbourg; thus, they were not without concrete models from which he could draw. Like Aquinas, Bucer believed that human law was derived from divine law, which served as the guiding principle.[356] Bucer wrote:

> The kingdom of our Savior Jesus Christ is that administration and care of the eternal life of God's elect, by which this very Lord and King of Heaven by his doctrine and discipline, administered by suitable ministers chosen for this very purpose, gathers to himself his elect, those dispersed throughout the world who are his but whom he nonetheless wills to be subject to the powers of this world. He

---

[355] Pauck, p. 167.
[356] Pauck, p. 164.

incorporates them into himself and his church and so governs them in it that, purged now fully day by day from sin, they live well and happily both here and in time to come"[357]

Bucer emphasized again concepts we have discovered repeatedly in his theology, that we are *incorporated* into Christ, the ever-present underlying presupposition of election, the role of the Christian ministry, sanctification, and the happiness of the Christian in the properly organized and restored Christian community. Only in the concept of incorporation into Christ do we find a different emphasis from Calvin, who usually followed Bucer closely. Calvin preferred to stress rather the imputation of Christ's righteousness.

Because of the significance of the work, we shall include here a summary of the chapters with some comment on significant points. Generally, the book may be divided into laws on (1) religious education, (2) sanctification of Sunday and holidays, (3) sanctification of church buildings, (4) the reformation of the ministry, (5) the protection of church property, (6) the relief of the poor, (7) marriage and divorce, (8) public education and the conquest of idleness through a proper training for the professions and crafts; supervision of industry, commerce, and agriculture; and the proper ordering of hostelries, inns, theaters, and public entertainment, (9) foods, (10) civil legislation, (11) the civil service, (12) the courts, (13) the penal system, and (14) penal law and capital punishment.[358] Bucer's work was comprehensive indeed! And it is astonishing to think that he could compose it so quickly. But lengthy and thorough writings done quickly had characterized Bucer's entire career. Obviously, Bucer aimed at the reform of the whole of life and society, and not just of the church.[359]

Book One

Chapter I: Names of the Kingdom of Christ

---

[357] *De Regno Christi,* tr. Pauck, p. 225.
[358] Pauck, p.162.
[359] Pauck, p. 163.

Chapter II: What the Kingdom of Christ and the Kingdom of the World Have in Common and What They Do Not.

In this second chapter, Bucer launched into the prime importance of the pastoral care of souls, emphasizing to the king that his consideration of the spiritual welfare of his people should be of first priority. That care of souls is to be shared by both church and state, and the state should see to it that no one would be deprived of hearing the saving doctrine of Christ and of instruction in Christian piety.[360]

Chapter III: Some More Eminent Passages of the Holy Scriptures Concerning the Kingdom of God in Christ, in the Light of Which What We Have Purposed Can be Better Understood.

Bucer based his comments in this chapter on Isaiah 2:2-3, the establishment of the Lord's kingdom as the mountain of the Lord's temple that is exalted above the other mountains, to which the nations of the world come to be taught of his ways and to walk in his paths. He describes the true Church of Christ as characterized by the faithful preaching of the gospel and praise of God in worship.

Chapter IV: The Various Periods of the Church

Bucer endorsed Constantine and Theodosius for having set up a Christian community and utilized the resources of the state to support the preaching of the gospel and the care of Christian souls. He referred to the Roman Catholic Church as the anti-Christ, but admitted that God had many citizens living in it, though they were involved in grave and serious errors and weakness of faith.[361] Bucer refused ever to deny that Catholics were Christians, and, of course, for a long time held forth the possibility of reunion. He emphasized the need for discipline in the restored churches and complained about those who were willing to renounce the anti-Christ and endorse justification by faith but not give themselves to good works and Christian discipline:

> Hence let us learn that the Kingdom of God does not remain, or even exist, where fruits, i.e., the works of all piety and

---

[360] *DRC*, p. 190.
[361] *DRC*, p. 209.

righteousness, are not manifested. And when this sterility of good works publicly prevails in some nation, the Lord transfers his Kingdom, i.e., the administration of man's salvation through pure doctrine and his salutary discipline, to another one.[362]

Bucer's comment is quite interesting in view of Christian history, in particular the change in the location of the strength of the church through the years. One has but to compare the contemporary spiritual condition in Europe with that of Bucer's day!

Chapter V: What the Kingdom of Christ Is, and What Is Necessary for Its Restoration

Bucer stressed the preaching of the word by capable ministers, discipline, catechism of baptized children, and the confirmation ceremony when the child reaches an age to confess his faith publicly.[363]

Chapter VI: The Dispensation of the Doctrine of Christ

Bucer emphasized that everything that is taught must be derived from Holy Scripture. He again discussed the importance of catechizing children.[364] Bucer himself was the author of several catechisms.

Chapter VII: The Administration of the Sacraments

His view of the sacraments as more than symbol is developed in this chapter. Christ administers and the saved receive the supreme benefit of salvation, the forgiveness of sins, and the inheritance of eternal life mysteriously through the sacraments of baptism and the Lord's Supper.[365] Bucer always held that faith was necessary for the effective reception of the grace conveyed through the sacraments.

Chapter VIII: The Ministry of the Discipline of Life and Manners

Chapter IX: The Ministry of the Discipline of Penance

---

[362] *DRC*, p. 220.
[363] *DRC*, p. 229.
[364] *DRC*, p. 232.
[365] *DRC*, p. 237.

Chapter X: Reforming the Church's Ceremonies: First, the Hallowing of Church Buildings

Chapter XI: Setting Aside Certain Times for the Worship of God: The Importance of Lord's Day Worship

Until 1536 Bucer considered as superstition the observation of any other day than Sunday, but he broadened his limitations in later years to admit Christmas and other Christian holidays.[366]

Chapter XII: Lent and Other Fasts, and the Taking of Food

He discussed whether or not Lent was introduced by the apostles, pointing out that scholars divide on the matter. He asserted that prescribing fasting as necessary for salvation cannot be allowed.[367]

Chapter XIII: The Regulation of Ceremonies

Chapter XIV: Care for the Needy, Almsgiving

Chapter XV: How Salutary It Is for All Men to Have the Kingdom of Christ Firmly Restored Among Them and How Necessary It Is for Salvation that Every Christian, According to His Place in the Body of Christ and the Gifts He Has Received from Him, Aim and Work toward this with Deepest Concern

In this chapter Bucer wrote, "A solid restitution and reception of the Kingdom of Christ is truly salutary and necessary for all happiness."[368] This goal would be achieved by being faithful to the words of Christ and not adding or subtracting anything or fabricating a ministry of religion other than what is delivered to us.[369] "We cannot knowingly and prudently neglect or omit any of these things for any reason without despising and repudiating Christ himself and all his sovereignty."[370]

---

[366] *DRC*, p. 251, n. p. 252.
[367] *DRC*, p. 253.
[368] *DRC*, p. 259.
[369] *DRC*, p. 263.
[370] *DRC*, p. 265.

Book Two

Chapter I: By What Ways and Means the Kingdom of Christ Can and Should be Reformed by Devout Kings

Chapter II: Who Are to be Used for the Reestablishment of Christ's Kingdom

Bucer suggested to King Edward that he identify capable leaders by their fruits as people endowed beyond others with special knowledge of the love of the Kingdom of Christ.[371]

Chapter III: The Kingdom of Christ Must be Renewed Not Only by Edict but also by Devout Persuasion

Of course, Bucer strongly encouraged King Edward both to issue edicts and devoutly persuade the people of England toward the renewal of the kingdom

Chapter IV: Approved Evangelists Must be Sent Out to All Parts of the Realm

Chapter V: The Kingdom of Christ Must be Reformed by Devout Persuasion and an Accurate Preaching of the Gospel, rather than by Decrees

Chapter VI: Where Suitable Evangelists Are to be Sought and the Matter of the Reformation of the Schools of Higher Learning

Bucer was quite concerned about Oxford and Cambridge becoming centers of the Reformation. He was upset about the lingering Catholic influence in these schools, and urged the restoration of the colleges as soon as possible. He spared no words in labeling the Roman Church as anti-Christ.[372]

Chapter VII: The Source and Support of the Evangelists and Pastors of the Churches

He was concerned that evangelists and pastors receive proper pay for their services, and he considered that it was the responsibility of the king to oversee this matter.[373]

---

[371] *DRC*, p. 267.
[372] *DRC*, p. 276.
[373] *DRC*, p. 279.

Chapter VIII: How the Full Restoration of Religion Must be Advocated and Enacted

He provided Edward with a plan to select qualified men who would advocate and command in the king's name the reformation of the churches.[374]

Chapter IX: The First Law: Children Must be Catechized and Educated for God

Chapter X: The Second Law: The Sanctification of Holy Days

Bucer appeared to be more concerned that the other Reformers that holidays, especially the Lord's Day, be kept sacred. He suggested to the king laws prohibiting labor, pleasures, and spectacles on holy days.[375] In many regards, English Puritans did not agree with Bucer, but in this area we can identify a point with which they would be in complete accord.

Chapter XI: The Third Law: The Sanctification of Churches

He suggested that the king restrict by edict the use of the churches to holy matters alone.

Chapter XII: The Fourth Law: The Restoration of the Ministries of the Church

Here we can find an area where Bucer was willing to make concessions for the sake of unity in a matter he did not consider an essential. In Germany his general practice, as we have discussed, was to organize churches under a Presbyterate, an eldership. However, recognizing the importance of the English Episcopal tradition, he was willing to consider the bishop as the chief elder, and he quoted copiously from the early church fathers to support this view. He stressed that the requirement of celibacy and the addition of the papacy was added later. He found no fault with the English system of having a bishop, a council of presbyters, and deans.[376]

Chapter XIII: The Fifth Law: Claiming Ecclesiastical Goods for Christ the Lord, and their Pious Use

---

[374] *Ibid.*
[375] *DRC,* pp. 281-282, n. p.282.
[376] *DRC,* pp. 285-286, p. 288.

Bucer urged the king to remove all simony and annates, and the practice of requiring the churches to help financially in public matters, and for him to be sure that the clergy was well paid and the poor relieved. Church funds should be used only for church purposes, although churches should be subject to a reasonable tax. Churches who have an abundance of wealth should share with poor people in churches that lack sufficient funds, and the king should stop the pillaging of church property.[377]

Chapter XIV: The Sixth Law: Poor Relief
The king should see that each church has deacons in charge of poor relief. The poor were to be provided for so that no one would go begging, which Bucer believed should be forbidden.[378] He advocated that alms would be given to and through the church rather than privately, and that to avoid poverty and begging, the churches provide training for all baptized people into skills.[379]

Chapter XV: The Seventh Law: The Sanctification and Regulation of Marriage

Chapter XVI: What Must be Established Concerning the Contracting and Entering of Holy Marriage, All according to God's Will

Chapter XVII: Which Reason It Is Proper to Join in Matrimony

Chapter XVIII: Marriages Should Not be Held Valid Which Are Contracted Without the Consent of Those Who Have Power Over the Ones Who Make the Contract, or Without Suitable Advisors
Bucer advocated that children should do things only by consent of their parents, including marriage. Yet children should not be embarrassed to ask the parents to approve their marriage to certain parties. Magistrates should interfere in cases where the parents were

---

[377] *DRC*, pp. 296, 299, 300, 301, 306.
[378] *DRC*, n. p. 311.
[379] *DRC*, pp. 314-315.

known to be harsh or abusive to their children.[380] Bucer continued to look out after the welfare of children and emphasize their importance and sanctity in the kingdom.

Chapter XIX: Whether It May be Permitted that the Promise of Marriage May be Rescinded before It is Fulfilled

He stated that the king would have power to so rescind a marriage arrangement, especially in cases where the marriage was not consummated.[381]

Chapter XX: The Celebration of Nuptials

Bucer advocated that the service be meaningful, understandable, and done reverently.[382] These three principles are in line with what Bucer consistently stressed regarding any Christian services.

Chapter XXI: The Preservation of Holy Marriage

Here he suggested to King Edward that the church should watch and investigate if husbands were treating their wives properly. (Bucer was also quite concerned about the welfare of women, another trait that showed him to be ahead of his times.) If they were mistreating their wives, they should be reported to the magistrates. Lay elders should be considered guardians of marriage, charged with the responsibility of investigating marital conduct.[383]

Chapter XXII: What the Ancient Churches Thought About Legitimate Divorce

This and the following twenty-four chapters were translated by John Milton, but not by Wilhelm Pauck. By the titles one can discern again Bucer's much more lenient view toward divorce, a manifestation of his strong feelings about safeguarding the happiness and well-being of the family and all its members, and his opposition to discrimination against women.

He assigned to the civil magistrates the control of the process, but he left them with the strong suggestion that people should have the right of divorce and remarriage for other reasons than adultery.

---

[380] *DRC,* p. 323.
[381] *DRC,* p. 325.
[382] *DRC,* p. 326.
[383] *DRC,* p. 327.

He substantiated his assertions by an appeal to the early fathers and a careful analysis of Jesus' teaching in Matthew 5:31-32.[384]

Chapter XXIII: The Ancient Fathers Allowed Marriage Even After the Vow of Celibacy

Chapter XXIV: Who of the Ancient Fathers Allowed Marriage after Divorce

Chapter XXV: A Discussion of the Sayings of our Lord and of the Holy Spirit through the Apostle Paul concerning Divorce

Chapter XXVI: God in his Law did not only Grant but also Command Divorce to Certain Men

Chapter XXVII: What the Lord Permitted and Commanded to his Ancient People concerning Divorce Applies also to Christians

Chapter XXVIII: Our Lord Christ Intended Not to Make New Laws of Marriage and Divorce or of Any Civil Matters

Chapter XXIX: It Is Wicked to Strain the Words of Christ beyond their Intent

Chapter XXX: All Narrations of the Gospels must be connected to One Another

Chapter XXXI: Whether the Lord in his Words which the Evangelists Matthew, Mark, and Luke Record Allowed Final Divorce because of Fornication

Chapter XXXII: A Manifest Adulteress ought to be Divorced and cannot be Retained in Marriage by any True Christian

Chapter XXXIII: Adultery must be punished by Death

Chapter XXXIV: Whether it is Permissible for Wives to leave their Adulterous Husbands and to Marry Someone Else

---

[384] Pauck, n. p. 328.

Chapter XXXV: An Exposition of the Holy Spirit concerning Divorce given to us in Writing through the Apostle Paul

Chapter XXXVI: Although in the Gospels our Lord appears to allow Divorce only in the Case of Adultery, He nevertheless allowed Divorce also for Other Causes

Chapter XXXVII: To which Men and Women Divorce is Granted in the Code of Civil Law

Chapter XXXVIII: An Exposition of those Passages of Holy Scripture wherein God explains to us the Nature of Holy Wedlock

Chapter XXXIX: A Definition of the Characteristics of Holy Wedlock

Chapter XL: Whether the Crimes listed in Civil Law Dissolve Matrimony in the Sight of God[385]

Chapter XLI: Whether a Deserted Husband or Wife may marry Someone Else

Chapter XLII: Incurable Inability to Perform the Duties of Marriage is a Just Ground for Divorce

Chapter XLIII: To grant Divorce for all the Causes which have so far been listed agrees with the Words Christ has spoken against Divorce

Chapter XLIV: To those who are legally Divorced a Second Marriage ought to be permitted

Chapter XLV: There are some Men so destined for Marriage by the Lord that it is repugnant to God's Decree that anyone should forbid them Marriage for any Reason.

Chapter XLVI: An Exposition of the Words of the Holy Spirit in Praise of Celibacy[386]

---

[385] I.e., the crimes he discusses in Chapter XXXVII.
[386] i.e., 1 Corinthians 7.

Chapter XLVII: Conclusion of the entire Tract on Marriage

Bucer urged the king to act against the perversion of God's laws on marriage and divorce by the anti-Christ. And he asserted that it was pernicious to forbid marriage to those who cannot live without this remedy.[387] He stressed that chastity and the sanctity of life must be publicly restored first in individual homes and the marriage contract treated responsibly and preserved in good faith. Marriage can and should be dissolved when unhappiness of the partners demands it, and legitimate remarriage allowed.[388]

Chapter XLVIII: The Eighth Law: The Civil Education of Youth and the Suppression of Idleness

Here Bucer stated that "every state and commonwealth should educate, form, and train its children for Him with utmost care, and adapt each of them to those skills and activities for which the Lord Himself has created each to be most suited."[389]   He went on to comment that the Christian state should not tolerate anyone who does not dedicate himself to honest work.[390]

Bucer, like all the other Reformers, advocated the establishment of schools. Yet Bucer's stress on education is probably the most pronounced among the Reformers. He suggested that the state determine who is gifted for higher education and who should be directed toward the crafts.[391]

Chapter XLIX: The Restoration of Various Crafts and honest Pursuits of Profit

This chapter is particularly interesting because it reveals Bucer's economic philosophy and its relationship to the overall scheme for the community. He had a great appreciation for "the blessings of wool and woolen," and he advocated that women should learn the skill of spinning, which would not only benefit society but keep the female sex from idleness.[392] He appreciated good soil and a good climate for farming, and thus manifested a high regard for

---

[387] *DRC, p.332.*
[388] *DRC,* p. 333.
[389] *DRC,* p. 334.
[390] *Ibid.*
[391] *DRC,* p. 334, pp. 336-337, n. p. 336.
[392] *DRC,* pp. 337-339.

agricultural pursuits. But the king should make laws not only to suppress idleness, but to guard against the greedy and profiteers. Thus the kingdom, through the king's legislation in these matters, feeds itself, defends itself (he discusses provision for training some for the military), and avoids luxury and idleness.[393]

He also suggested that paper be made from worn out rags! Bucer was truly concerned about frugality and avoidance of wastefulness. He went on to suggest that from childhood every individual citizen be assigned the pursuit of some special skill, and the nobility should be a shining example to the common people.[394]

Chapter L: The Reform of Marketing

He continued to set forth his economic philosophy: "Marketing is a business which is honest and necessary for the commonwealth if it confines itself to the export and import of things that are advantageous to the commonwealth for living well and in a holy way, but not those which encourage and foster impious pomp and luxury."[395] He was opposed to the greed and wickedness of merchants, and "looked on all business and trade carried on for the sake of profit with great suspicion and even hostility because he believed them to be irreconcilable with Christian morality."[396] Bucer showed himself much in line with the general Reformed view of pursuing one's calling to the glory of God, and of a comprehensive Christian world view that extended to all of life.

Chapter LI: The Care of Public Inns entrusted to Men of Piety, Chastity, and Decency

Chapter LII: Those who have no Aptitude for honorable Skills should be reduced to manual Labor and humble Tasks

Chapter LIII: Prefects must be appointed for Skills and Labor

---

[393] *DRC*, p. 340.
[394] *DRC*, p. 341.
[395] *DRC*, pp. 342-343.
[396] Pauck, n. p. 343.

These prefects Bucer envisioned to be guardians or overseers for assigning citizens definite virtuous lines of work, whether philosophical or mechanical.[397]

Chapter LIV: Honest Games

Bucer suggested to the king that he make provisions for relaxations from work and study, for the recreation of strength of spirit and body in play and games. The games he proposed were to be derived from musical and gymnastic art. He suggested modest dances and expressions of our joy as Christians:

> Certainly if we belong to Christ, if he is our life, and eternal salvation is from him and about him, every cause of joy and gladness ought to be ours; and complete exultation both of spirit and of body should be aroused, something which anyone will acknowledge who has experienced but a little of what it is 'to love God with your whole heart, your whole mind, and with all your strength,' indeed, who has ever known any of the power of human love and exultant gladness.[398]

Bucer suggested that youth could engage in drama as a useful means of entertainment, honorable and contributing toward an increase in piety, but composed by devout and wise men.[399] Bucer was willing to allow even comedies, and he suggested that the Bible be used as a source for drama, illustrating examples of biblical themes. It would also be possible to use stories and occurrences from daily life as dramatic themes. He advocated sports that contributed to physical health, the preservation of the body, and would help to render men fit for military service.[400]

Chapter LV: The Ninth Law: Controlling Luxury and Harmful Expenses

In this chapter Bucer dealt with scriptural arguments in favor of modest attire and urged the king to give vestiary and sumptuary laws that would control luxury in housing, dining, dress, and adornment. These laws would arouse, promote, and strengthen a necessary

---

[397] *DRC,* p. 346.
[398] *DRC,* p. 348.
[399] *DRC,* p. 349.
[400] *DRC,* pp. 350-351.

modesty in Christians and frugality among his people, avoiding extravagant luxuries.[401]

Chapter LVI: The Tenth Law: On the Revision and Elaboration of Civil Law

He clarified here the laws regarding the communication of obligations and the exchange of goods among men, suggesting to the king that these laws be based on the Decalogue.[402]

Chapter LVII: The Eleventh Law: The Appointment of Magistrates

Bucer advised the king, in an extremely lengthy and detailed recommendation, that the magistrates should excel in knowledge and zeal for the Christian religion.[403]

Chapter LVIII: The Twelfth Law: The Establishment and Correction of Tribunals and Judges

He insisted here that the king must not have judges who would be hostile to or even neglect pure religion, and that the number of judges should be increased, that the rights of the plaintiff should always be respected, and that the judges always abide by the law.[404]

Chapter LIX: The Thirteenth Law: The Custody of Accused Persons

Bucer urged the king to avoid harsh and unjust imprisonment of accused people and to allow them a quick hearing.[405]

Chapter LX: The Fourteenth Law: The Modification of Penalties

Bucer, like the other Reformers, agreed to the practice of capital punishment as biblical, and he listed those who legitimately might be put to death: (1) those who injured the worship of God by false and impious doctrines, (2) those blaspheming the name of God, (3)

---

[401] DRC, p. 357.

[402] DRC, p. 360.

[403] DRC, p. 362.

[404] DRC, pp. 374-375.

[405] DRC, p. 377. In his oration at Bucer's funeral, Haddon mentioned that during his stay in Cambridge, Bucer took a personal interest in the fate of prisoners., Pauck, n. p. 377.

those violating the Sabbath, (4) those who despised the authority of parents and lived wickedly, (5) those unwilling to submit to the sentence of the supreme tribunal, (6) those guilty of bloodshed, (7) those guilty of adultery, (8) those guilty of rape, (9) those guilty of kidnapping, and (10) those who bore false testimony in a capital case.[406] He further urged Edward to enact laws with sufficient penalties so that he would drive away and stamp out every attempt to harm one's neighbor.[407]

In his final and concluding chapter, Bucer admitted to the king that his words were many, but urged him to consider the vices currently present in the administration of church and state. He stated that he knew some would criticize him for what he said, and some would accuse him of trying to design some kind of Platonic republic, but he asked that people judge and estimate what he offered, not on the basis of the judgment of men, but on the immutable word of God.[408]

Several points should be noticed before concluding this survey of Bucer's *De Regno Christi.* Not only does it present his mature, comprehensive program for the reform of church and state and the creation of his concept of a genuine Christian community, but it reflects the underlying presuppositions that Bucer held and that he would pass on to future generations of Protestant leaders. True doctrine, Christian piety, and a Christian world view realized in the context of the Kingdom of Christ stand forth as the basic principles of the work, and these became the basic principles of evangelical Christianity, in particular, of the Reformed faith. That the definition of the Kingdom was far broader than church, that it included state as well, and that all those who lived under the Christian king should be regulated by a Christian set of laws, were beliefs held dear by all the leaders of the Reformation at this time. That dream has become past history in the twenty-first century, and many of his ideas will seem quaint and outmoded. Yet they reflect the principles of God's law,

---

[406] *DRC,* pp. 378-379.
[407] *DRC,* p. 383.
[408] *DRC,* pp. 384-385.

which Christians admit to being fundamental to living a life of holiness in a fallen world.[409]

End of the Journey

Bucer was in the middle of his lectures on the book of Ephesians at Cambridge when, on February 13, 1551, he was taken ill. The lectures were never finished, for he died on the twenty-eighth. His last lecture concerned once more his interpretation of the Lord's Supper, that subject that occupied so much of his time and energy through his career. It included these words:

> Now it has always been acknowledged in the Church, and the Scripture also manifestly teaches, that Christ's body and blood are not the food and drink of the body, nor are they bestowed literally by these [words], to be eaten and drunk, but by a similitude, and therefore metaphorically. For as the bread eaten, and the wine drunk, nourish the body, and support strength and life; so the body and blood of the Lord, received by faith and by the inward working of the Holy Spirit, nourish a man unto new life, support the strength for this life and the life itself, the life in which the just live by their faith..."[410]

Peter Martyr and John Bradford remained with him through the final days of his illness. His wife, who had returned to Germany, was summoned; the Duchess of Suffolk came as well. Peter Martyr described the final suffering of Bucer:

> It was a grievous spectacle for us, and indeed miserable also for his own household, when from the extreme debility of his

---

[409] Cf. John Witte, Jr., *Law and Protestantism: The Legal Teachings of the Lutheran Reformation* (Cambridge: At the University Press, 2002), pp. 153-154, 228-229; Amy Nelson Burnett, "Church Discipline and Moral Reformation in the Thought of Martin Bucer," *Sixteenth Century Journal,* Vol. 22 (1991), pp. 440-445.

[410] Cited in Smyth, p.172; cf. *The Heidelberg Catechism,* questions 75-80. This catechism was written in 1563, twelve years after Bucer's death, in an effort to arrive at the formula on which Lutherans and Reformed Christians could agree, the very formula that Bucer sought elusively for so many years. The wording is almost the same.

whole body, the enervation of his limbs, the difficulty of digestion, and a perpetual choking for his breath, he was in such great pain, that he could hardly bear to see or talk with anyone. Not that either his kindness towards us or his piety towards all was in any degree diminished: but he felt...that his hour was at hand...When Bradford...was going [out] to preach, and said that he wished to be remembered in his prayers, [Bucer] said, weeping, 'Cast me not away, O Lord, in the time of my old age, when my strength has failed': then he added, 'Let him stoutly chastise me, yet he will never cast me away, he will never cast me away...' Now I ought to mention that the physicians and his other friends were afraid lest when the moon waned [in eclipse], his strength too might wane, and he might be overcome by the strength of his disorder: when on the following day he seemed a little better, Bradford came to him as usual and explained to him the fear of the physicians and the anxiety of his friends on account of that eclipse of the moon and perturbation of the heavenly bodies, and he is said to have held up three fingers and, raising his eyes to that eternal heaven, cried, 'It is he, it is he who ruleth and ordaineth all things...' No tearful words escaped him, no complaint of his illness, no sorrowful cry. Thus constantly and patiently he bore the cruelty of his continuous pain. His death was like his life: if you know how he lived, you cannot be ignorant how he died...Even as he lived, as no man better; so he died, as no man more blessedly: even as he bore his illness, that no man might see him lament; so he passed away, that no man could perceive him dying...[411]

When Calvin was informed of Bucer's death, he was disappointed because he had hoped that Bucer would live long enough to exercise an even greater influence on the development of the Reformation in England: "We lament our lot and that of the Church in being deprived of a man not only very useful but inexpressibly necessary for the Lord's work."[412] Calvin went on to

---

[411] Cited in Smyth, p.174.
[412] Smyth, p. 175.

say, "I feel my heart almost like to break when I think of the great loss the church of God has sustained in the death of Bucer...He would have been very useful in England. I was hoping still more from his writings than all he had accomplished up till now."[413]

Fuller gives the following account of Bucer's death:

Martin Bucer ended his life (and was buried in St. Maries) several Authours assigning sundry dates of his death. Martin Crusius, part 3a. *Annal. Suev. Lib.* II. Cap. 25. makes him to die 1551 on the second of February. Pantaleon, *De Viris Illustribus Germaniae,* makes him expire about the end of April of the same year. Mr. Fox, in his *Reformed Almanack,* appoints the 23 of December, for Bucer his Confessourship. A printed table, of the Chancellours of Cambridge, set forth by Dr. Perne, signeth March the tenth 1550 for the day of his death. Nor will the distinction of old and new-style (had it been then in use) help to reconcile the difference. It seems by all reports that Bucer was sufficiently dead in our about this time. Persons, the Jesuite, tell us, that some believed that he died a Jew (meerly, I conceive, because he lived a great Hebrician) citing Surius, Genebrand, and Lindan (ask my fello if I be a lier) for this report. Sure I am, none of them were near him at his death, as Mr. Bradford and others were. Who when they admonished him in his sicknesse, that he should arme himself against the assaults of the Devil, he answered, that he had nothing to do with the Devil, because he was wholly in CHRIST. And, when Mr. Bradford came to him, and told him, that he must die, he answered, *Ille, ille regit, et moderator omnia,* and so quietly yielded up his soul. What good man would not rather die like a Jew with Martin Bucer, then like a Christian with Robert Persons? He was a plain man in person, and apparel; and therefore, at his own request, privately created Doctour, without any solemnity: a skillfull Linguist, whom a great Critick (of a palate not to be pleased with a common gust) stileth *Ter Maximum Bucerum,* a commendation which he justly deserved.[414]

---

[413] *Ibid.*
[414] Fuller, p. 130.

Sir John Cheke, tutor of Edward VI and friend and admirer of Bucer, wrote to Peter Martyr when he heard of his death: "We are deprived of a leader than whom the whole world would scarcely obtain a greater, whether in knowledge of true religion or in integrity and innocence of life, or in thirst for study of the most holy things, or in exhausting labour in advancing piety, or in authority and fullness of teaching, or in anything that is praiseworthy and renowned."[415]   What an appropriate summation of the life and character of Martin Bucer!

Bucer's funeral was held March 2, 1551, in the choir of Great St. Mary's.   Another friend whom he had made in England, Matthew Parker, delivered the eulogy in English. He commented:

> I commend Doctor Martin Bucer whom for the sincerity and truth of his doctrine grounded upon the sure foundation of the word of God, upon the confession of the Apostolic and Catholic church of Christ...[and for his] great pains and labors to expound, to be helpful, ever asking...to have our advice in the order of his labors...[we] his weak disciples...He powdered his lessons with weighty exhortations to godly life...he was marvelous in the moderation of our public disputations in the common schools and overmuch painful in attending them, though his immoderate pains in the great rigor of the winter...I fear was the cause of our untimely mourning for him at this time...with quiet spirit he would rather teach the truth than to contend with young divines in vanity of words...[he compiled] certain works of grave importance...[he was] also busied in diligent preaching the Word of God....[he] had also a special eye or desire to the politic and Christian order of the whole township in the respect of the civil society an...order thereof...Verily he was an incomparable ornament.[416]

Parker and Walter Haddon were appointed Bucer's executors, and as such they turned over 380 pounds to his widow, Wibrandis Bucer. The king and the University of Cambridge gave her money

---

[415] TA, prefactory 'Iuducia Doctissimorum, in Hall, in Wright, p. 144.
[416] Sigs. E ii, Ev, Eiii. TA, pp. 892-8, in Hall, in Wright, p. 147.

also, and she returned to Strasbourg at the end of April. Conrad Hubert and Ulrich Chelius were appointed guardians of Bucer's children and Wendelin Richel as trustee. Edward kept his manuscripts in England, and as a result many survive today to make up his *Opera Omnia*. The Duchess of Suffolk purchased most of the works, which would account for their survival. Cranmer purchased the remainder.[417] Unfortunately, after the works were hidden from Queen Mary, who would most certainly have burned them had she been able to put her hands on them, when they were uncovered, it was found that many had deteriorated and been gnawed by rats. Also Bucer's handwriting is notoriously bad.[418]

Bucer's position as Regius Professor of Theology at Cambridge was kept vacant until 1553 when the king offered it to Melancthon. However, it was in that eventful year that the young king, always unhealthy, died, and his elder sister, the Catholic Mary, ascended the throne. During her persecution and execution of the leaders of the Reformation in England, in 1556 she had the bones of Bucer and Fagius dug up, taken out of their graves, placed on a cart, with his books, and denounced. However, in July 1560 Queen Elizabeth ordered Bucer and Fagius to be restored to their former honors when she received letters from Archbishop Parker. A great memorial service of re-consecration was held in Great St. Mary's. Ironically, it was Perne of Peterhouse, Vice-Chancellor of Cambridge, who presided at both ceremonies, both his burning and his restitution.[419]

---

[417] Eells, p. 413.
[418] Hopf, p. 33.
[419] Smyth, p.177.

Conclusion

Martin Bucer, "the other Martin," was born in poverty; Martin Luther was born of wealthy, yet peasant-stock parents. Both men became monks, Bucer a Dominican and Luther an Augustinian, and subsequently left their vows and monastic life to embrace the Reformation. Luther defined the Biblical doctrine of forensic justification, and Bucer accepted it. Luther and his colleague Philip Melancthon organized a reformation in Germany with the distinct characteristics that survive in the Lutheran Church. Bucer worked with a far broader constituency and traveled far more extensively than did Luther, and his efforts, codified, systematized, and clarified by the genius of John Calvin and those who studied under him at Geneva, resulted in the Reformed Church. Bucer's parallel efforts in England with Cranmer helped to shape the Church of England. Both Martins were mighty instruments of God in a critical moment in the unfolding and building of Christ's church, but one is relatively, though not sufficiently, known, and the other rests in comparative obscurity.

Martin Bucer came to Strasbourg in 1523 fleeing from persecution from a Roman Church angry and disappointed in his behavior; he left Strasbourg in 1549 once again fleeing from an angry Roman Church as well as a furious German emperor. He took refuge in a land where there was hope that reform might take root, but England was foreign to him in every way, and he died disappointed, broken in body and spirit, but working for what he believed was right and true to the very end. He had suffered financial distress and much personal loss in the death of a beloved wife and so many of his children. He had been misunderstood and denounced, not only by Catholics whom he thought would be reasonable and work for reform of abuses, but also by most of his fellow Protestants who frequently found him too willing to compromise principles of doctrine for the sake of a unity they thought impossible. The powerful prince who held such hope for bringing about reform throughout Europe disappointed him when he lost his influence due to his personal conduct. He had to deal with Anabaptists, Separatists and licentious Epicureans who managed to carve out areas of considerable power and influence. He witnessed the death of so many brave and capable colleagues who could have helped him so greatly had they continued to live. From so many points of view, Bucer's life was a failure.

Yet Strasbourg had its moment of glory when all of Protestant Europe could look to this city on a hill as an example of a true Christian community, and as a safe haven of refuge for those who experienced persecution. And from Strasbourg the foremost leader of the next generation of the Reformation whose name everyone knows went to Geneva to replicate Strasbourg and to create the new center for training pastors who would go out from there to plant evangelical churches all over the world; quite literally all over the world, for Protestants brought their faith to the Americas and Protestant missionaries spread the doctrines of the gospel of grace wherever they went. Bucer provided the basic interpretation of theology and the blueprint for a Christian community that would characterize the evangelical faith generally and the Reformed faith in particular. Bucer left a significant mark on the doctrines of the Church of England, and his spirit of flexibility and emphasis on essentials has helped that church to adapt to the religious disposition of the English people and to have the flexibility that has characterized it through the years.

Bucer contributed ideas that, although they were not appreciated completely by Calvin, have proven to be valuable in the contemporary church as it seeks for identity and relevance in twenty-first century culture. He taught that Christian leaders should seek the essentials of the faith and not be weighed down by the indifferent points; he emphasized the rights of women, and saw the defining role of love and mutual commitment in marriage, and the pain and hopelessness of people living in unhappiness simply because they are taught that divorce is sinful. His emphasis on pastors' caring for their flock and on the obligation of Christians to place priority above everything else on genuine love for their neighbors are points of emphasis that the church is beginning to realize had been neglected and must be implemented. That pastors and teachers must be taught and equipped for the ministry, and that they need to tailor their teaching to meet the spiritual needs of the people and speak to them in understandable terms is certainly relevant today.

Although we are beyond the time of hoping for a "city of God" today and have acquiesced to a secular society, Bucer as a diplomat who developed connections with the people of political power in his day and worked tirelessly to bring about a Christian society through them, reminds us that Christian leaders, and Christian laity, for that matter, cannot live in isolation from the world, but must be involved in it. The state, after all, whether it is distinctly Christian or not, is ordained by God. Bucer's willingness to jump into the political arena as well as in to the arena of ecclesiastical leadership is a model to the church of today not to abandon efforts to inculcate principles of righteousness even into a pagan world. Bucer is an example and incentive to men like Billy Graham and the Reverend Jesse Jackson, even to Pope John Paul II, all of whom have had the courage to face political leaders and work for what each of them has believed to be moral and right. Thus Christian ministries today are often emboldened to enter the political arena and speak out on issues concerning human rights and the protection of the rights of Christians.

Bucer is likewise the exemplar for those who see the importance of working to maintain the unity of the Spirit in the bond of peace. Although, like Bucer, all those who work for unity will be accused of going too far and compromising principles in so doing, Bucer showed that the quest should never be abandoned. Those who have seen the harm caused to Christian souls by denominational controversies, by legalistic wrangling over fine points of doctrine and practice, and the image presented to the world by a fractured Christendom must imbibe, to some degree, the spirit of Bucer. They need to know of his work. Further, both the critics of those who seek unity and those who passionately do so should be well aware that at the root Bucer held tenaciously to the principles of the gospel, to the basic and fundamental doctrines of evangelicalism, and that he was willing to draw a line that he would never cross. That line is best defined by the doctrine of justification by faith, and its corollaries would be the necessity of basing all upon the Word of God, of doing everything to the building up of the Kingdom of Christ, which certainly involved the welfare of its people, and the absolute necessity of always acting in love. There were places that Bucer simply would not go for the sake of unity, but that did not stop him from being, as Margaret Blaurer called him, "the fanatic for unity."

Martin Bucer can also set an example for a leader in the church of today because his testimony was never obscured or diminished by any lack of his personal integrity. He did not make the mistake that Philip of Hesse did. He was a loving, devoted, and faithful husband and father. He was mighty in prayer, and practiced strict personal spiritual discipline. He observed Sunday rigorously. Even his worst enemies could not accuse him of any immorality, and that is always the test of integrity. Though he seldom joked, he believed that Christian joy should characterize every moment of one's life, and so it did his. He was a good friend, and he sought out people to make acquaintance with them in order that he could make them into his friends, so that he could be a friend to them. He answered his letters promptly. Young men who as yet were unknown and without influence would seek out Bucer's help to get a start, and Bucer was always eager to help and to recommend those he considered promising. He lost some friends, but it was not until after he had done all in his power to keep them. He never sought the accolades of people, and he never allowed differences of opinion or even criticism and reproof to affect his friendships. He spoke frankly, but always in a spirit of brotherly love, unlike the other Martin who was given to outbursts of anger and scathing, personal attacks. He bore no grudges, he was no tyrant, and he never sought to be a prelate. All the Strasbourg reformers, including Zell, Capito, and Hedio understood that he was always their comrade and friend, even when there were disagreements. He spent much time with his close friends like Philip Sailer and Ambrose Blaurer, but he never despised any of his friends. He always took an interest in them and in people in general for their own sakes, not for his. Think of what a difference it made in Calvin's life to have a friend like Bucer![420] It surely may be said of Martin Bucer that, in the words of the writer of the epistle to the Hebrews, here was a man of whom the world was not worthy.

---

[420] Eells, p. 421.

Appendix I:
The Works of Martin Bucer

The Opera Omnia of Martin Bucer is contained under his Latin and German writings, with the Latin works, *Martini Buceri Opera Latina,* abbreviated BOL and the German works, *Martin Bucers Deutsche Schriften,* BDS.[421] Most of his theological works are in Latin, while his letters are in German.

Bucer wrote about 150 volumes; consequently, a complete list would be of little interest to most readers. Calvin wrote: "Bucer is too verbose to be read quickly by those who have other matters to deal with…..He does not know how to stop writing." He also wrote with a notoriously poor handwriting, so much so that the English bishop Edmund Grindal said that a conjurer was needed to decipher it.

Many of Bucer's short treatises were written in response to some challenge he confronted. I have tried to include his most significant works, using D.F. Wright's selections as a general guide.

1523: *Das Ym Selbs (That no one should live for himself...)* His first work, on the primacy of love for one's neighbor[422]
1523: *Summary*: Summation of his theological beliefs at time of entrance into Strasbourg.[423]
1523: *Verantwortung*: Bucer's autobiography used as defense before Strasbourg City Council. Also known as *Apologia pro vita sua.*[424]
1524: *Against Treger*: Response to the Catholic antagonist Conrad Treger[425]

---

[421] *Martin Bucers Deutsche Schriften,* Internationals Kommittee zur Herausgabe der Werke Martin Bucers: Francois Wendel, Ernst Staehelin, Robert Stupperich, Jean Rott, Rodolphe Peter (Guetersloh: Guetersloher Verlagshaus, 1960).
[422] BDS I, pp.2-67.
[423] BDS I, pp. 69-147.
[424] BDS I, pp. 149-184.
[425] BDS II, pp. 15-173.

1524: *Grund und Ursach* (Foundation and Reason, or Foundation and Cause) His proposal for worship in Strasbourg[426]

1526: *Psalter*[427]

1526: *Apologia*

1527: *Commentary on St. Matthew* (A translation into French has been done by Jacques Couvoisier: Paris: Librarie Félix Alcan, 1933.)

1527: *Preface*[428]

1527: *Getrewe Warnung* (Sincere Warning or Admonition): Bucer's account of his disputation with the Anabaptist Hans Denck at Strasbourg.[429]

1527: *Commentary on Ephesians* (The commentaries of 1527 had a great influence on the development of John Calvin's theological beliefs, as well as those of Peter Martyr and others.)

1528: *Berner Predigt*[430]

1528: *Commentary on St. John*

1528: *Vergleichung*: Bucer's attempt to show that there existed essential agreement between Luther and Zwingli over the meaning of the Lord's Supper.[431]

1528: *Commentary on Zephaniah*

1529: *Gutachten*

1529: *The Marburg Religious Discussion*[432]

1529: *Tetrapolitan Confession*: The confession of four cities (Strasbourg, Lindau, Memmingen, and Konstanz) accepting Bucer's definition of the meaning of the Lord's Supper and incorporating many of the *Marburg Articles.*[433]

1529: *Commentary on the Psalms:* One of his most popular and effective works

1529: *Strasbourg Confession*

1530: *Ursach*

---

[426] BDS I, pp. 185-278.
[427] BDS II, pp. 175-223.
[428] BDS II, pp. 259-275.
[429] BDS II, pp. 225-258.
[430] BDS II, pp. 277-294; ed. H.-G. Rott, BDS IV, pp. 15-158.
[431] BDS II, pp. 295-383.
[432] BDS IV, pp. 323-364 (unpublished).
[433] BDS III, pp. 13-185.

1530: *Gospels*
1530: *Preface*
1531: *Quomodo*
1531: *Arrangement for the Church in Ulm*[434]
1531: *Confutatio*
1531: *Zwei Predigten*
1531: *Apologie der Confessio Tetrapolitana*[435]
1531: *Gutachten*[436]
1532: *Schweinfurt Confession*
1533: *Handlung gegen Hoffman*[437]
1533: *Quid de Baptismate*
1533: *Augsburg Summary*
1533: *Furbereytung zum Concilio*[438]
1534: *Bericht auss der Heyligen Geschrift*[439]
1534: *Kirchenordnung*[440]
1534: *Catechism*
1535: *Dialogi*
1536 *Commentary on Romans*
1537: *Shorter Catechism*
1538: *Benfelder Predigten*
1538: *Von der waren Seelsorge*; (On the True Care of Souls) Bucer's philosophy of pastoral care
1539: *Ziegenhainer Zuchtordnung*
1539: *Kasseler Kirchenordnung*
1541: *Abusuum ecclesiasticorum*
1541: *Acta colloqui*
1541: *Constans Defensio:* Bucer's defense of Herman von Wied after he was dismissed as Archbishop of Köln.

---

[434] BDS IV, ed. E.-W Kohls,.pp. 183-305.
[435] BDS III, pp. 187-317.
[436] BDS IV, pp. 409-448 (unpublished): concerns his opinion regarding the negotiations for compromise on the controversy over the Supper taking place in Schweinfurt and Nürnberg, his opinion concerning the *Augsburg Confession,* and his opinion regarding *the Schweinfurt Articles.*
[437] BDS V, pp. 43-108, ed. Robert Stuppereich.
[438] BDS V, pp. 259-364, ed. Wolfgang Hage.
[439] BDS V, pp. 109-258, ed. Robert Stuppereich.
[440] BDS V, pp. 15-42, ed. Robert Stuppereich.

1542: *De vera ecclesiarum*

1544 (?) *Judges*

1545: *Bestendige Verantwortung*

1546 : *Von der Kirchen mengel und fähl*

1548: *Ein Summarischer vergriff,* Bucer's defense of his teaching before the Strasbourg council, translated into French by François Wendel as *Resumé Summaire de la Doctrine Chrétienne,* Universitaires de France, 1951.

1550: *De Regno Christi, (On the Kingdom of Christ),* his model of a Christian community for King Edward VI

1550: *De vi et usu*

1550: *Ephesians*

1550: *Censura*: Bucer's critique of the 1549 edition of *The Book of Common Prayer*, most of which was utilized by Cranmer in the 1552 edition. It has been translated by E.C. Whitaker, M.A. (Alcuin Club Mayhew: McCrummon, Great Wakery, 1974).

Appendix II: The Status of Bucer Research

Interest in Bucer and his work has intensified in recent years, especially since the 1950's when Robert Stupperich began work on his collection of Bucer's works entitled *Bucer and His Time (Bucer und sein Zeit)* and research is ongoing in a number of areas. Bucer's works cover more than 150 titles, and they have been published as a part of the *Opera Omnia* in three sections.

The first section was under the direction of Robert Stupperich and underway by 1952 including Bucer's German works. Six volumes appeared between 1960 and 1975. There are now seventeen volumes.

The second section included his Latin works, the first two volumes of which were edited by François Wendel of the University of Strasbourg. His Latin works are now available in five volumes.

The third section, and most recent, include the approximately 2500 letters that Luther wrote, the first volume of which made his letters up to 1524 available and was edited by Jean Rott. I have noted in Appendix I specific works that are available in English translation.[441]

The international committee for the publication of the works of Martin Bucer is composed of Peter Brooks of Cambridge, Pierre Frankel of Geneva, Martin Greschat of Giessen, Gerald Hobbs of Vancouber, Marc Lienhard of Strasbourg, Gerhard Müller of Braunschweig, Jean Rott of Strasbourg, Willem Van't Spijker of Apeldoorn, and Robert Stupperich of Münster.

Robert Stupperich prepared a bibliography with an extensive list of Bucer's published works (*Bibliographia Bucerana: Schriften des Vereins fuer Reformationsgeschichte,* N. 169, Jahrgang 58, heft 2, 27-96. He followed with a bibliographical review "Stand und Aufgabe der Butzer Forschung" in *Archiv fuer Reformationsgechitchte,* XLII (1951), 244-59, and supplemented by "Bucerana" in the next volume, XLIII (1952), 106-07. Another listing of Bucer's materials was produced by Karl Schottenloher in

---

[441] Martin Buceri, *Opera Omnia Latina*, Vol. I, ed. Cornelis Augustin, Pierre Fraenkel, and Marc Lienhard, (Leiden: E.J. Brill, 1982), vii-viii.

Bibliographie zur deutschen Geschichte im Zeitalter Glaubensspaltung, 1517-1585 (Leipzig, 1933-1940) Vols. I, II, and V.[442]

Hastings Eells biography of 1931, of which I have made extensive use in this work, is remarkably detailed and informative. However, no English biography involving the whole of Bucer's life and work has appeared since, and Eells book is probably too tedious for most modern readers. There have been some biographical sketches, however, such as Alfred Erichson's *Martin Bucer* (Strasbourg, 1951) and François Wendel's French work published the same year in Strasbourg. Both of these works commemorated the 400th anniversary of his death.[443]

Several Reformation scholars have produced works that analyze the influence of Bucer on Calvin, Bucer's definition of the doctrine of the spiritual presence in the Lord's Supper growing out of the controversy between Luther and Zwingli, Bucer's efforts at unity, his work as reformer, pastor, and educator, his relationship to Erasmus and the humanist movement, and his work in England and subsequent influence on Cranmer and the development of the English Church.[444]

Recently Amy Nelson Burnett has published an impressive number of articles on Bucer and the reformation in Strasbourg, emphasizing especially the subject of his view of discipline, which is the subject of her book, *The Yoke of Christ.*[445] D.F. Wright's book consisting of essays on several significant aspects of Bucer's work, especially relating to his views of church and community, as reflected in his title, has brought together the work of some of the foremost Bucer scholars of today. An English translation of Martin Greschat's biography of Bucer (1990) by Stephen Buckwalter appeared in 2004.

Bucer research in Germany is underway at the University of Erlangen, headed by Andreas Puchta, working with Bucer's letters.

---

[442] Bard Thompson, "Bucer Study Since 1918," in *Church History,* Vol. 25, no. 1, March 1956, pp. 63-64..

[443] Thompson, p. 64.

[444] See Thompson, pp. 64-81.

[445] The list of her publications is available online at www.unl.edu/history/faculty/Burnett_Amy.html.

They have concentrated on Jean Rott's work which involved deciphering about seventy percent of Bucer's letters prior to his death in 1998. There is also a group in Heidelberg at work editing his German language treatises and memoranda. Involved in this study group are Thomas Wilhelmi, Stephen Buckwalter, and several assistants. When I contacted Professor Puchta and Stephen Buckwalter at these two German centers, I received enthusiastic cooperation and encouragement in my efforts. It is personally gratifying to me to be aware of an an awakening of interest in Bucer and of the work of these capable scholars on both continents. All of us are deeply concerned that Bucer's work be edited and preserved and that the story of his significant contributions to the Reformation be known.

Appendix III: Chronology of the Life of Martin Bucer

1491	Birth of Martin Bucer in Schlettstadt, now Selestat
1506	Joined Dominican Order at Schlettstadt
1516	Bucer moved to Dominican Order at Heidelberg to study
1516	Bucer moved for a very short time to Mainz
1517	Bucer returned to Heidelberg and matriculated
1518	Heard Luther to defend his theses at Heidelberg; converted to evangelicalism
1519	Bucer made a disputation that nearly caused him to be stoned
1520	Appeared before Inquisitor Jacob Hoogstraten at Köln
1520	Bucer left monastery, stayed in hiding in Speyer with Maternus Hatten
1521	Relieved of monastic vows, Bucer became a secular priest
1521	Bucer at Ebernburg
1522	Chaplain for Franz von Sickingen at Landstuhl; married Elizabeth Silbereisen.
1522	Pastor in Landstuhl
1522	Bucer pastor in Weissembourg
1523	Bucer excommunicated; he and Elizabeth fled to Strasbourg
1523	Began Latin lectures in Strasbourg
1523	Defense before Strasbourg city council
1524	Gardeners of St. Auriole called Bucer as their pastor
1528	Disputation at Bern where Bucer favored Zwingli's views on Eucharist
1529	Marburg Colloquy where Bucer began to develop his own understanding
1530	Bucer drew up *Tetrapolitan Confession* (Strasbourg, Constance, Lindau, Memmingen) as formula for accord on Lord's Supper
1530	Bucer attended Diet of Augsburg; *Augsburg Confession*
1530	Bucer participated in two religious discussions concerning Lord's Supper

1531	Bucer and Oecolampadius worked to accomplish Reformation at Ulm
1531	Bucer and Oecolampadius worked for Reformation in Augsburg, Memmingen, and Biberach.
1531	Bucer dealing with Anabaptists and Michael Servetus.
1531	Bucer gave Grynaeus his advice about divorce of King Henry VIII.
1532	Bucer presented views to meeting of Protestant Estates at Schweinfurt and Nürnberg.
1533	Bucer attended the Synod in Zürich
1533	First session of Strasbourg Synod
1534	Bucer issued his *Larger Catechism*
1534	Bucer attended secret conferences at Augsburg, Konstanz, and Kassel
1536	Wittenberg Concord arranged by Bucer and Melancthon
1537	Calvin came to Strasbourg and worked under Bucer
1538	Worked with Jacob Sturm to establish Academy that became University of Strasbourg
1540	Colloquies of Worms and Hagenau: Meeting with Bucer, Melancthon, Calvin, and Contarini
1541	Bucer appeared at Regensburg Diet
1541	Death of Elizabeth; marriage to Wibrandis Rosenblatt
1542	Bucer attempted Reformation at Köln
1548	Cranmer invited Bucer to England
1548	Charles imposed Interim in Strasbourg; Bucer asked to leave
1549	Bucer fled to England
1550	*De Regno Christi* and *Censura*
1551	Death of Bucer
1556	Queen Mary exhumed Bucer's bones and burned at stake
1560	Queen Elizabeth restored Bucer

Biographical Index

Ascham, Roger, Supporter of Bucer's efforts while Bucer was in England.

Blaurer, Ambrose, Reformed pastor of Konstanz, friend of Bucer, follower of Zwinglian school

Blaurer, Margaret, Sister of Ambrose Blaurer, well-educated and passionately Reformed in theology, Zwinglian, called Bucer "fanatic for unity."

Bradford, John, Protestant who studied under Bucer while Bucer was in England; he was present at his death and described the event.

Brentius, Bucer's Greek instructor at the Dominican monastery in Heidelberg.

Butzer, Claus, Bucer's father. (Butzer is German spelling; Bucer is Latin)

Butzer, Eva, Bucer's mother. She was a midwife.

Bullinger, Heinrich, Zwingli's successor as pastor of Grossmünster in Zürich, leader of Zwinglian school of interpretation regarding Communion

Calvin, John, 1509-1564, protégé of Bucer, pastor of St. Peter's Church in Geneva, author of *Institutes of the Christian Religion.*

Capito, Wolfgang, Friend of Bucer and fellow pastor in Strasbourg.

Charles V of Hapsburg, Emperor of Holy Roman (German) empire 1519-1555, devout Catholic and avowed opponent of Reformation.

Cheke, John, Close supporter of Bucer while Bucer was in England. Cheke was a humanist scholar who embraced Protestant theology.

Coverdale, Miles, Protestant scholar who admired Bucer and used his works in his translation of the Bible into English.

Cranmer, Thomas, Archbishop of Canterbury under Kings Henry VIII and his son Edward VI, Reformed in theology, leader of Reformation efforts under Edward, author of *The Book of Common Prayer,* strongly influenced by Bucer. Cranmer invited Bucer to England after he was banished from Strasbourg.

Denck, Hans, Anabaptist who fled to Strasbourg for refuge. Bucer held several dialogues with him and treated him with respect.

Eck, John, Professor of theology at University of Ingolstadt, opponent of Luther, Bucer, and of all leaders of the Protestant Reformation. Eck was an excellent debater.

Edward VI, Son of King Henry VIII and his successor, ruled England 1547-1553, committed to Protestant cause, supported Cranmer and Bucer. Bucer dedicated his *De Regno Christi* to the young king.

Erasmus of Rotterdam, 1466-1536, humanist scholar who worked for a reform of the Church based on rational, Biblical principles. He exerted a strong influence on Bucer as a youth, but the two parted over Bucer's adherence to the Protestant cause and its theology.

Fagius, Paul, Pastor of St. Peter the Younger Church in Strasbourg who was exiled to England with Bucer. He was a devoted friend of Bucer and died in his arms in England.

Farel, William, Protestant pastor in Geneva who persuaded Calvin to join him there. He often cooperated with Bucer.

Francis I, King of France whom Bucer hoped to influence either to end persecution against the Protestants or perhaps to understand and support the Reformation.

Fuller, Thomas, Protestant in England, Bucer's friend while there, wrote history of time documenting Bucer's stay in England.

Gebweiler, Jerome, Bucer's teacher at the Humanist academy in Schlettstadt.

Granvelle, Bishop, Catholic leader who strongly opposed Bucer and Protestants.

Gropper, Bishop, Catholic leader who was initially more moderate and interested in working with Bucer for possible reunification and for reform in Catholic Church. He later turned against Bucer and the moderate platform.

Haddon, Walter, Co-executor of Bucer's estate.

Hedio, Kaspar, Fellow pastor (at Cathedral) and co-worker with Bucer in Strasbourg.

Henry VIII, King of England 1509-1547 who broke with the Papacy and established the Church of England with himself as head. He appointed Thomas Cranmer Archbishop of

Canterbury, but prevented Thomas from instituting a true Reformation, replacing Thomas' Protestant *Ten Articles* with his pro-Catholic *Six Articles.*

Hoffmann, Melchoir, Anabaptist leader who took refuge in Strasbourg.

Hoogstraten, Jacob, Catholic official involved with Dominicans who sought to censure Bucer when Bucer was first converted to Protestantism.

Hooper, John, Protestant leader in England during Edwardian Reformation who worked with Cranmer but supported Zwinglian interpretation and therefore opposed Bucer's influence.

Hubert, Konrad, Bucer's secretary in England and later appointed guardian of Bucer's children.

Lasco, John, Polish Protestant who was present with Bucer in England. He accepted the Zwinglian position.

Lenglin, John, pastor at St. William Church in Strasbourg

Luther, Martin, 1483-1546, Leader of Reformation in Wittenberg, Germany, who made initial break with Rome 1517-1521. Luther held to a literal view regarding the Lord's Supper, sparking the controversy with Zwingli that Bucer tried to mediate.

Marbach, John, Pastor of Old St. Peter's Church in Strasbourg.

Melancthon, Philip, Luther's colleague and fellow theologian at Wittenberg who authored the *Augsburg Confession* of 1530 and was always more inclined toward moderation than Luther. He worked closely with Bucer.

Motherer, Heinrich, Protestant co-pastor with Bucer at Weissembourg.

Musculus, Wolfgang, Protégé of Bucer whom he installed as pastor in Augsburg.

Oecolampadius, John, Reformed pastor of Basel, Switzerland who was closely involved with Bucer and his work in Strasbourg.

Myconius, Pastor in Basel after Oecolampadius.

Parker, Matthew, Protestant scholar in England during Bucer's stay; he delivered eulogy at Bucer's funeral and was executor of his estate.

Perne of Peterhouse, Vice-Chancellor of Cambridge who presided both at the desecration and re-consecration ceremonies for Bucer at Cambridge.

Philip, Landgrave of Hesse, Nobleman who supported the Protestant Reformation strongly and was good friend and supporter of Bucer.

He worked with Bucer to accomplish unity among Protestants, but was discredited after entering into bigamy.

Ridley, Nicholas, Protestant scholar in England, friend and supporter of Bucer.

Rosenblatt, Wibrandis, Bucer's second wife who was the widow of three Protestant pastors including Oecolampadius and Capito.

Sandys, Edwin, Protestant scholar in England who was one of Bucer's friends and supporters.

Schell, Conrad, Co-pastor at St. Thomas Church in Strasbourg.

Schwartz, Thiebaut, Pastor of Old St. Peter's Church in Strasbourg.

Silbereisen, Elizabeth, Bucer's first wife.

Sleidan, John, Respected historian, Protestant friend and supporter of Bucer while Bucer was in England.

Steinlin, John, pastor of St. Auriole in Strasbourg

Sturm, Jacob, Humanist and Protestant supporter of Bucer in Strasbourg. He held considerable influence over the Strasbourg city council.

Sturm, John, Humanist scholar whom Bucer employed to head the Academy of Strasbourg. John Sturm often accompanied Bucer to religious meetings.

Suffolk, Duchess of, Close friend and strong supporter of Bucer while Bucer was in England.

Treger, Conrad, Catholic leader who opposed and debated Bucer early in Bucer's career.

Von Hohestein, William, Bishop of Strasbourg who opposed Bucer and the Reformers.

Von Hutten, Ulrich, German humanist and nobleman who was converted early to the Protestant cause. He supported both Luther and Bucer, helping Bucer gain his appointment as court chaplain to Franz von Sickingen.

Von Sickingen, Franz, nobleman at Ebernburg who employed Bucer as court chaplain until his own military involvements necessitated Bucer's leaving.

Von Wied, Hermann, Catholic Archbishop of Köln who accepted the theology of the Reformation and asked Bucer to implement a Reformed community in Köln (Cologne). The efforts were forcibly halted by the Emperor.

Wimpheling, Jacob, Humanist instructor involved at Schlettstadt and elsewhere who exerted an influence on Bucer as a youth.

Wolfhard, Boniface, Protégé of Bucer whom he installed as co-pastor in Augsburg; later he accepted the Zwinglian position on the Lord's Supper.

Zell, Matthew, pastor of St. Thomas Church in Strasbourg before Bucer. He had laid a solid foundation of Protestant theology before Bucer's arrival.

Ziegler, Clemens, Anabaptist who fled to Strasbourg for refuge.

Zwingli, Ulrich, Protestant pastor of Grossmünster in Zürich, Switzerland, who held to the concept that the bread and wine in the Lord's Supper are only symbols of the body and blood of Christ.

Select Bibliography

d'Aubigne, Merle: *History of the Great Reformation in the Times of Luther and Calvin.* Milwaukee: A.A. Swanlund, 1901.

Bradford, John, MA: *Writings,* ed. Aubrey Townsend, B.D. Cambridge: at the University Press, 1853.

Brady, Thomas A. Jr: *The Politics of the Reformation in Germany: Jacob Sturm (1489- 1553) of Strasbourg.* Atlantic Highlands, NJ: Humanities Press, 1997.

Bouwsma, William J: *John Calvin.* New York: Oxford University Press, 1988.

Burnett, Amy Nelson: *The Yoke of Christ: Martin Bucer and Christian Discipline.* Kirksville, MO: Sixteenth Century Journal Publishers, Inc., 1999.

Eells, Hastings: *Attitudes of Martin Bucer toward the Bigamy of Philip of Hesse.* AMS Press, 2000.

_____: *Martin Bucer.* New Haven: 1931.

Fuller, Thomas: *The Church History of Britain from the birth of Jesus Christ until the Year 1648.* London: John Williams, 1655.

Greschat, Martin. *Martin Bucer: Ein Reformator und seine Zeit (1491-1551).* Munich: Beels, 1990; English translation Stephen E. Buckwalter, Louisville: Westminster John Knox Press, 2004.

Hopf, Constantin: *Martin Bucer and the English Reformation.* Oxford: Basil Bladewell, 1946.

Jensen, de Lamar: *Reformation Europe: Age of Reform and Revolution.* Lexington, MA: D.C. Heath and Co., 1992.

Krüger, Friedhelm: *Bucer und Erasmus: Eine Untersuchung zum Einfluss des Erasmus Auf die Theologie Martin Bucers (Bis zum Evangelien Kommentar von 1530).* Wiesbaden: Franz Steiner Verlag GMBH, 1970.

MacCullouch, Diarmaid: *Thomas Cranmer.* New Haven: Yale University Press, 1996.

Maxwell, William D: *An Outline of Christian Worship: Its Development and Forms.* London: Oxford University Press, 1963.

Müller, Johannes: *Martin Bucers Hermeneutik: Quelen und Forschungen zur Reformationsgeschichte.* Band XXXII. Güterslohere Vorlagshaus Gerd Mohn, 1965.

Pauck, Wilhelm: *Melancthon and Bucer.*

Pollet, J.V: *Martin Bucer: Etudes sur la Correspondance.* Vol. I. Paris, 1958 ; Vol. II, Paris, 1962.

Selderhuis, Herman J: *Marriage and Divorce in the Thought of Martin Bucer,* tr. John Vriend and Lyle D. Bierma. Kirksville, MO: Thomas Jefferson University Press At Truman State University, 1999.

Smyth, C.H: *Cranmer and the Reformation under Edward VI.* Cambridge: at the University Press, 1926.

Stephens, W.P: *The Holy Spirit in the Theology of Martin Bucer.* Cambridge: at the University Press, 1970.

Spitz, Lewis: *The Religious Renaissance of the German Humanists.* Cambridge, MA: 1963.

Thompson, Bard: *Liturgies of the Western Church.* New York: World Publishing Co.,1961.

_____: *Humanists and Reformers: A History of the Renaissance and Reformation.* Grand Rapids: William B. Eerdmans Publishing Co., 1996.

van de Poll, G.J: *Martin Bucer's Liturgical Ideas: The Strasbourg Reformer and His Connection with the Liturgies of the Sixteenth Century.* Assen, Netherlands: Koninklijke Van Gorcurn & Comp. NV, 1954.

Van't Spijker, Willem: *The Ecclesiastical Offices in the Thought of Martin Bucer* in *Studies in Medieval and Reformation Thought,* ed. Heiko A. Oberman, vol. 57. Leiden: E.J. Brill, 1996

Wendel, François: *L'eglise de Strasbourg: sa constitution et son organization 1532-1535.* Paris, 1942.

Witte, John, Jr : *Law and Protestantism : The Legal Teachings of the Lutheran Reformation.* Cambridge: University Press, 2002.

Wright, D.F: *Martin Bucer: Reforming Church and Community.* Cambridge: at the University Press, 2002.

About the Author

J. David Lawrence is professor of history at Lipscomb University in Nashville, Tennessee and also teaches for Engedi Ministries. He has been involved in Christian ministry as a pastor and theology teacher for over fifty years. A graduate of Drury College in Springfield, Missouri and holding a master's degree in history from Wichita State University and a Ph. D. from the University of Kansas, Dr. Lawrence has published *Erasmus and the Renaissance Neo-Platonic Revival* (University of Kansas Ph. D. dissertation, 1984), a number of articles on Renaissance and Reformation theological topics and has reviewed several books for history journals. He taught for fifteen years at Wichita Collegiate School and has been on the Lipscomb faculty since 1986. He is married to the former Alice Davis, and they have two sons and three grandchildren.

Printed in the United States
104081LV00002B/1-48/P

9 781933 912097